Politics and Popular Culture

Politics and Popular Culture

Edited by

Leah A. Murray

CAMBRIDGE SCHOLARS

PUBLISHING

Politics and Popular Culture, Edited by Leah A. Murray

This book first published 2010

Cambridge Scholars Publishing

12 Back Chapman Street, Newcastle upon Tyne, NE6 2XX, UK

British Library Cataloguing in Publication Data
A catalogue record for this book is available from the British Library

ISBN (10): 1-4438-2259-0, ISBN (13): 978-1-4438-2259-6

TABLE OF CONTENTS

Introduction

Hollywood Politics:
The Popular Culture Factor
in 21st Century Politics

Leah A. Murray

In 2008 we saw a continuation and perhaps even acceleration in the trend of popular culture having a discernible effect on politics. From *The Daily Show* to Barack Obama's Blackberry to candidates' use of Facebook and MySpace, politics have opened up to new technologies as we come online for the next generation. Our political world has become popularized, or our popular world has become politicized. Politics has become a part of our daily lives in a new way, facilitated by the entertainment media and new technologies. This next generation will grow up in a politicized popular world where issues like torture are explored on shows like *24* and fictional presidents deal with real policy choices on shows like *The West Wing*. Also, our political news has adjusted as we see the amalgamation of politics and entertainment in society. Politicians appear regularly on *Saturday Night Live* and *The Colbert Report* to entertain the masses while they work to govern off camera.

This volume's authors attempt to make sense of the changing political popular world through a series of interdisciplinary essays that explore the ramifications of popular cultural depictions of politics drawing on literature in a variety of fields: political science, history, literature, fine arts and communications. We examine three major phenomena in a politicized popular culture. First, we explore the role that the entertainment media play in understanding politics. For example, we can understand deeply complicated political thought if we watch characters on *Lost* struggle with a state of nature; we can consider the ideas of a unitary executive divorced from our own partisanship if we engage *Battlestar Galactica*'s Laura Roslyn's decision making calculus; we see our American political soul reflected in movies and television shows and we are able to reflect on it.

What is interesting about our fictional political worlds is we are allowed, as a people, to consider different political ideals without the baggage of our last vote or our ideology. We can step outside ourselves and challenge the way we think on particular issues. We are opposed, for example, to torture but we root for Jack Bauer on *24*, so we can think about how we really feel about the use of torture to gain information. Second, we explore the real world of politics as it has been shaped over the last century of new technology. As powerful a medium television proved to be to politics, the latest technological breakthroughs have proved to be a paradigmatic shift. From Twitter to Facebook, our politicians are able to keep in almost constant contact with their constituencies, which has vast implications for the way political discourse will progress. If a Senator needs to respond within eight minutes to an event, that response will certainly be different from those in a time when he had a day or a week to respond. If the news media need to report in a 24 hour news cycle, competing not only with other news sources but with amateur journalists with digital cameras, the gatekeeping function of our political media is drastically affected as all news is almost instantaneous. Third, we explore what happens when the real world and media collide. Entertainment media change their messages when major political events happen. For example, spymaster tropes had to evolve when 9/11 changed the international dynamic in a fundamental way. Robert Ludlum's Jason Bourne series had to be conceptualized on film in a new way after this event. The influence goes in both directions as politicians and the political world adjust when media coverage changes. When *Saturday Night Live* ran its impersonation of the 2000 presidential debates, the Gore campaign watched to see how to advise its candidate for the next round.

These three phenomena are explored using both theoretical and empirical methods throughout the volume, organized into three major topical sections. First, we examine the use of popular culture as an explanation of political theory. Consumers of these media products are learning political theory, indeed advanced political theory in some cases. The authors in this section each grapple with how political theory and political popular culture intersect. First, Gerry Canavan examines the seeming incongruity of 2008, a year that celebrated the hope and optimism of Obama's presidential campaign message and also delivered box office records to the message of death and negativity found in the character of the Joker in *Dark Knight*. He argues that this culture's drive toward disruption is the common appeal and that 21st century America is looking for change. Second, John Freie takes a historical look at the image of the presidency to demonstrate that the way presidents govern has substantially changed since Neustadt's seminal work *Presidential Power and the Modern Presidents* laid out a model for understanding the presidency, often known in the literature as the modern presidency. Freie argues that we have shifted from a modern paradigm to a postmodern governing structure and that we need a new understanding of the use of popular culture by politicians, specifically the president. How Obama governs looks very different given this new paradigm and we need to adjust our expectations accordingly. Third, a current popular show, *Lost*, is seemingly designed to teach social contract theory to the masses. Every character is a referent to some major political work. Scott McDermott fleshes out the connections between the plot lines and characters and age old Enlightenment ideas. He enters what is a well traveled conversation about the purpose of the show and adds to our understanding of the phenomenon. McDermott demonstrates that *Lost* deliberately teaches its viewers the basic tenets of social contract theory in its characters and story arcs. Fourth, Hugo Torres examines the intersection of entertainment media and ideology as both are influenced by 9/11. Torres explores how conservatives find a home in a post-9/11 understanding of interacting with enemies in *24* while liberals are more attracted to *Battlestar Galactica*. He argues that each show demonstrates a different value orientation toward terrorism and asks different questions about our war against terrorism while still having a common faith in democracy. Viewers of these shows would find compelling arguments for each ideological perspective. Finally, in this section, I explore the role leadership plays in political judgment as demonstrated in *Battlestar Galactica*. Using Weber's leadership archetypes, I argue that this show implicitly makes a case for the vocational politician, or civil servant, being a hero when all else fails. The idea that a civil servant can make the best decisions in a post-apocalyptic world is depicted throughout the show's characters and storylines. The authors in these chapters demonstrate the power of popular culture in understanding politics, whether it is through entertainment media or through the perception of governing by presidents in a world where popular culture plays a much larger role.

In the second section, we grapple specifically with the dynamics of popular culture and the presidency. The 2008 election brought many new media to bear as well as much interaction between facets of popular culture and politics, especially as it pertained to Obama. These authors examine the relationship the presidency specifically has with changes in popular culture, be it technology or product placement. First, Jeffrey Crouch and Richard Semiatin argue that changing technologies have affected the nature of presidential discourse, most especially as we transition from a political theater based on party to must see entertainment based on individual personality. They specifically look at those times in debate history when candidates fail and how those failures are so important to political discourse. As presidential debates are a moment in political time when prime time popular culture and real-time politicians interact, understanding how they have evolved over time is an important piece to the puzzle when gaining knowledge of the mutual influence of popular culture and politics. Second, Lilly Goren and Justin Vaughn examine how the presidential image is marketed and consumed. These authors argue that the presidential image has become a market force in popular culture – that the Obama image has economic value. When the First Lady wears a specific brand of clothing, people across the nation go out to buy the same dress. Thus politics has become about product placement. Third, Gwendelyn Nisbett and Lindsey Harvell look at the 2008 presidential election and the role popular culture played in affecting young people's politics. Using focus groups, these authors found that while the newer non-traditional media play a role in forming political opinions, young people still rely more on interpersonal relationships. They are more likely to cite their family and friends than any technology when discussing where their opinions were formed. Finally, LaChrystal Ricke explores the role of the relatively recent political phenomenon of YouTube. She looks specifically at the 2008 election and finds that the political use of YouTube facilitates collective action and creates knowledge. Thus, political communication has been drastically changed by the introduction of YouTube, much the same way the Nixon-Kennedy debate fundamentally changed politics fifty years ago. We can only guess at the potential possibilities for politics as the use of YouTube is embraced by more campaigns. Presidential politics, the authors in this section demonstrate, has changed in both the nature of our consumption of it and also in our political discourse. These chapters indicate that we have experienced a major paradigm shift in how presidential politics play out. In much the same way people neither anticipated nor predicted how television media would change the way we think of our presidential candidates, we are just beginning to understand how the intersection of politics, popular culture and new media will affect presidential politics in the long term.

Finally, in the third section, we look at the effects when popular culture and politics very specifically interact due to specific catastrophic events. These authors examine the influence of focusing events of politics and popular culture, whether the result is fiction, satire or news coverage. First, Karen K. Burrows examines the effect 9/11 has on politics in popular culture. In her chapter, Burrows argues that America is searching for its post-9/11 identity and that popular culture plays a role. Looking at two television shows that bookend 9/11 in the United States, *Alias* and *La Femme Nikita*, Burrows argues that these shows grapple with spying as a career demonstrating the way America conceives of itself in a "war on terrorism" world. Thus, this acts as a natural experiment as we see how America thought of itself through the lens of the spy genre prior to 9/11 and then following; the two series depict very different ideals. Also examining the role 9/11 has had on Americans' perception of themselves, Jacobus Verheul argues that *24* informs our conversation about torture as a tool in our war on terrorism as well as our use of preemptive violence. Popular culture has helped us morally justify our use of tools that previous to 9/11 would not have been acceptable. We root for Jack Bauer in a way that we would not have in the 1990s. Third, Betty Kaklamanidou examines the populist politics of the political documentary. She argues that through the use of documentary filmmaking, Michael Moore has become the unofficial regulator of popular politics. In this way, we see popular culture used as a threat in political movements giving quite a bit of power to the media. Thus Moore is no longer reporting on political phenomena, but creating them and manipulating them. In fact, his presence as a reporter at the 2008 Republican National Convention made news itself. Kaklamanidou explores what happens when popular culture becomes politics, which then becomes popular culture. Finally, Chapman Rackaway, Kevin Anderson, Michael A. Smith and Ryan Sisson examine where media coverage of events becomes political by looking at those moments in our political world when candidates die. They demonstrate that there is a "eulogy effect" in a number of relatively recent cases. Thus a major event affects media coverage of politics *writ large* which then affects the political world. The authors in this section demonstrate that popular culture plays a role in our struggle with our conceptions when a catastrophic event changes the playing field. As our world becomes more intimate with everyone being able to know every detail of every event, our popular culture world reflects those struggles. Media coverage is affected by and affects our understanding of ourselves and our politics.

The relationship between popular culture and politics has a long history because politics make the best stories. Some of most well known and sexiest scandals in history happen in political circles. Entertainment media going at least as far back as Greek drama have explored political questions. The authors in this volume not only make interesting arguments about the mutual relationship of politics and popular culture in the modern day, they open up new questions about where we will head in the future.

Given all the new media and technology, the interaction between politics and popular culture will only increase in both intensity and importance.

POPULAR CULTURE AS POLITICAL THEORETICAL EXPLANATION

PERSON OF THE YEAR:
OBAMA, JOKER, CAPITALISM, SCHIZOPHRENIA

GERRY CANAVAN

How then does one explain the fact that capitalist production is constantly arresting the schizophrenic process and transforming the subject of the process into a confined clinical entity, as though it saw in this process the image of its own death coming from within? Why does it make the schizophrenic into a sick person not only nominally but in reality? Why does it confine its madmen and madwomen instead of seeing in them its own heroes and heroines, its own fulfillment?
—Deleuze and Guattari, *Anti-Oedipus*

If 2008 had a person of the year, it had two: Barack Obama on the one hand and Heath Ledger's Joker on the other. Each in his own way was a spectacular image made flesh—the spectacle of hope, change, and progress against that of disaster, dread, and death—and each in his own way embodied his moment. *The Dark Knight*, a cultural sensation, shattered records, including $67.2 million in a single day, the biggest single-day opening ever; the largest opening weekend, $150 million; $100 million in two days, $200 million in five days, $300 million in ten days, and $400 million in 43 days—all records, the last achieved with twice the speed of the previous record holder.[1] The film's total gross has now crossed a billion dollars worldwide after its release on DVD and a subsequent re-release in theaters in January 2009.[2] For its part, the Obama campaign, aided by an acute awareness of mimetic branding and viral marketing, and fueled by unprecedented use of online fundraising and social networking tools, set its own monetary records throughout the primary and general election season, including $133 million dollars in the first quarter of 2008 and $150 million dollars in a single, record-smashing September[3] that included $10 million dollars in one night after Sarah Palin's speech at the Republican National Convention.[4] In all Obama had millions of donors, with approximately half that number giving less than $200. Obama's stump speeches regularly drew crowds of 50,000 people or more, with 33.6 million people tuning in to watch a campaign-paid *infomercial* a week before Election Night.[5] By the end of the election the

Obama campaign had collected 13 million email addresses, a million cell-phone numbers and half a billion dollars from three million people over the Internet, the vast majority in increments of $100 or less.[6] All this, and he won too.

At first glance the sheer fact of this paradox appears ludicrous, but we cannot escape it. It was the power of this juxtaposition that gave Australian artist James Lillis instant fame when he chose to parody Shepard Fairey's iconic HOPE campaign posters (vaguely reminiscent of the iconic "Che" print) with JOKE, a image of the-Joker-as-Obama that circulated quickly on the Internet and is still (as of this writing) available as a T-shirt.[7] How can the country that elected Obama on a rhetoric of "hope" and "change" *at the same time* revel so completely in the Joker's pure negativity and aura of death? What can explain the appeal of *The Dark Knight* to countless numbers of Obama supporters, donors, and volunteers, many of whom must have gone from working for the campaign during the day to seeing the film that night? How could any cultural moment be attracted to such polar opposites simultaneously? This chapter will argue, through reference Deleuze and Guattari's category of the schizophrenic, that despite their surface differences the Obama campaign and *The Dark Knight*'s Joker in fact drew their tremendous popular appeal from a common source: a projected desire for a revolutionary reconfiguration of the conditions of life in twenty-first century American capitalism.

Secret Identities and Missing Birth Certificates

Almost two decades ago, in *Super Heroes: A Modern Mythology,* Richard Reynolds noted the essential passivity of all superheroes, who take on the role of foil or antagonist against the active engine of plot in their stories, the figure who formally speaking is the protagonist: the villain.[8] This has never been truer than in *The Dark Knight.* Naturally, Batman is the nominal hero of this film, but in this, more than any other film in the franchise—befitting the first movie in the series to forgo his name in its title—he is neither the film's star nor its object of primary interest. Indeed at times he is something of an afterthought to a war of wills between the Joker and Harvey Dent, able to be returned to a place of honor in his own franchise at the end of the film only because Dent has the bad luck to be half-doused in gasoline.

This is the Joker's film, and had been ever since its predecessor (*Batman Begins* [2005]) ended with its tease of the Joker's "calling card." The Joker is whom we have come to see, the Joker what we have been waiting for, the Joker who generates nearly all of the pleasure of the film. So we must be careful to resist readings of *The Dark Knight* as an uncomplicated, one-to-one mapping of the major players in the War on Terror into comic-book terms. That is to say that the Joker is not best understood as "a terrorist," though characters in the film call him such repeatedly. The wishful thinking of some right-wing commentators aside,[9] the film is not a grand apologia for the Bush presidency, despite the presence of torture and fanciful domestic spying subplots and its apparent Jack Bauer ethos of legal exceptionalism. It is, instead, a kind of macabre pageant, a celebration of the violent revolutionary excess of the Joker himself that is legitimized by the disciplining presence of Batman— delight in destruction made ideologically safe because it is (a) not "real" and (b) eventually (if nominally) "punished."

More so than even Jack Nicholson's turn in the iconic 1989 Tim Burton film, this is a film that lives and dies by Heath Ledger's performance. The film's advertisers were surely aware of this when they crafted the "Why So Serious?" viral advertising campaign dedicated to his performance, as well as the various Alternate Reality Games and online promotions crafted towards uncovering images that tease the Joker. This is why the frenzy of media speculation that greeted Ledger's death immediately translated into free advertising for the film.

However, the lingering aura of Ledger's death has a consequence: it significantly deforms the audience's ability to read this film correctly. That Ledger died just after filming—that initial reports blamed *the role itself* for his (as it turned out, incorrectly assumed) "suicide"—in some ways threatens to transform *The Dark Knight* into a kind of snuff film. As an unnamed "studio insider" told Variety after news of the actor's death broke:

> "The Joker character is dealing with chaos and life and death and a lot of dark themes," one insider with knowledge of the campaign said. "Everyone is going to interpret every line out of his mouth in a different way now."[10]

It was in this context that early media reports in the wake of Ledger's death inevitably turned to a cryptic statement from Jack Nicholson, the Joker in Tim Burton's 1989 *Batman*: "I warned him."[11] Or, as David Denby put this point in his review of the film in *The New Yorker:*

> When Ledger wields a knife, he is thoroughly terrifying (do not, despite the PG-13 rating, bring the children), and, as you're watching him, you can't help wondering—in a response that admittedly lies outside film criticism—how badly he messed himself up in order to play the role this

way. His performance is a heroic, unsettling final act: this young actor looked into the abyss.[12]

This question—which Denby "can't help wondering," which dominated both public and critical reception of the film—is precisely the question that *we are not supposed to be able to ask of the Joker.* The film is quite clear that the Joker has no history, and can have no history. This is why he tells multiple versions of the story of how he got his scars depending on whom he hopes to terrify, and if the point isn't clear Jim Gordon is sure to drive it home: "Nothing. No matches on prints, DNA, dental. Clothing is custom, no labels. Nothing in his pockets but knives and lint. No name, no other alias..." The Joker's violence cannot be located in an identity or a personal subjectivity. It must originate from and out of nothing, *out of the shadows of Gotham itself*; that is the entire point.

Precisely the opposite could be said of Bruce Wayne, who is *all* history—who builds his own assemblage of gadgets, disguise, gravelly voice, and affectless persona precisely because his father and mother were murdered in Crime Alley, whose entire life grows out of and *is* a (frankly insane) response to that singular event. But it is true of Batman; like the Joker himself, Batman appears suddenly as an irruptive force of no apparent origin, without history or explanation, which disrupts the ordinary flows of mafia capital in Gotham City. Batman, too, must necessarily have no history: to locate even a shred of history in Batman, as the Joker does regarding his relationship with Rachel Dawes, is to cripple him almost beyond repair.

To link the Joker to Heath Ledger's death, therefore, does devastating interpretive violence to the figure of the Joker as such; it is an attempt to inject with history something that has no history, that is frightening and terrifying but also liberatory and powerful—"out-of-control" in both its senses—precisely because it has no past, no desires, no agenda, and no future. It is an attempt to make sense out of what is insensible, what is multiple, what is (in Deleuzean terms) purely schizophrenic:

The schizo has his own system of co-ordinates for situating himself at his disposal, because, first of all, he has at his disposal his very own recording code, which does not coincide with the social code, or coincides with it only in order to parody it. The code of delirium or of desire proves to have an extraordinary fluidity. It might be said that the schizophrenic passes from one code to the other, that he deliberately scrambles all the codes, by quickly shifting from one to another, according to the questions asked him, never giving the same explanation from one day to the next, never invoking the same genealogy, never recording the same event in the same way. When he is more or less forced into it and is not in a touchy mood, he

> may even accept the banal Oedipal code, so long as he can stuff it full of
> all the disjunctions that this code was designed to eliminate.[13]

This question of history is similarly inescapable with regard to Barack Obama, who has managed to draw such a superfluity of history to himself that one hardly knows where to begin. He has positioned himself variously as a kind of self-conscious Oedipus seeking a lost father—*Dreams of My Father*—and as the voice of a "new generation" he predates by ten to twenty years, as a reformer/revolutionary, a reconciler, and also as the fulfillment-through-return of a particular sort of American greatness. He even possesses in his own way a kind of doubled identity—the Barry he grew up as becomes "Barack" in adulthood, who in turn becomes the hidden truth behind a opaque public image ["Barack Obama"] which has no history, which is widely perceived to have come out of nowhere, almost to have sprung suddenly into existence on the second night of the Democratic National Convention in 2004. Obama, too, came from nowhere, irrupting on the scene to impossibly defeat the best-known establishment figures in both political parties, first the Clintons, then the Bush and McCain—winning both the primary and the election despite his youth, his race, his relative lack of name recognition, his comparative inexperience, and his surface similarities to the "latte-sipping, arugula-eating" Northeastern liberals who had lost in 1980 (Kennedy to Carter), 1988 (Dukakis to Bush), and 2004 (Kerry to Bush II).

Accordingly, the greatest threats to Obama's political viability came in attempts to linking the meteoric Candidate Obama to some real, flawed person, for instance the man who had attended Rev. Jeremiah Wright's church, or the man who once lived in the same neighborhood as former Weather Underground leader Bill Ayers. Even now, a significant portion of the right wing has invested itself in the so-called "birther" movement, which denies the reality of Obama's citizenship and insists instead that he was actually born in Kenya. These are all hyperbolic, if futile, efforts to locate Obama's "true" past, his "real" history—his secret identity—and thereby depower him. That there exist no photographs of Candidate Obama smoking cigarettes during the long 2008 campaign, despite his quiet admission that he did so, is proof enough of the power of his carefully honed public mask, beneath which we can never see.

Like Batman, like the Joker, Barack the man has been overwritten completely, overcoded by Barack the Utopian fantasy of a break with history. Here, it was break from both eight long years of Bushism and from the troubled racial history of the nation itself, in particular as the sudden and unexpected fulfillment of Martin Luther King's longed-for dream—which, we were soberly assured by media figures on both

Election Night and Inauguration Day, turns out to have been specifically and exclusively about the presidency all along.

'Change'

The Joker's parodic self-representation of his own history—"Wanna know how I got these scars?"—is only the most salient example of his schizophrenic powers of complication and recombination. What the Joker seeks to do—all he seeks to do—is break down codes:

TWO-FACE
It was your men, your plan!
THE JOKER
Do I really look like a guy with a plan? You know what I am? I'm a dog chasing cars. I wouldn't know what to do with one if I caught it. You know, I just... do things. The mob has plans, the cops have plans, Gordon's got plans. You know, they're schemers. Schemers trying to control their little worlds. I'm not a schemer. I try to show the schemers how pathetic their attempts to control things really are.

This is as political as the Joker gets, and as expected it is an apolitics of pure negation, an insistent rejection of all status quos. The Joker decenters, he decodes, he disrupts flows. He queers all hierarchies and subverts all norms. He swaps hostages for hostage-takers, school buses for getaway cars, recodes scotch as poison and police protection as death, scrambles the map of the city, turns a DA into a killer, creates a network of Joker acolytes to rob a bank and then murders them, gathers all the capital of Gotham's mafia-corruption complex to himself and then burns it. Consider his various remappings of the dead man's switch—to kill him kills you, *or* to do nothing kills, *or* saves some *and* kills others, except when he decides to blow the switch anyway, *or* when the locations have been switched, *or, or, or*. There is nothing to hold onto with the Joker—he deterritorializes everything, even the terms of his own murderous games. His violence is deeply and inescapably recombinative—it is never the same thing twice, and we are never the same afterwards.

What does it mean, then, for us to *like* the Joker, to indeed *prefer* the Joker to either Batman or Dent or anybody else in the film? What does it say that we do not *care* that he kills Rachel, Bruce Wayne's barely-there love interest, that he corrupts the already-doomed-by-sixty-years-of-comics-canon Harvey Dent for our amusement? What are we to make of the Joker's undeniable appeal? This is a film that draws its power not from the repetitious narrative staging of hero vs. villain—a manifest staging that the audience, on the level of the latent, rejects—but from the audience's delight in pure, anarchistic violence. This is divine violence, to borrow Walter Benjamin's term from his "Critique of Violence" (1920): messianic violence that does not found or preserve the law but overturns it.[14]

So, to rephrase the question, what does it mean to (in this sense) *approve* of the Joker? To root for him? To see his "point," such as it is? Because, I think, we do. When we retheorize the film around the Joker we recognize that he is in every sense its creative engine, its vital force. Thinking in Deleuzean terms, the Joker is the film's embodiment of the unstoppable creative force of the nomadic war machine of *A Thousand Plateaus*—even, as one of his henchmen describes, wearing not makeup but "war paint." And it was this drive towards disruption that was the barely sublimated subtext of Campaign 2008, not just in Obama's slogan of CHANGE but in McCain's counter-meme of MAVERICK—the gambling anti-hero, the hotshot fighter pilot who doesn't play by the rules. Even the planned title for the autobiography of ex-Governor Sarah Palin, McCain's vice-presidential candidate, suggests the continued appeal of the Joker's vital force: *Going Rogue.*

The Joker seeks to disrupt a system of overlapping codes, flows, and conventions that is often unjust, inequitable, stultifying and suspect—and while naturally we must disapprove of his *methods* we must admit there is something of a revolutionary Utopian impulse in him that we can surely *recognize*, if not exactly admire. The Joker, when all is said and done, wants CHANGE too. And does that not suggest the possibility that we too might be Jokerized, that there is something essential about the Joker we dare not see lost?

Near the end of the film, dangling upside down the Joker says to Batman: "I think you and I are destined to do this forever." (Note how the camera slowly adjusts itself to his positionality in this moment, against "absolute gravity", suggesting both the Joker's thematic centrality and his essential weightlessness.) And of course they are. We see that in this film, unlike 1989's, the Joker cannot be killed: this time Batman—that is to say, Bruce Wayne, über-capitalist, master of the reterritorializing power of capitalism who has remade himself so entirely—must *save* the Joker in his fall off the skyscraper. Without the Joker Batman is obsolete, as he is already obsolete when the film begins. This time, we find, he (and we) need the Joker to live. Batman's productive powers as the defender of the Gotham City status quo stand in the same relation to the Joker as capitalism does to schizophrenia; the Joker can never be killed because he provokes, and embodies, Batman's own creative excess.[15] In this way the Joker is the truth of the Batman; he is Batman's exterior limit, that line towards which he is continually drawn towards and perpetually—structurally—unable to resist. The Joker is the force that gives Batman life. Without the Joker Batman is essentially self-negating; he defeats the mobsters, ends corruption, and then hangs up his cowl and gadgets, totally supplanted. Without the Joker, that is to say, Batman exhausts himself. It is only through the schizo-flows generated by the Joker and the other supervillains who will infest Gotham in sequel after sequel (and comic after comic) that Batman's creativity and heroism can be continually reborn and revitalized—that Batman himself can continue to exist. Batman is indeed only as good as his villain, and they do, in fact, need each other—the Joker to push the limit and the Batman to recoil/chase/follow.

There is a lesson here for Barack Obama, or really for the supporters who have created an image of him in their minds as a kind of redeemer superhero. The disruptive drive for CHANGE—the Joker's drive—was the recombinative schizo-fuel both for Obama's campaign and his immense popularity. It is what allowed him to build that unprecedented, multifaceted network of dedicated and industrious volunteers, allowed him to channel new media technologies to handily beat better-known establishment figures in both parties. CHANGE was the fuel that drove those six million donations, that launched a thousand blogs, and that made 2008's historic election and 2009's equally historic inauguration possible.

That CHANGE is a highly adaptive buzzword meaning nothing and everything briefly fed the fantasy that 52% of the country now agreed on some soon-to-be-enacted radical program of change—but now we know better. This is to say that Obama achieved the presidency through a largely content-free, Joker-like demand that the applecart be overturned and the flows of our own military-industrial-mafia-corruption complex be disrupted, and that this demand has, paradoxically, catapulted him to a Batman-like office where his job is to *preserve*, not disrupt, capital's flows.

'Socialism'

In summer 2009, only a few months after Barack Obama's inauguration, a digitally altered image of Obama began to appear as graffiti on overpass walls, first in Los Angeles and then in other major American cities, including Boston and Atlanta. The striking image, drawn from an October 23, 2008, *Time* magazine cover, depicts a snarling Obama made up as Ledger's Joker, with heavily made-up white skin, green hair, heavy eye shadow, and scarred cheeks highlighted by wildly excessive red lipstick. The image was created with Photoshop in January 2009 by a twenty-year old Chicago art student, Firas Alkhateeb, and had sat in digital obscurity on the storage site Flickr[16] until borrowed by an unknown party and repurposed for protest against Obama administration policies. The artifacts of the original *Time* magazine context were digitally stripped away, leaving only the doctored image of Obama, and below the portrait was added a one-word caption suggesting the field of this supposed Obama-Joker equivalence: SOCIALISM.

The reaction to the Obama-as-Joker image was immediate, with wide discussion on political blogs in both the left and right corners of the blogosphere trickling upwards into discussion on talk radio and television. The image was adopted by members of the Tea Party movement and appeared at related protests throughout the summer, appearing on protest signs at health-care-reform "town halls" and the "9/12 Movement" protest on the Mall in Washington, D.C., which had been spearheaded by prominent conservative talking-head Glenn Beck and heavily promoted by the Fox News Channel. At the same time the image was pilloried by liberals and the left, which found itself perplexed by the hyperbolic caption—isn't Obama clearly governing as a centrist? Isn't the Joker more of a radical Libertarian?—and disturbed by the racial connotations of the whiteface makeup. In a *Washington Post* editorial, Philip Kennicott argued that the image's evocation of Ledger's Joker was calculated to suggest an ideological stereotype of violent, black urbanity that (the artist's apparent argument goes) is quite literally coded in Obama's genes. These racial and perhaps racist connotations were likewise noted by a blogger who helped catapult the image to national prominence, Steven Mikulan at LAWeekly.com, who drew attention to the whiteface makeup's photo-negative reflection of blackface minstrelsy and concluded "The only thing missing is a noose."[17]

But the provenance of the image suggests something besides race is also at work. In an interview with the *Los Angeles Times*—the news outlet that finally tracked him down—Alkhateeb describes himself as neither a Democrat nor a Republican, and admits that while he didn't vote in November, if he *had* voted it would have been for Ohio's Dennis Kucinich, widely understood as the Democratic primary candidate furthest to the left.[18] In one interview, Alkhateeb expressed ambivalence about the SOCIALISM caption not readily admitted by partisans on the left: "It really doesn't make any sense to me at all," he said. "To accuse him of being a socialist is really ... immature. First of all, who said being a socialist is evil?" For Alkhateeb, it seems, Obama's bait-and-switch was not SOCIALISM at all, but rather the short-lived paucity of CHANGE.

But such attempts to engage the anonymous poster as if it were making some earnest political claim only draw us deeper into its trap. No matter what you throw at it, the poster has but one reply: "Why So Serious?" Like the spectacle of the "tea parties," like the chaotic disruptions at health-care town halls, like Rep. Joe Wilson's unprecedented heckling of the president during a televised address to Congress, like any prank, the poster has no real argumentative content. A prank doesn't *mean* anything; it just disrupts.

The right, it seems, may have learned the lessons of Campaign 2008 better than the left.

There was always something of the Joker's revolutionary mania lurking just beneath Obama's campaign appeals, a schizophrenic drive to scramble the system as it currently exists. And it is only this Utopian impulse towards the ecstasy of disruption that can fuel a successful Obama presidency—whether you call it CHANGE, SOCIALISM, JOKE, or whatever else you like. It is not surprising that Obama's sky-high approval numbers have sharply dipped since his inauguration; it is Obama himself who has returned to Earth as his ambition, his taste for CHANGE, has been tempered by the duties of the office he now holds. There is only one way for Obama to retain his vitality and his creative energy as a political actor—to remain in his own way, if you'll forgive me, Batmanesque. He must let himself dance with the Joker, pushing on and being pushed by the limits of CHANGE. He cannot grow complacent; he will have to, in the Joker's words, let a little chaos in. And to the extent that he cannot, to the extent that *any* person in his position will necessarily become the champion not of change but of continuity, it will be up to those who supported him—those who are psychologically invested in Obama's success but who at the same time want to see the flows at last disrupted and the old codes finally overturned, who want in the end CHANGE (whatever that means)—to reassert their impossible demand for a Utopian break from history, to push the limits, to resist the schemers, to Jokerize themselves in opposition.

Notes

[1] "IMDb: The Dark Knight," Internet Movie Database, http://www.imdb.com/title/tt0468569/faq, Accessed 26 January 26, 2009.
[2] "Box Office Mojo: The Dark Knight," Box Office Mojo, http://www.boxofficemojo.com/movies/?id=darkknight.htm, Accessed 26 January 2009.

[3] Christopher Cooper, "Obama Takes in a Record $150 Million, But McCain Narrows Gap in Some Polls," WSJ.com, 20 October 2008, http://online.wsj.com/article/SB122441294251948009.html?mod=googlenews_ws, Accessed 12 August 2009.

[4] Nico Pitney, "Obama Raises $10 Million After Palin Speech," HuffingtonPost.com, 4 September 2008, http://www.huffingtonpost.com/2008/09/04/obama-raises-8-millionaf_n_124023.html, Accessed 12 August 2009.

[5] David Bauder, "Barack Obama Informercial Ratings: 33.6 Million Watched Across All Networks," HuffingtonPost.com, 30 October 2008, http://www.huffingtonpost.com/2008/10/30/barack-obama-infomerical_n_139263.html Accessed 12 August 2009.

[6] Jose Antonio Vargas, "Obama Raised Half a Billion Online," WashingtonPost.com, 20 November 2009, http://voices.washingtonpost.com/44/2008/11/20/obama_raised_half_a_billion_on.htm, Accessed 26 January 2009.

[7] See, for instance, an interview with Lillis at Lewis Wallace, "Dark Knight Fan Cooks Up 'Audacity of Joke,'" Wired.com, 4 November 2008, http://www.wired.com/underwire/2008/11/dark-knight-fan/, Accessed 5 October 2009.

[8] Richard Reynolds, *Super Heroes: A Modern Mythology,* Jackson: University Press of Mississippi, 1992, 50-52.

[9] See, for instance, Andrew Klaven, "What Bush and Batman Have in Common," WSJ.com, 25 July 2008, http://online.wsj.com/article_print/SB121694247343482821.htm, Accessed 25 July 2008.

[10] Diane Garrett, "Heath Ledger Dies at 28," Variety.com, 22 January 2008, http://www.variety.com/article/VR1117979502.html?categoryid=1236&cs=1, Accessed 12 August 2009.

[11] Joe Neumaier, "Jack Nicholson warned Heath Ledger on 'Joker' role." NewYorkDailyNews.com. 24 January 2008. Last accessed 26 January 2009. <http://www.nydailynews.com/news/2008/01/24/2008-01-24_jack_nicholson_warned_heath_ledger_on_jo.html>
"Jack Nicolson Says He 'Warned' Heath Ledger." FoxNews.com. 24 January 2008. Last accessed 26 January 2009. <http://www.foxnews.com/story/0,2933,325208,00.html>

[12] David Denby, "Past Shock," NewYorker.com, 21 July 2008, http://www.newyorker.com/arts/critics/cinema/2008/07/21/080721crci_cinema_denby, Accessed 12 August 2009.

[13] Gilles Deleuze and Félix Guattari, *Anti-Oedipus,* Trans. Robert Hurley, Mark Seem, and Helen R. Lane, Minneapolis: University of Minnesota Press, 1977, 15.

[14] See Walter Benjamin, "Critique of Violence," Trans. Peter Demetz and Edmund Jephcott, republished in *On Violence: A Reader,* Ed. Bruce B. Lawrence and Aisha Karim, Durham: Duke University Press, 2007: 282-285. "If mythical violence is law-making, divine violence is law-destroying; if the former sets boundaries, the

latter boundlessly destroys them; if mythical violence brings at once guilt and retribution, divine power only expiates; if the former threatens, the latter strikes; if the former is bloody, the latter is lethal without spilling blood."

[15] See Deleuze and Guattari 1977, 34: "What we are really trying to say is that capitalism, through its process of production, produces an awesome schizophrenic accumulation of energy or charge, against which it brings all its vast powers of repression to bear, but which nonetheless continues to act as capitalism's limit."

[16] The original image is still available at http://www.flickr.com/photos/khateeb88/.

[17] Steven Mikulan, "New Anti-Obama 'Joker' Poster," LAWeekly.com, 3 Aug. 2009, http://blogs.laweekly.com/ladaily/politics/new-anti-obama-joker-poster/inde x.php. A followup post on Aug. 13 (http://blogs.laweekly.com/ladaily/community/obama-poster-all-about-race/) contextualizes his claim of racial appeal alongside the various racist email forwards and talk-radio parodies popularized by opponents of Obama since the election. Another early commenter on the image was Jonathan Jerald of BedlamMagazine.com, who notes the image's "malicious, racist, Jim Crow quality." Jonathan Jerald, "Mystery Obama/Joker Poster Appears in L.A.," BedlamMagazine.com, 25 April 2009, http://bedlammagazine.com/06news/mystery-obamajoker-poster-appears-la.

[18] Mark Millian, "Obama Joker artist unmasked: A fellow Chicagoan," LATimes.com, 17 Aug. 2009, http://latimesblogs.latimes.com/washington/2009/08/obama-joker-artist.html.

THE POSTMODERN PRESIDENCY

JOHN FREIE

News reporters, political pundits, and even academics have been puzzled by presidential behavior over the last 30 years. Frustrated by Ronald Reagan's ability to maintain his popularity while pursuing policies a majority of Americans disapproved of, many reluctantly concluded that image has become more important than substance. Puzzled by how Reagan could say one thing and then pursue policies that contradicted what he said, academics have referred to his presidency as a "the Reagan paradox"[1]. Unable to explain how a president who seemed to possess the kind of personality well-suited to the presidency, but who vacillated between effective leadership and uninhibited adolescent behavior, one academic has characterized Bill Clinton as possessing a Zelig-like personality with "a constellation of traits that vary in their ascendancy depending upon the circumstances in which he finds himself".[2] Those less sympathetic attacked Clinton as immoral and corrupt and only became increasingly angry and frustrated when his popularity increased even in the midst of his impeachment trial. Recognizing that this anomaly runs counter to our previous understanding of how citizens evaluate presidents, political scientists have attempted to revise their model of presidential popularity and have cynically concluded that the public has adopted a Machiavellian view of presidential behavior where "morality is irrelevant to the achievement of political results".[3]

Yet, all this pales in comparison to the chorus of criticism that was heaped upon George W. Bush. Tracing the expansion of presidential power throughout history, one recent book claims that the Bush administration has so expanded presidential power that the presidency now threatens democracy.[4] Even less sympathetic, one presidential scholar concluded that Bush's claim of executive authority "is an honest reading of the Constitution only if the reader is standing on his or her head at the time".[5] In their study of unilateral presidential actions, Mayer and Price, while not suggesting that the modern presidency model should be discarded, nonetheless conclude that "students of the American presidency should revise the prevailing view of presidential power".[6]

In a satirical attempt to summarize the foibles of recent presidencies, the *Washington Monthly* gathered a group of political pundits into a pseudo-nominating committee to identify the most serious "fibs, deceptions, and untruths" spoken by the last four presidents. The list was then submitted to another panel of judges composed of other pundits who rated each president to create a "mendacity index" (George W. Bush won, but barely).

Throughout American history politicians have always been accused of being liars, of deceiving others for political gain, or of simply being corrupt. It is, to some extent, a facet of our political culture. Yet, the intensity and depth of hostility from not just the partisan press, but from political opinion leaders and academics seems unprecedented. It is the argument of this article that something more fundamental is occurring other than the personal mendacity or political failures of a series of presidents.

The paradigm that has been used to assess presidential behavior—the modern presidential model (sometimes referred to as the strong presidency)—has failed to adequately explain recent presidencies. Nonetheless, those who watch the presidency continue to employ that outdated model to assess behaviors that, in fact, can best be explained using an alternative model—the postmodern presidency.

The Modern Presidency Paradigm

The dominant paradigm used to explain and evaluate presidential behavior is referred to as the modern presidency. Although its roots can be traced to the presidencies of Theodore Roosevelt and Woodrow Wilson, it is commonly accepted that it came of age during the presidency of Franklin Roosevelt and was most clearly articulated in Richard Neustadt's book *Presidential Power* which was written as a primer for president-elect John F. Kennedy. Over the years, modest changes in the model have been made, but the general framework for explaining presidential behavior remains much as it was outlined by Neustadt.

Following are the key elements of the modern presidency model:

The president activates the system. The modern presidency perspective begins with the belief that the constitutional structure and the nature of the political party system have produced a politics prone to inaction and gridlock. Every place a president turns, his power is checked by competing powers. The danger is not, as some would claim, that government will become too powerful and too oppressive, rather, it is that government will be unable to act decisively to address problems. Government inaction is a greater challenge to democracy than government oppression.

The president should be the initiator of action because he is the only public official who has been elected by the entire nation. The president "creates the issues for each new departure in American politics by his actions and by his perceptions of what is right and wrong".[7] Representing a national constituency, the president uses his power on behalf of everyone. Early formulations of the modern presidential model even went so far as to fuse presidential power with protection of the national interest. As Neustadt somewhat naively put it: "what is good for the country is good for the President, and *vice versa*" [emphasis in original].[8]

Legislative leadership. Legislating is a slow and methodical process, frustrating those who want change and often leads to gridlock. Consequently, the modern president must take an active role in legislative policy formation and set the congressional agenda. "The president has become a driving force within the legislative system....this force works to produce policy output, which is why Congress looks to the president for new initiatives and why it tolerates his influence".[9]

The formal powers of the president assure only that a president will be a clerk. To be successful a president must be a skilled politician who can persuade others to support his initiatives: "A president's job is to get congressmen and other influential members of the government to think his requests are in their own best interests".[10] A modern president must be willing and able to bargain and negotiate with legislators. Whether it is leading through partisan appeals, bipartisanship pleas, twisting arms, making personal appeals, offering pork to obtain votes, or even going over the heads of legislators to appeal to the public to pressure their legislators, a modern president should be an active participant in the legislative process.

Presidential character. Character is associated with a group of traits that have significant social, ethical, and moral qualities. It involves both a mastery and development of the self as well as the extension of the self into society to shape culture. A person with good character is a person who is oriented toward hard work and productivity, is flexible and pragmatic, is adaptive, rational, courageous, and possesses high self-esteem; above all, he or she is a person of integrity. Confident in knowing who he is a president seeks power not to satisfy deeply hidden needs to compensate for his own insecurities, but because the exercise of power makes it possible for him to improve the nation and the world.

The presidency, probably more than any other national political office, is affected by the character of its occupant. White House staffers, politicians themselves, quickly assess the best ways of approaching a president by observing his likes and dislikes, his work habits, and the manner in which he approaches his job, whether he seeks out problems or avoids them, whether a president is active or passive—are all orientations that stem from character and affect the operation of an administration.

The electoral process as a winnowing process. Although the nomination and election processes appear haphazard, messy, and lacking an internal logic, they actually emphasize and reward the skills and talents needed to be a good president. As presidential candidates proceed to collect delegate votes in the caucuses and primaries, the lesser qualified candidates and the ones who fail to create a vision for the country fall by the wayside until only two, one Democrat and one Republican, remain standing. The contest between the Democratic and Republican nominees is the final struggle between two visions of what America should be like at that particular time in history. The campaigns involve significant portions of the electorate resulting in a legitimization of the person who is eventually chosen while providing citizens with a means to express their interests.[11]

Presidential reputation. One of the critical resources a president has is his reputation. Politicians in the "Washington community" keep a keen eye on the president to examine his judgment as he goes about making decisions, looking for patterns of behavior. A president does not have to be concerned his day-to-day performance, but he has every reason for concern about the residual impressions that accumulate in the minds of those who watch him. His political advantages lie in what others think of him; his professional reputation alone will not persuade, but it makes persuasion easier.[12]

The plebiscite president. Early formulations of the modern presidency emphasized the relative stability of public support for the president as presidential decision-making was seen as remote from the lives of Americans. Only when events touched upon the everyday lives of people would opinion shift: "The moving factor in prestige is what men outside Washington see happening to *themselves*" [emphasis in original].[13]

Revisions of the modern presidency have added a plebiscitary character to the model. Kernell documents how presidents have developed strategies of "going public" whereby "a president promotes himself and his policies in Washington by appealing directly to the American public for support",[14] thus putting pressure on members of Congress to cooperate with presidential initiatives. Constrained by weak political parties and structural barriers which create checks on presidential actions, presidents have used the modern mass media to forge direct links with the public and, by doing so, build legitimacy and political capital.[15]

This model has been used to explain, predict, and even justify presidential behavior. Presidents themselves often believe that their actions can be justified because they are linked to the assumptions of the model. Yet, its ability to adequately account for behavior is increasingly falling short of providing satisfying explanations of presidential behavior.

An Emerging Postmodern Critique

Over the last three decades scholars from a wide range of disciplines have articulated a postmodern vision and at least one has claimed that present-day America is the ideal of postmodernity.[16] Indeed, the scope of postmodern analysis has extended to art, architecture, literature, economics, philosophy, religion, technology, social criticism, psychology, but ever so reluctantly to political science, particularly to analyses of contemporary politics.

While it seems obvious to even the most casual observer that politics today is much different from politics in the past, postmodern analyses of the American presidency have been rare.[17] Presidential scholars in particular have made only very modest forays into using postmodernism to explain presidential behavior. Of the few, only two have argued that recent changes are so fundamental as to constitute paradigmatic change.[18] Neither have been well-received and presidential scholars remain unconvinced that postmodern structural changes have occurred.

An equally modest, but more accepted, body of literature analyzes presidential personality and rhetoric from a postmodern perspective. As might be expected, this research has focused on President Bill Clinton. In what is perhaps the most influential research yet on the postmodern presidency, Bruce Miroff describes Bill Clinton as a man with a shape-shifting personality who possessed no core moral values and governed through the use of symbols, gestures, and rhetoric rather than substance. Following the advice of his political advisor Dick Morris, "Clinton became increasingly adept at dominating the terms of political debate, demonizing his political enemies, and reinventing his own political personae. He was increasingly expert at pleasing the public with his shifting stances on issues large and small and at impressing the public with the skill of his performance on the job".[19]

The work of Parry-Giles and Parry-Giles also focuses on Bill Clinton. Recognizing a new era of postmodern American politics they refer to as "hyperreality," they claim that Bill Clinton was able to navigate difficult waters because he used the art of image-making to throw off his political opponents and garner public support. They focus not on the personality of Clinton, but on the construction of the images that he created and their consequences. For Parry-Giles and Parry-Giles Bill Clinton is the harbinger of a new form of postmodern presidential politics where hyperreal images dominate the political landscape.

The Transition to Postmodernism

Since postmodernism contains elements of both the modern as well as the postmodern, it is difficult to determine exactly when and where the modern paradigm ends and the postmodern begins. Indeed, no clear line representing such a change exists. Although some have traced threads of the postmodern presidency as far back as Nixon,[20] this study starts with Reagan because it was his presidency that first realized the power of the image—one of the most fundamental aspects of the postmodern presidency.

In what has become a classic story in the world of image manipulation then CBS correspondent for "60 Minutes" Leslie Stahl often tells audiences of the time in 1984 when the program decided to challenge the Reagan administration on the disjunction between its policy actions and the re-election campaign it was conducting. In an unusually long report (almost 8 minutes) Stahl narrated an expose which showed pictures of Reagan visiting homeless shelters, glad-handing African-Americans, and interacting with school children. While these images were presented, a voice-over attacked Reagan for reducing funding to homeless shelters, opposing affirmative action, and making massive cuts in school funding. As anticipated, the next day she received phone calls from White House staffers. To her surprise however, they called not to criticize her, but to thank her. "What!" she exclaimed. "I spent eight minutes on prime time television attacking you. Why are you thanking me?" She then learned a lesson in image manipulation. One staffer told her that people don't *listen* to the news, they *watch* it and she had provided the White House with "golden images" which they couldn't have produced better had they done it themselves. This story captures the major theme of the Reagan administration: pursue a consistent ideologically conservative policy while projecting favorable images of the president in a variety of settings.

Although the George H. W. Bush presidency followed the Reagan presidency chronologically, Bush's behavior once in office was more in the mold of the modern presidency. Where Bush's behavior was consistent with postmodernity, however, was in his first campaign in 1988. Wanting to desperately win, he took advice from a cadre of advisors honed in postmodern politics. Bush emphasized image over issues, developed a symbolic theme of "1000 points of light," promised that he would not raise taxes ("read my lips, no new taxes"), and viciously attacked his opponent as an unpatriotic supporter of criminals.

During his four years in office, however, Bush behaved more like a modern, than a postmodern president. He was comfortable using bargaining, negotiation, and persuasion tactics behind closed doors, rather than building and appealing to the public for support. Not fully appreciating the new form of politics that was engulfing Washington, Bush made a crucial tactical error in 1990 by compromising with Democrats who controlled Congress to produce what he believed was a responsible budget, even though it resulted in tax increases which violated his no new taxes campaign promise. While in some respects Bush demonstrated responsible, even courageous, leadership by compromising with a hostile, Democratic Congress, he was unable (or unwilling) to manage public expectations and experienced one of the largest reversals of public approval of any president. He failed to advance the postmodern presidency not so much because of the nature of the times, but rather because of his own political inclinations and a personality that was poorly suited for the postmodern political environment.

Clinton, taking his cues more from the Reagan presidency than the Bush presidency, expanded the postmodern presidency. More attuned to the public nature of the presidency, he embraced the idea of the permanent campaign—the idea that effective governance was tied to maintaining high popularity on an almost daily basis. As postmodern guru Dick Morris advised Clinton: "Today, a politician does not just need public support to win elections, he needs it to govern".[21] In order to curry support among the public Clinton embarked on an ambitious campaign of, in the words of Samuel Kernell, "going public."[22] Realizing that the Washington media were far too cynical, Clinton spent a considerable amount time outside of Washington giving small, targeted speeches and making appearances throughout the country. Local reporters, flattered by being able to actually meet a president, were far more likely to provide favorable coverage than were the "cynical establishment media."

Clinton advanced the postmodern presidency in other ways as well. Still focused on policy in the vein of modern presidents, Clinton, however, viewed policy far differently. Over the years, presidents who have had such broad, national visions have packaged their policies into comprehensive programs linked by a defining theme such as the New Deal, the Fair Deal, the New Frontier, or the Great Society. But, in postmodernity broad, comprehensive visions are problematic. Instead, the postmodern president advocates narrow micro-policies ("small-bore" issues) targeted at niche constituencies. "[T]he era of *the big issue* has left us. It went the way of big government. No overarching ideological redesign of our basic economic, social, or tax systems is going to galvanize today's voters" [emphasis in original].[23]

In order to determine which policies to support the Clinton administration subjected them to the "60 percent rule." If, according to public opinion polling, 60 percent of the American people supported a policy, so too would Clinton.[24] Morris explains how this process worked in the Clinton White House: "It has been Clinton's great strength that his endlessly fertile mind is constantly inventing new alternative programs to reach his goals and quickly grasps the possible arguments for and against each idea. He briefs his pollsters for hours on the options he wants them to probe. A good pollster then tests each specific alternative, examining the arguments for and against to measure public support".[25] Policies and issues were not things to be avoided; indeed, they were embraced as a way of revealing presidential character and establishing an emotional connection with the citizenry. Clinton advanced the postmodern presidency by realizing that support can be obtained by linking policies to citizens by appealing to their emotions rather than their intellect, much as Reagan had done.[26]

"Small-bore" policies were pursued not only because of their public appeal, but also because a new postmodern vision of the role of government was emerging. For the modern president the role of the government was to identify problems, initiate policy to address those problems, and then create a bureaucracy which would implement the solutions. But the reality of the administrative state changed in the postmodern age. Today's challenges occur amongst a political environment characterized by decentralization, diffusion, dispersion, and fragmentation of authority and responsibility. Responsibility and authority moves upward, downward, and horizontally through private, public, and nonprofit organizations. The Clinton administration recognized these changes and attempted to redefine the federal government in the role of "facilitator" to bring together a variety of groups to solve problems on narrowly focused issues in an initiative called the reinvention of government headed up by Vice President Al Gore.

The Bush Presidency: A Maturing Postmodernism

Although Bill Clinton advanced the postmodern presidency from its early beginnings in the Reagan White House, it fell to the George W. Bush administration to implement a more fully developed postmodern model. To a large extent Bush's postmodern orientation is summed up in a quote of a senior White House aide who put a *New York Times* reporter in his place with the following: "We're an empire now, and when we act, we create our own reality. And while you're studying that reality—judiciously, as you will—we'll act again, creating other new realities, which you can study too, and that's how things will sort out". It is this fundamental postmodern orientation—that reality is malleable and can be created and recreated—that has allowed the Bush presidency to become the embodiment of the postmodern presidency. Building upon the public relations advances of the Reagan White House and the extension of public relations into the policy arena innovated by Clinton, the Bush presidency has revealed additional dimensions of the postmodern presidency.

The George W. Bush presidency pushed the presidency even further in the direction of the postmodern presidency by building popular support and, at the same time, expanding power through unilateral actions. Both were trends begun under earlier presidents. Bush not only built upon those precedents, but he more fully integrated them into the day-to-day operation of the White House and, in the process, developed a more coherent (though more controversial) view of presidential power.

Early in his presidency George W. Bush embraced Reagan and Clinton's strategy of going public to obtain political support. In his first three years in office Bush shattered all previous presidential records in terms of the number of public appearances he made outside of Washington, easily surpassing the record set by his predecessor Clinton. Although claiming that his presidency would not imitate the Clinton presidency, Bush learned early on that maintaining public approval was a resource critical for presidential action. While such a belief could be viewed as part of the modern presidency model, Bush added a new wrinkle which pushed the presidency more into the realm of postmodernism.

For the modern presidency, public support is maintained in order to obtain political pressure to influence other political actors (most commonly members of Congress). But the Bush administration *fully* integrated public opinion into the policy making process, not just at the time when other political actors might be pressured to accept the policy. In the modern presidency model policy making is created in the executive branch—through complex interactions between the White House staff and the bureaucracy—and through interaction and input from advisors outside of government and members of Congress. After the broad outlines of the policy are forged, questions about how to build support for the policies become the focus. But the postmodern president injects public opinion concerns into the policy making process from the very start. In the Bush administration this was accomplished with the creation of the Office of Strategic Initiatives headed by Karl Rove. Political consultants and pollsters were included in initial policy meetings and their advice was sought before policy discussions even began. In this way, developing a strategy for the selling of policies became an integral element of the policy process itself.

The second area where the Bush administration advanced the postmodern presidency was in the expansion of unilateral action. Although prior presidents have often taken unilateral action to achieve specific, targeted objectives, the George W. Bush administration expanded the use of unilateral actions in unprecedented ways. Through the use of executive orders, signing statements, extraordinary renditions, and the cloak of secrecy the Bush administration has expanded the power of the presidency arguably beyond Constitutional bounds, creating a new vision of presidential power called the unitary executive theory. This questionable theory of presidential power claimed that the president was the ultimate and final authority in the operation of the executive branch and that his actions were nonreviewable by other branches of government.[27]

An additional area of unilateral action during the Bush administration was the attempt to politicize the bureaucracy. All presidents have had difficulty controlling the bureaucracy and indeed, there is reason to believe that aspects of the bureaucracy were, in fact, designed to thwart presidential control. Postmodern presidents, even more than modern presidents, have sought to exert political control over the bureaucracy. Bush pursued this strategy in two ways: first, by relying on the White House and Executive Offices to develop and oversee policy initiatives, and second, by expanding the use of partisan political appointments within departments to obtain bureaucratic responsiveness.[28]

The Postmodern Presidency Paradigm

As is often the case with the presidency, precedent sets the tone for future presidential behavior. Since the Reagan presidency, the precedents that have been most compelling have been those that have pushed the presidency in the postmodern direction. This has happened to such an extent that the modern presidential paradigm has been distorted beyond recognition. This becomes obvious when scholars attempt to employ the modern paradigm to explain presidential behavior. It is only by shifting the paradigm that we can understand presidential behavior in the 21st Century. What is described below is a shift in the assumptions and beliefs that guide presidential behavior, not merely a reflection of particular personalities who have occupied the office.

A key element of the postmodern presidency is the president's relationship to the American people. Postmodern presidents cultivate public support on a daily basis and strategies to obtain public support are fully integrated into the workings of the policy process. Narrow, "small-bore" issues which emotionally appeal to niche voters are identified and government resources are employed in an effort to facilitate solutions. The issues selected are chosen on the basis of how well they lend themselves to the strategic use of spectacle as well as their public opinion payoff. At the same time, policy initiatives that can be achieved through the use of unilateral action are pursued. Less visible, unilateral actions allow the president to define the policy agenda and often achieve more controversial objectives.

The specific elements of the postmodern presidential model include the following:

The president activates the system with unilateral action. Like the modern president, the postmodern president is seen as the primary political actor on the national stage. With the increasing polarization of national politics the political system is even more fragmented, checked, and decentralized than the modern analysis claims. Special interests have increased in influence and power and American public opinion has become increasingly concerned with narrow interests rather than the common good. Congress, a decentralized body by creation, has become dramatically more decentralized as seniority rules have been undermined, representatives have become more interested in constituent service, and an overall democratization, and hence fragmentation, of Congress has occurred. In this environment it has become even more imperative that presidential action occurs.

Yet, the president's ability to bargain and negotiate with other political actors has become increasingly difficult. Politicians have become more ideological and more subject to direct (with the Internet almost immediate) citizen influence. As the transparency of legislative actions has occurred and as citizen mobilization has increased, political actors have less flexibility to negotiate behind closed doors. At the same time, presidents enter office having made substantial campaign promises. The pressure to act, and to act quickly and decisively, often results in the use of unilateral action to set the political agenda.

While Neustadt claimed that presidents who resort to command are indications of failure, the postmodern president sees unilateral action (sometimes command) as, at times, an effective political strategy. Recent presidents have increased their use of national security directives (policies that are not made public), have embarked upon literally hundreds of military actions without congressional authorization, have liberally made use of use of presidential signings, have participated in extraordinary renditions of terrorism suspects to other countries to be tortured, have issued a large number of "significant" executive orders,[29] and have operated under a veil of secrecy. Many of these actions have been designed to circumvent, rather than negotiate, with Congress.[30]

The postmodern president does not totally reject the modern perspective that other political actors should be negotiated with, and because of that there is a tendency to believe that the modern model is still operative. However, postmodern presidents are far more willing to employ direct action when negotiation falters and are far more willing to strategically position themselves for the use of unilateral action in the future. What's more, much of that unilateral action is "hidden" from public view in the form of executive agreements, presidential signing statements, and the like which are seldom reported by the media.

Legislative leadership/issues. Modern presidents pursued comprehensive legislative agendas to address a host of social problems (e.g., the New Deal, the New Frontier, the Great Society). Such approaches are no longer feasible in the fragmented postmodern political environment. "Just as the era of big government is dead, for now, the era of the big issue is over as well. Any big new idea is sure to be picked apart by the special interests".[31] Although issues are critical for the postmodern president, "big" ideas run counter to the postmodern vision of a fragmented public.

Postmodern presidents (and in the presidential campaign, postmodern candidates) select issues to pursue for two reasons. First, issue positions are short-cuts to reveal one's personality and values. Issues are important for the citizenry not because they are necessarily "real" problems that they are dealing with, but because the issues reveal something about the president's values and philosophy. If those values emotionally "connect" with citizens, the president will obtain support. "Issues become a form of symbolic speech, an opportunity to speak to a candidate's character and attributes".[32] But even more, it is not so much the position that a postmodern president takes that is the crucial factor. Instead, the position must be presented is such a manner that it activates positive emotions.

"Politics *are* related to voting, but not directly. Policies matter *to the extent that they influence voters' emotions*" [emphasis in original].[33]

Second, the issues selected are determined not so much on the basis of the needs of the citizenry, as they are determined by an empirical assessment of their support with narrowly target publics—niche audiences—usually determined through polling. Polling is used extensively to determine the issues, but perhaps more importantly, to determine the manner in which the issues are presented to the demographic that is interested in the issue. Postmodern presidents are continually concerned about maintaining at least majority support on an almost daily basis: "a politician does not just need public support to win elections; he needs it to govern. . . . When he dips below 50 percent, he is functionally out of office".[34] To do this the postmodern president patches together a pastiche of small-bore issues designed to obtain support from niche groups.

Public support. Modern presidents have made use of public support to put pressure on political actors in order to obtain concessions. Still arguing within the modern president paradigm, Kernell refers to this as "going public"—going directly to the American people to encourage them to contact their representatives to support or oppose specific policy initiatives. Postmodern presidents rarely employ such a strategy. Instead, conducting a public relations campaign about policy issues has become fully integrated into the president's efforts to create policy. It is not unusual for postmodern presidents to attempt to shape public opinion as an *initial* step in the policy process in an effort to shape, rather than mobilize, opinion. This is in contrast to the modern president who was warned by Samuel Kernell to carefully weigh when to go public: "When presidents adopt intensive public relations as their leadership strategy they render bargaining increasingly difficult. The decision to go public at one juncture may preclude and undermine the opportunity to bargain at another, and vice versa".[35] In contrast, postmodern presidents go public on a regular basis.

Presidents no longer feel an obligation to work *with* Congress. For a postmodern president, the check that is more important than Congress (or even the Constitution) is public opinion. If a president can shape public opinion he can feel comfortable pursuing policy initiatives even in the face of congressional opposition. George W. Bush embraced this strategy: "Bush is hardly the first president to do an end run of Congress in an attempt to build public support for his programs. But his administration may be the first to make modern campaign tactics—stump speeches, political ads, email bursts, war rooms—into a routine part of the legislative process, and a higher priority than cultivating disaffected rank-and-file legislators".[36]

Spectacles. The postmodern president attempts to build support by establishing emotionally linkages with the public through the use of symbols which tap into deeply held beliefs. This is most effectively done by staging spectacles. "[T]he most distinctive characteristic of a spectacle is that the actions that constitute it are meaningful not for what they achieve, but for what they signify. Actions in a spectacle are gestures rather than means to an end".[37]

Because the emphasis of the postmodern president is on spectacle rather than reasoned discussion and debate, postmodern presidents have employed those who possess expertise in television and the entertainment industry. Spectacles are staged performances with the president in the starring role surrounded by aides who help produce the performance— write the script, design the stage, create the props, direct the action, etc. The media become, at best, theater critics, and at worse merely broadcasters of the performance, and the citizenry plays the role of the passive audience. If the spectacles are compelling they will be widely broadcast and the president will enjoy public support; if they are poorly done, reporters will criticize the president for not being a leader or not having a vision. To successfully perform this task a president must be a skilled actor.

Presidential personality. Ideally, a president operating in a postmodern environment possesses a personality that is compatible with the dictates of this new environment. An effective postmodern president must posses the ability to appear to be one thing to one audience and another thing to a different audience, without appearing to be contradictory to either. Miroff claimed that the personality characteristics of such a person would be a person who "lacks a stable identity associated with ideological and partisan values and who is, thereby, free to move nimbly from one position to another as political fashion dictates".[38] Without disagreeing with Miroff, other personality types—those who can become detached from the action—might also be effective.

The neoadministrative presidency. While, on the one hand, the postmodern president employs unilateral action, at the same time, such actions are of only limited effectiveness. This is because of a fundamental change in the nature of the administrative state. This evolution is referred to as the "neoadministrative state".[39] It is characterized by a growing executive branch no longer capable of making or implementing policy. "Rather, these agencies arrange, coordinate and monitor networks of public, private, and nonprofit organizations that pursue these things with or for them. In turn, these complex, nonhierarchical, and loosely coupled networks operate within ever-expanding discretionary bounds, with federal agencies able to affect their structures, budget, personnel decisions, priorities, and decisions rules only marginally".[40] Yet, most postmodern presidents have failed to attempt the kind of fundamental change necessary to address this challenge. Under pressure to create solutions quickly, presidents have, at best, developed symbolic responses to this postmodern problem. This remains an area to be addresses by future postmodern presidents.

Conclusion

On November 24, 2008 *Time* magazine's cover presented a picture of the face of recently elected Barack Obama on the body of Franklin Roosevelt seated in an unmistakable FDR-like pose in a car riding in a motorcade. In typical postmodern image-making fashion one did not have to read the inside story to understand the meaning of the message—Barack Obama had an opportunity to be the next transformative Democratic president and reinvigorate liberalism. But for our purposes it probably would have been more appropriate to place Obama's head on the body of Ronald Reagan, for it was the transformation of the presidency by Reagan that made the Obama presidency possible.

Obama ran a campaign of image over substance by convincing voters that he was the candidate of change and McCain was aligned with Bush, he was "McSame." However, what specific issues president Obama would embrace and what particular policies he would pursue remained vague even after a campaign that lasted almost two years. While our analysis cannot predict the particular ideological direction Obama will take, the manner in which he behaves is more predictable. President Obama will rely on spectacles to connect with the public, will employ symbols that tap into deeply held American beliefs, and he will dominate the national political stage. He will make extensive use of unilateral actions in policy areas of greatest importance to him—on military decisions about the wars in Iraq and Afghanistan, on the economy, and on actions that bear directly on niche groups critical for his re-election political coalition.

But the larger questions about the postmodern presidency relate to the extent to which these developments enhance or undermine democracy. As evidenced by past presidents, the potential for manipulation of the public is great. Yet, postmodernism also offers the possibility of opening new avenues for citizen activity. It remains to be seen which direction the postmodern presidency will lead us.

Notes

[1] Bell, Coral. 1989. *The Reagan Paradox: US Foreign Policy in the 1980s.* New Brunswick: Rutgers University Press.

[2] Greenstein, Fred I. 1998. "There He Goes Again: The Alternating Political Style of Bill Clinton," *PS: Political Science and Politics*, Vol. 31: 178-181, 178.

[3] Harvey, Dianne Hollern. 2000. "The Public's View of Clinton," in *The Postmodern Presidency: Bill Clinton's Legacy in U. S. Politics*, ed. Steven E. Schier. Pittsburgh: University of Pittsburgh Press, 124 -142, 142.

[4] Genovese, Michael A. and Lori Cox Han (eds). 2006. *The Presidency and the Challenge of Democracy.* New York: Palgrave Macmillan.

[5] Spitzer, Robert J. 2006. "The Commander in Chief Power and Constitutional Invention in the Bush Administration," in *The Presidency and the Challenge of Democracy*, eds. Michael A. Genovese and Lori Cox Han. New York: Palgrave Macmillan, 115.

[6] Mayer, Kenneth R. and Kevin Price. 2002. "Unilateral Presidential Powers: Significant Executive Orders, 1949-99." *Presidential Studies Quarterly* 32: 367-386, 380.

[7] White Theodore H. 1962. *The Making of the President 1960.* New York: Pocket Books, 436.

[8] Neustadt, Richard E. 1980. *Presidential Power: The Politics of Leadership From FDR to Carter.* John Wiley & Sons: New York, 136.

[9] Wayne, Stephen J. 1978. *The Legislative Presidency.* New York: Harper & Row, 23.

[10] Cronin, Thomas E. 1979. "Presidential Power Revised and Reappraised," *The Western Political Quarterly,* Vol. 32: 381-395, 383.

[11] Pomper, Gerald M. 1975. *Elections in America: Control and Influence in Democratic Politics.* New York: Dodd, Mead & Company.

[12] Neustadt, Richard E. 1980. *Presidential Power: The Politics of Leadership From FDR to Carter.* John Wiley & Sons: New York.

[13] *Ibid.*, 73.

[14] Kernell, Samuel. 2007. *Going Public: New Strategies of Presidential Leadership.* 4th ed. Washington, D. C.: CQ Press, 1-2.

[15] Rimmerman, Craig A. 1993. *Presidency by Plebiscite: The Reagan-Bush Era in Institutional Perspective.* Boulder: Westview Press.

[16] Baudrillard, Jean. 1988. *America.* Trans. Chris Turner. London: Verso.

[17] Fontaine, Juston K. 2003. "Beyond the Modern Era?: An Analysis of the Concept of the Postmodern Presidency." Master of Arts thesis. Virginia Polytechnic Institute.

[18] Barilleaux, Ryan. 1988. *The Post-Modern President: The Office After Ronald Reagan.* New York: Praeger and Rose, Richard. 1991. *The Postmodern President.* 2nd. Ed. Chatham, N.J.: Chatham House Publishers.

[19] Miroff, Bruce. 2000. "Courting the Public: Bill Clinton's Postmodern Education," in *The Postmodern Presidency: Bill Clinton's Legacy in U. S. Politics*, ed. Steven E. Schier. Pittsburgh: University of Pittsburgh Press, pp. 106-123, 120.

[20] Cammarano, Joe. 2009. "From Substance to Symbol: Head Start and the Change From Modern to Postmodern Presidents," paper presented at the 2009 meeting of the American Political Science Association conference, Toronto, Canada.

[21] Morris, Dick. 1999. *The New Prince*. Los Angeles: Renaissance Books, 71.

[22] Kernell, Samuel. 2007. *Going Public: New Strategies of Presidential Leadership.* 4th ed. Washington, D. C.: CQ Press.

[23] Morris, Dick. 1999. *The New Prince*. Los Angeles: Renaissance Books, 58.

[24] Stephanopolous, George. 2000. *All Too Human: A Political Education*. Boston: Back Bay Books.

[25] Morris, Dick. 1999. *The New Prince*. Los Angeles: Renaissance Books, 84.

[26] Westen, Drew. 2007. *The Political Brain: The Role of Emotion in Deciding the Fate of the Nation.* New York: Public Affairs.

[27] Spitzer, Robert J. 2006. "The Commander in Chief Power and Constitutional Invention in the Bush Administration," in *The Presidency and the Challenge of Democracy*, eds. Michael A. Genovese and Lori Cox Han. New York: Palgrave Macmillan, pp. 93-117.

[28] Campbell, Colin. 2006. "Presidents, Prime Ministers, and the Civil Service, in *The Presidency and the Political System,* ed. Michael Nelson. Washington, D.C.: CQ Press, pp. 430-454.

[29] Howell, William G. 2003. *Power without Persuasion: The Politics of Direct Presidential Action.* Princeton, New Jersey: Princeton University Press.

[30] Deering, Christopher J. and Forrest Maltzman. 1999. "The Politics of Executive Orders: Legislative Constraints on Presidential Power," *Political Research Quarterly*, Vol. 52, pp. 7676-783.

[31] Morris, Dick. 1999. *The New Prince*. Los Angeles: Renaissance Books, 179.

[32] *Ibid*, 176-177.

[33] Westen, Drew. 2007. *The Political Brain: The Role of Emotion in Deciding the Fate of the Nation.* New York: Public Affairs, 120.

[34] Morris, Dick. 1999. *The New Prince*. Los Angeles: Renaissance Books, 71.

[35] Kernell, Samuel. 2007. *Going Public: New Strategies of Presidential Leadership.* 4th ed. Washington, D. C.: CQ Press, 4-5.

[36] Wilner, Elizabeth. 2005. "This President Hits the Road, Not the Phones," *The Washington Post* (May 29), p. B1.

[37] Miroff, Bruce. 2006. "The Presidential Spectacle," in *The Presidency and the Political System,* ed. Michael Nelson. Washington, D.C.: CQ Press, pp. 255-282, 247.

[38] Miroff, Bruce. 2000. "Courting the Public: Bill Clinton's Postmodern Education," in *The Postmodern Presidency: Bill Clinton's Legacy in U. S. Politics*, ed. Steven E. Schier. Pittsburgh: University of Pittsburgh Press, pp. 106-123, 106.

[39] Durant, Robert F. 1998. "Agenda Setting, the 'Third Wave,' and the Administrative State," *Administration & Society* 30: 211-247.

---

[40] Durant, Robert F. and Adam L. Warber. 2001. "Networking in the Shadow of Hierarchy: Public Policy, the Administrative Presidency, and the Neoadministrative State," *Presidential Studies Quarterly* 31: 221-244, 222.

LOST IN AMERICA:
IN SEARCH OF A SOCIAL CONTRACT[1]

SCOTT MCDERMOTT

When Oceanic Flight 815 crashed on a mysterious island, its survivors sought only to find rescue. But in the early episode of *Lost* called "Tabula Rasa," some characters began to grasp the possibilities the island held out to them. "Tabula Rasa," of course, recalls John Locke's theory that the mind is a blank slate which can reason its way to moral knowledge only through experience. But in the context of the show, *tabula rasa* suggests that all the characters have been given a fresh start. "Three days ago we all died," Dr. Jack Shephard told Kate Austen. "We should all be able to start over." But another castaway, Sawyer, realized the situation even more completely. Caught looting the plane's fuselage, Sawyer informed Jack, "I'm in the wild."[2]

Sawyer understood that the crash survivors had been suddenly thrust into a state of nature, a crucial concept of enlightenment political philosophy. And Americans have been there before. In September 1774, Patrick Henry told the First Continental Congress that "Government is dissolved....We are in a state of nature, sir."[3] So the Founding Fathers did as enlightened philosophy taught them. They formed a new social contract based on the "Laws of Nature and of Nature's God," as the Declaration of Independence put it. Congressional delegate Oliver Wolcott hoped that the American Revolution would provide "a Government founded in Compact, Express and Clear."[4] John Adams later wrote that the American polities were "perhaps, the first example of governments erected on the simple principles of nature."[5]

Lost presents citizens of the American global empire, struggling to maintain civilization by creating a new social contract. The names of the island's residents – John Locke, Danielle Rousseau, Desmond David Hume, and Juliet Burke – indicate *Lost*'s debt to enlightened political philosophy. But have the show's creators simply tossed in these names as a red herring? This reading of *Lost* will make sense of its allusions to enlightenment political thought. The show's enlightenment references are more than simply random memories of Government 111; in fact, *Lost* reveals a highly sophisticated grasp of enlightened ideas. Each character who bears the name of an enlightened *philosophe* brings that thinker's ideas into the project of constructing a new social contract. As these ideas play out, however, the contradictions and deficiencies of enlightenment thought become manifest. Nevertheless, we can also discern which enlightened ideas may prove useful to the survivors as they cobble together a social contract suitable for the postmodern world.

The Enlightenment Political Theory

Enlightened thinkers, and the American Founding Fathers, operated within the same framework of political concepts derived ultimately from the Middle Ages. Prior to society, people lived in a state of nature. They were governed only by God's laws of nature, which gave each individual executive power to defend his natural rights. At some point, they agreed to form a social contract and establish government. They ceded their political prerogatives to a sovereign power in return for security. The sovereign, however, was obliged to respect natural law and natural rights. Any sovereign who commanded his subjects to violate natural rights became a tyrant. This meant he abdicated sovereignty, which returned to the people, who could depose the sovereign, exercising the right of resistance. In the ensuing vacuum of legitimate authority, the people had to establish a new contract of government. They acted as a second cause on behalf of God, the First Cause, who legitimized the new regime. In turn, the new sovereign had to obey God's natural laws and honor natural rights. Although each nation had a social contract, there was no international social contract. Rather, each nation was in a state of nature relative to all others. Just war theory explains how nations can defend themselves according to the law of nature.

Even as they retained this conceptual model, enlightened thinkers tended to emphasize certain elements at the expense of others, distorting the overall picture. Liberals like John Locke placed the accent on natural rights, especially the right to property, at the expense of the common good. Others like Jean-Jacques Rousseau promoted the "general will" or state power to the detriment of personal rights. Not all enlightened philosophers retained the idea of a personal Divine Lawgiver. The Anglo-American enlightenment which the Founding Fathers inherited, however, was both liberal and theistic. In the Declaration's deposition of George III and the Constitution's creation of a new government, we see the broad outlines, still intact, of the enlightened political consensus.

Yet today's Americans, to the extent they are aware of their social contract at all, wonder how relevant it is to postmodern conditions. *Lost* depicts Americans' anxious exploration of critical political questions. Have globalism and pluralism eroded the basis for our social contract? Have we reverted to a state of nature, with no consensus on social ethics? Is it possible or desirable to establish a new social contract – or are these enlightenment terms simply antiquated and meaningless? Have we lost our national soul because of the moral compromises involved in the "war on terror" or because of "life issues"? And to what extent must any reconstruction of society involve an encounter with the divine?

John Locke

Jack Shephard, the "man of science" who emerged as the castaways' leader in season one, evaded the question of the divine. Refusing the role of the island's spiritual leader, Jack based his call for social reorganization on pragmatic concerns. "It's time to start organizing. We need to figure out how we're going to survive here....If we can't live together, we're gonna die alone."[6] But the islanders soon realized that the spiritual world could not be ignored. They encountered mystical manifestations, especially the baffling "smoke monster." This apparition initially called to mind the pillar of cloud that guided the Hebrews during the Exodus. But if the smoke was a theophany of some sort, it clearly represented a punitive concept of God. The smoke monster killed the unrepentant Mr. Eko[7] and defeated Martin Keamy's "freighter folk" commandos.[8]

Only one survivor, John Locke, had a vital connection with the smoke theophany. Encountering it for the first time, John told Jack that "I've looked into the eye of this island, and what I saw was beautiful."[9] Shortly before Eko's demise, John reported that "I saw [in the black cloud] a very bright light. It was beautiful."[10] Because of his special link with the island's fearsome avenger, John became the show's proverbial "man of faith." This is in keeping with the most advanced scholarship on the historical John Locke. [In order to avoid confusion, I will refer to the philosophers by their surnames, and the characters by their first names. So the philosopher John Locke will be Locke, and the character who shares his name will be called John.] Jeremy Waldron has underlined the centrality of a personal Divine Lawgiver to Locke's theory of natural rights.[11] Recent scholars like Richard Tuck and Mark Goldie have emphasized Locke's commitment to the idea of God as an essentially punitive being, enforcing the natural law against offenders.[12] This "authoritarian element"[13] in Locke has frequently surfaced in the character

John. In season four John declared, "You may think this is a democracy, Kate, because of the way Jack ran things. But this is not a democracy." He then informed Miles, "I learned something yesterday. No use having rules if there's no punishment for breaking them."[14] Compare Locke's statement that "there is no law without a lawmaker, and law is to no purpose without punishment."[15]

Current scholarship also exposes other aspects of Locke's thought which undermine his progressive credentials. Locke helped draft the "Fundamental Constitutions of Carolina," which set up a decidedly feudal scheme of government, run by potentates called "landgraves" and "caciques." Locke himself became the first landgrave of Carolina. The Constitutions gave Carolina's feudal proprietors absolute power over their slaves, while Locke himself favored punitive action against Indians who killed whites, in keeping with just war theory.[16] For a long time historians saw Locke's involvement in the Carolina experiment as an aberration which had no effect on Locke's mature political theory, as found in the *Second Treatise of Government.* But David Armitage has shown that Locke was writing the *Second Treatise* in 1682 while still amending the Fundamental Constitutions.[17] The *Treatise* reflects Locke's American adventure in several examples drawn from the colonial experience and in his famous remark that "in the beginning all the world was America"[18] – that is, a state of nature. Locke's "labor theory of value" justified settlers' appropriation of "unused" Indian land by mixing their labor with it. Settlers could then defend their right to this newfound property by force.[19] Sawyer's aggressive appropriation of unclaimed goods in the plane wreckage epitomizes the labor theory of value. Sawyer declares, "it was mine when I took it."[20]

Locke's theories of a punitive God and an assertive right to property are problematic, therefore, for the island's inhabitants – indeed, much more problematic since the identity of the "smoke monster" as the sinister "man in black" has been revealed. Nevertheless, only Locke's insistence on a personal Divine Lawgiver can account for the island's intense spiritual atmosphere. This suggests that Locke's philosophy may yet play an indispensable role in the reconstruction of society on the island.

Anthony Cooper

But John's backstory complicates his relationship to any Father-God. Most of the characters have "daddy issues,"[21] but John's are extreme – his father pushed him out of an eighth-story window, rendering John paraplegic.[22] The island cured John's legs, but the "tabula rasa" is far from completely blank. John is haunted by memories of his father, Anthony Cooper. This name offers one of *Lost's* most obscure and significant enlightenment allusions. The first earl of Shaftesbury, a political leader of Locke's era, and the third earl, an enlightened eighteenth-century philosopher, were both named Anthony Ashley Cooper. Indeed, John Locke was intimately connected with both Shaftesburys. Locke served the elder Shaftesbury as secretary, beginning in 1667, and later tutored the earl's grandson, the future philosopher. The first Shaftesbury got Locke involved in Carolina.[23] Locke, also Shaftesbury's physician, operated on the earl's liver.[24] This found an echo on *Lost* when Anthony swindled John into donating a kidney to save his life.[25] If John Locke wrote his *Treatises* to refute the paternalistic philosophy of Robert Filmer's *Patriarcha*, then the character of Anthony Cooper represents the return of repressed patriarchal authority in Locke's thought.

Making Anthony Cooper John's father is doubly ironic, however, because the philosopher Shaftesbury rejected Locke's idea of a punitive Divine lawgiver. He saw the idea of future rewards and punishments as a base and selfish motive for doing good works. Rather, Shaftesbury emphasized natural human benevolence and sociability. He originated the concept of a "moral sense," the intuitive feeling that something is morally right.[26] By bestowing Shaftesbury's name on their least moral and benevolent character, Anthony Cooper, *Lost's* creators seem to ridicule the idea of basing morality on feelings. But Anthony's name becomes more appropriate when we consider Shaftesbury's major theoretical innovation, the assimilation of morality to aesthetics.[27] For Anthony Ashley Cooper, goodness and beauty are identical; all should strive to "become artists."[28] And Anthony is a peculiarly American kind of artist: a con artist.

Sawyer

There is, of course, another con artist on *Lost*. Sawyer chose his name and career as a con man to emulate Anthony, who under the literary name "Tom Sawyer" caused the death of Sawyer's parents. The island's most dedicated reader, Sawyer illustrates how Shaftesbury's aesthetic was applied to American conditions. Sawyer's season one episode called "Confidence Man" alludes to Herman Melville's novel *The Confidence-Man: His Masquerade*. Melville's book demonstrates the influence of Shaftesbury's moral sense thought in the early American republic. His main character reads a Shaftesburyan work entitled "Pleasures of Imagination."[29] Sawyer exemplifies an important American literary trope of the nineteenth century: the American Adam. Thrust into a state of nature, the American Adam combines Lockean ideas of property with themes from the Book of Genesis.[30] As an American Adam, however, Sawyer proves more interested in property than theology. "It's Lord of the Flies time now," he proclaims at one point.[31] And he denounces Jack's short-lived cave colony: "I don't know what kind of commie share-fest you're running in Cave Town, but down here, possession's nine-tenths."[32]

Thus *Lost* takes a dim view of the potential contribution of Shaftesbury, a.k.a. Anthony Ashley Cooper, to its new social contract. However, Shaftesbury's emphasis on natural sociability may yet provide an intellectual resource for the survivors.

Rousseau

In Danielle Rousseau, or the "French chick" as Sawyer dubs her, the dark side of enlightenment emerges even more starkly. Her name evokes the enlightened *philosophe* Jean-Jacques Rousseau, who avoided the individualistic tendencies of Locke's thought. His concept of the "general will"[33] was an extreme statement of the primacy of the common good. Rousseau taught that the general will of society must change human nature; recalcitrant individuals must be "forced to be free."[34] Rousseau radically revised natural law theory, reducing it to two principles: self-preservation and the unwillingness to see others suffer.[35] This innovation produced Rousseau's weird combination of totalitarianism and sentimentality,[36] reflected in Danielle's behavior. She tortures Sayid with electric current and then tells him, "I can't let you go. Don't you understand? To have someone to talk to, to touch."[37]

Under the social contract, according to Rousseau, "life is no longer a mere bounty of nature, but a gift made conditionally by the state."[38] Not surprisingly, then, Danielle frequently brings American anxieties over the "life issues," especially euthanasia, infanticide, and abortion, into play. Shipwrecked on the island, Danielle euthanized her companions.[39] She is obsessed with reclaiming her daughter Alex, kidnapped by the Others as a baby (an intriguing connection with the life of Rousseau, whose children with Thérèse Lavasseur were raised by others, as orphans).[40] Yet Danielle advocates infanticide for Aaron, Claire's baby, seemingly "infected" by the Others.[41] Rousseau opposed infanticide and abortion, and called the family the "first model of political societies."[42] But the contradictions in Rousseau's theories allow *Lost*'s creators to raise the specter of infanticide through Danielle. Nevertheless, Rousseau's ideas, especially the primacy of the common good, may not prove irrelevant to the island's new social contract. Danielle herself dies nobly, proclaiming her love for her daughter.[43]

Hugo (Hurley) Reyes

Lost's invocation of Hugo Grotius, the enlightened thinker who pioneered international law, seems very tentative. Hugo Reyes bears only Grotius' first name, and most of the time he goes by "Hurley." Moreover, Hugo's last name, which suggests the Spanish monarchy, contradicts Grotius' strong support for Dutch independence from Spain. But Hugo's personality resembles the public image of Grotius as a peaceable, irenic statesman and humble Christian.[44] Hurley shies away from conflict, promoting sharing and harmony among the survivors. He touts "all the good stuff that comes from being a part of this society."[45] Even when Hugo decides to "lay down the law," his method is to take a census.

But Boone's reaction to the census, which he compares to the PATRIOT Act, signals that there is more to Grotius' thinking than peace and flowers. Grotius valued Christianity primarily for its power to support the modern state.[46] He declared that "it is better to be a good citizen than a good Christian."[47] Grotius ruled out almost all justifications for resistance to tyranny.[48] His international law, which sees all nations in a state of nature relative to each other, leaves many openings for colonialist wars of "self-defense." Grotian theory, like Locke's ideas, were used to justify war against indigenous peoples in colonial territories.[49] Grotius' version of just war theory resonates with American anxieties over the war on terror, which *Lost* has extensively explored through the character of Sayid, a former torturer for Saddam's Republican Guard. The survivors have also debated the rationale for war against the island's indigenous Others.[50] In Grotius, as in Locke, natural law justifies imperial expansion[51] (Hurley's rapacious appetite, and pilfering from the survivors' food supply, is symbolic here).

Furthermore, Grotius' suppressed last name, in its Dutch form, surfaces in Karen and Gerald de Groot, who founded the creepy Dharma Initiative.[52] The term *dharma* may be translated as "natural law."[53] Does Dharma – like the thought of Grotius – represent natural law sundered from its Christian theological roots?[54] Even so, Grotius' thought may be of some benefit to the survivors as they construct a new society under pluralistic postmodern conditions. *Dharma* reminds us that natural law, as a potential basis for a new social contract, has meaning for non-Christian cultures as well as Westerners.

Desmond David Hume and Juliet Burke

I have suggested that the survivors' new contract must account for the Divine. The philosopher David Hume, a skeptic, hardly seems a promising resource. But in choosing Henry Ian Cusick to play Desmond David Hume, *Lost*'s producers disputed the stereotyped notion of Hume. Cusick portrayed Jesus in the film *The Gospel of John*. Desmond manifests religious faith on numerous occasions. He says that if Jack heals Sara's paralysis, it would be "a miracle," and then takes leave of Jack with the words "see you in another life, yeah?"[55] Desmond later says the same thing to John, and crosses himself while turning the "failsafe key."[56]

Examining Hume's take on faith will help us to understand Desmond's faith. Hume recommended a type of fideism, that is, an irrational faith based solely on revelation, not reason. Hume did not possess such a faith, but saw its utility for social peace. For Hume, custom and opinion were the basis of society, and these were primarily formed by passion, not reason.[57] The Scottish thinker said that societies should be governed by the "moral attraction, rising from the interests and passions of men."[58] These interests and passions were primarily expressed through the family, the primordial social principle.[59] Desmond's religious belief, like that of Hume, is not rationally grounded; his intuitive flashes may be seen as a manifestation of Hume's version of the "moral sense." Desmond believes in miracles, luck, and fate, not a personal Divine Lawgiver. His character further suggests that the private affections which Hume celebrated cannot unify society in general. Once Desmond is reunited with Penny, his sole concern is his family; unwilling to return to the island in season five, Desmond is eventually brought back only by force.

All these aspects of Hume's thought were taken up by another enlightened thinker mentioned on *Lost*, Edmund Burke. (Dr. Juliet Burke's ex-husband was named Edmund.)[60] Like Hume, Burke emphasized the primacy of custom and personal affections. But Burke took Hume's reverence for the family even farther, into a clear analogy between the state and the domestic sphere. "We have given to our frame of polity the image of a relation in blood, binding up the constitution of our country with the dearest domestic ties, adopting our fundamental laws into the bosom of our family affections."[61] Burke's emphasis on the family, with its positive and negative results for society, appears in the character of Juliet, a fertility doctor. The Others brought Juliet to the island to seek a cure for the syndrome which causes all the island's women to miscarry during their second trimester.[62] Juliet is willing to take any step, ethical or not, to promote live births. In one experiment she made a male field mouse pregnant.[63] The Others' chieftain Richard Alpert tells Juliet, "you created life where life isn't supposed to be. You have a gift."[64] Clearly, Juliet "plays God" in her research and thus offends the spiritual powers of the island.

Burke's and Hume's emphasis on custom is hardly a live option for the survivors as they reconstruct society; in the postmodern scene they inhabit, all organic customs have long since been destroyed. However, both Juliet's and Desmond's commitment to family affections, when it has been purified of anti-social elements, will doubtless play a part in the islanders' social synthesis.

"Jeremy Bentham"

John told Jack, "you're a man of science...I'm a man of faith."[65] Jack's ethic is Kantian, motivated by duty rather than compassion,[66] while John attempts a Kierkegaardian leap of faith. Thus one could see Jack as the purely "ethical" man Kierkegaard criticized in *The Sickness unto Death*.[67] In my opinion, however, the dialectic between Jack and John, science and faith, has been greatly overblown. John's leap of faith was rather mediocre from the beginning. He helped the heroin-addicted Charlie with banal advice,[68] but refused to destroy the heroin-filled Mary statues because he was "superstitious."[69] John bestowed more Oprah-esque wisdom on Hurley: "change is good."[70] John's faith is without content, like Eko's discovery of a hollowed-out Bible that contained only a Dharma training film.[71] John belittled baptism as "spiritual insurance."[72] Like the Dharmas, John represents natural law divorced from the Divine personal Lawgiver.[73] As he said in season three, "I'm on my own journey now."[74]

John is alienated from himself because he has "lost" the sense of a just Father-God which was so important to him. Thus it comes as no surprise when in season four he takes on a new identity – "Jeremy Bentham." This post-enlightened philosopher developed the hedonism – that is, an ethics based on pleasure and pain – implicit in Locke's emphasis on Divine rewards and punishments. But in his utilitarian theory, which turns politics into the quest for "the greatest happiness of the greatest number,"[75] Bentham rejected Locke's entire scheme of natural rights and social contract. He attacked the "pretended law of nature"[76] and ridiculed natural rights as "nonsense upon stilts."[77] Bentham also caustically observed that the Carolina constitution Locke penned "has never been spoken of in any other character than that of a failure."[78]

Bentham correctly pointed out that if one eliminates the Divine giver of the natural law, one must also discard natural rights. But according to

Bentham, natural rights are chiefly touted by those enlightened philosophers "by whom the existence of a divine law and of a divine lawgiver are equally denied." Therefore, "a natural right is a son that never had a father."[79] According to Bentham, Lockean natural rights are not based on a personal Divine Lawgiver; this leaves Lockean natural law, like John on the show, a fatherless orphan. John's metamorphosis into "Jeremy Bentham" signals his loss of faith, his increasing cynicism, his devolution to a shallow utilitarianism and hedonism. The "man of science"/"man of faith" dialectic has collapsed. John and Jack are utilitarian doubles, Tweedledum and Tweedledee. The dialectic can never achieve synthesis. And in a further devastating commentary on Lockean theory, John's corpse has been inhabited since the end of season five by the smoke monster himself, clearly revealed as a force of evil.

The New Dialectic of Science and Faith

Have the survivors been forced to abandon their project of reconstructing a viable society? What resources remain on which to base it? One purely "faith-based" possibility centers on the child Aaron, named after the Old Testament priest, Moses' brother. Aaron, surrounded by messianic portents from the womb,[80] is baptized by Eko.[81] Sun Kwon experiences another miraculous conception and birth.[82] She names her baby Ji Yeon, which has the Marian meaning "Flower of Wisdom." Will Aaron and Ji Yeon be the Christ and Mary figures of a restored island civilization?

However, I would suggest that *Lost*'s ultimate solution will have to incorporate science as well as faith. This is in keeping with the American national character. Henry F. May has described the American propensity "to believe at once in social and even scientific progress and in unchanging moral principles."[83] Or as William McLoughlin put it,

> American culture has at its core a congeries of conceptions that we have already identified: the chosen nation; the covenant with God; the millennial manifest destiny; the higher (biblical or natural) law, against which private and social behavior is to be judged; the moral law (the Ten Commandments, the Sermon on the Mount); the laws of science, presumed to be from the Creator....[84]

Particularly important is the rapprochement of science and faith in the first American contract. Americans tended to follow Isaac Newton and Robert Boyle in their insistence on a mechanistic universe which was nevertheless actively regulated by a personal Creator.[85] Any revision of the American social contract would have to include these two sides of the American mind and character. If natural law is to be a part of the new system, a Divine personal Lawgiver – perhaps a resurrected Jacob? – must be acknowledged, one more in keeping with theological truth than Locke's dispenser of rewards and punishments.

I believe *Lost*'s solution – which I eagerly await – will emerge from the new dialectic of science and faith which has appeared in the characters of Daniel Faraday and Eloise Hawking. Daniel seems to be a second "man of science," while Eloise, his mother, has clear links to the supernatural -- among other things, her picture appeared on the desk of Brother Campbell, Desmond's superior at his monastery.[86] Through Eloise and Daniel, the science/faith dialectic may at last be synthesized into a stable social system. Daniel's (apparent) murder by Eloise has certainly cast a damper on hopes from this quarter. But *Lost* still has four episodes remaining, as of this writing, in which to save the world – or at least to constitute a remnant of civilization. Meanwhile, the producers and writers of *Lost* have already performed a great service for the American polity, simply by reminding Americans (who have almost entirely "lost" the political heritage of our founding) about our social contract and its philosophical origins.

Notes

[1] I dedicate this essay to my sister Kelly McDermott, who introduced me to *Lost*, and with whom I have spent many happy hours watching and discussing *Lost*. I am also indebted to Adam Hoose for communal viewings and valuable insights. Luke Ritter and Tim Ivancic also offered extremely helpful comments.

[2] "Tabula Rasa," *Lost: The Complete First Season*, 7 DVDs. (Burbank, CA: Buena Vista Home Entertainment, Inc., and Touchstone Television, 2005) [hereinafter Lost 2005].

[3] William Wirt Henry, ed. *Patrick Henry: Life, Correspondence and Speeches* (New York: Charles Scribner's Sons, 1891), I:221. Google Books. http://books.google.com.

[4] Paul H. Smith et al., eds. *Letters of Delegates to Congress, 1774-1789* (Washington, DC: Library of Congress, 1976-2000), IV:16-17. American Memory. http://memory.loc.gov.

[5] Charles Francis Adams, ed. *The Works of John Adams* (Boston: Little, Brown, 1865), IV:292. Google Books. http://books.google.com.

[6] "White Rabbit," Lost 2005.

[7] "The Cost of Living," *Lost: The Complete Third Season*, 7 DVDs. (Burbank, CA: Buena Vista Home Entertainment, Inc., and Touchstone Television, 2007) [hereinafter Lost 2007].

[8] "The Shape of Things To Come," *Lost: The Complete Fourth Season*, 6 DVDs.

(Burbank, CA.: Buena Vista Home Entertainment, Inc., 2008) [hereinafter Lost 2008].

[9] "White Rabbit," Lost 2005.

[10] "The Cost of Living," Lost 2007.

[11] Jeremy Waldron, ed. *"Nonsense Upon Stilts": Bentham, Burke and Marx on the Rights of Man* (London: New York: Methuen & Co., 1987), 13; Jeremy Waldron, *God, Locke, and Equality* (Cambridge: Cambridge University Press, 2002), 12, 101-102, 242.

[12] Richard Tuck, *Natural Rights Theories: Their Origin and Development* (Cambridge: Cambridge University Press, 1979), 168-169; Mark Goldie, ed. *Locke: Political Essays* (Cambridge: New York: Cambridge University Press, 1997), xxiii, 113, 303.

[13] Frederick Copleston, SJ, *A History of Philosophy*, vol. V, part I: *Modern Philosophy: The British Philosophers: Hobbes to Paley* (Garden City, NY: Image Books, 1964), 182.

[14] "Eggtown," Lost 2008.

[15] "nulla enim lex si nullus legislator, aut frustra si nulla poena." John Locke, *Essays on the Law of Nature*, W. von Leyden, ed. (Oxford: Clarendon Press, 1954), 174.

[16] Barbara Arneil, *John Locke and America: The Defence of English Colonialism* (Oxford: Clarendon Press, 1996), 5, 69; Goldie, *Locke*, 162-163, 166, 180, 272.

[17] David Armitage, "John Locke, Carolina, and the Two Treatises of Government,'" *Political Theory* 32:5 (October, 2004), 602, 610, 614-615.

[18] John Locke, *The Second Treatise of Government and A Letter Concerning Toleration* (Mineola, NY: Dover Publications, 2002), 22.

[19] Arneil, 18, 79, 81, 147. On the labor theory of value, see Locke, *Second Treatise*, 6, 15-16, 22, 56; see also Forrest McDonald, *Novus Ordo Seclorum: The Intellectual Origins of the Constitution* (Lawrence, KS: University Press of Kansas, 1985), 63-64; Richard Davies in Sharon M. Kaye, ed. *Lost and Philosophy: The Island Has Its Reasons* (Malden, MA: Oxford: Blackwell Publishing, 2008), 182; James Tully, *An Approach to Political Philosophy: Locke in Contexts* (Cambridge: Cambridge University Press, 1993), 144.

[20] "Enter 77," Lost 2007.

[21] "All the Best Cowboys Have Daddy Issues," Lost 2005.

[22] "The Man from Tallahassee," Lost 2007.

[23] Tully, 63; *Oxford Dictionary of National Biography Online*, s.v. "Cooper, Anthony Ashley, first earl of Shaftesbury," http://www.oxforddnb.com (accessed July 21, 2009).

[24] Peter S. Fosl in Kaye, 161; Peter Reill and Ellen Wilson, eds. *Encyclopedia of the Enlightenment*, Revised Edition (New York: Facts on File, 2004), 349.

[25] "Deus ex Machina," Lost 2005.

[26] Anthony Ashley Cooper, *Characteristics of Men, Manners, Opinions, Times* (Cambridge: Cambridge University Press, 1999), 268, 270-271, 283.

[27] Copleston V:I, 186.

[28] Cooper, 327, 332.

[29] Herman Melville, *The Confidence-Man: His Masquerade*, Hershel Parker, ed. (New York: W.W. Norton, 1971), 22; Elizabeth S. Foster, *Herman Melville's* The Confidence Man*: Its Origins and Meaning* (PhD diss., Yale University, 1942), 152. Dissertations & Theses: Full Text. http://proquest.umi.com.

[30] R.W.B. Lewis, *The American Adam* (Chicago: University of Chicago Press, 1955), passim.

[31] "In Translation," Lost 2005.

[32] "Confidence Man," Lost 2005.

[33] Jean-Jacques Rousseau, *The Social Contract and Discourses*, G.D.H. Cole, trans. (Ontario, Canada: Fitzhenry & Whiteside, 1973), 192; "volonté générale," Jean-Jacques Rousseau, *Du Contrat Social*, Pierre Burgelin, ed. (Paris: Garnier-Flammarion, 1992), 40.

[34] Rousseau, *Social Contract*, 195; "on le forcera d'être libre," Rousseau, *Du Contrat Social*, 43. On the general will changing human nature, *Du Contrat Social*, 65, 91.

[35] J.W. Gough, *The Social Contract: A Critical Study of Its Development*, 2nd ed. (Oxford: Clarendon Press, 1957), 166.

[36] Julián Marías, *History of Philosophy* (New York: Dover Publications, 1967), 266.

[37] "Solitary," Lost 2005.

[38] Rousseau, *Social Contract*, 208-209; "sa vie n'est plus seulement un bienfait de la nature, mais un don conditionnel de l'État." Rousseau, *Du Contrat Social*, 60.

[39] "Solitary," Lost 2005.

[40] Reill and Wilson, 524.

[41] "Maternity Leave," *Lost: The Complete Second Season*, 7 DVDs (Burbank, CA: Buena Vista Home Entertainment, Inc., and Touchstone Television, 2006) [hereinafter Lost 2006].

[42] Rousseau, *Social Contract*, 121, 182; Rousseau, *Du Contrat Social*, 30; Jean-Jacques Rousseau, *Discours sur l'Origine et les Fondemens de l'Inegalité parmi les Hommes* (Amsterdam: Marc Michel Rey, 1755), 212. Google Books. http://books.google.com.

[43] "Meet Kevin Johnson," Lost 2008.

[44] see Jan Paul Heering in Henk Nellen and Edwin Rabbie, eds. *Hugo Grotius Theologian: Essays in Honor of G.H.M. Posthumus Meyjes* (Leiden: New York: E. J. Brill, 1994), 45.

[45] "Raised By Another," Lost 2005.

[46] Grotius Committee of the Royal Netherlands Academy of Arts and Sciences, *The World of Hugo Grotius (1583-1645): Proceedings of the International Colloquium* (Amsterdam: Maarssen: APA – Holland University Press, 1984), 51; see also G.H.M. Posthumus Meyjes, ed. *Hugo Grotius, Meletius, Sive de Iis Quae inter Christianos Conveniunt Epistola* (Leiden: New York: E.J. Brill, 1988), 128-129.

[47] "Prius est, bonum civem esse, quam bonum Christianum." quoted in Grotius Committee, 63.

[48] A.C. Campbell, ed. *The Rights of War and Peace, Including the Law of Nature an;d of Nations, Translated from the Original Latin of Grotius* (Westport, CT:

Hyperion Press, 1979), 67-69; John Neville Figgis, *Political Thought from Gerson to Grotius, 1414-1625* (New York: Harper & Brothers, 1960), 242.

[49] Arneil, 53.

[50] "The Hunting Party," Lost 2006; "One of Them," Lost 2006.

[51] Richard Tuck, *The Rights of War and Peace: Political Thought and the International Order from Grotius to Kant* (Oxford: Oxford University Press, 1999), 195-196.

[52] "?," Lost 2006.

[53] Kaye, 173, 200.

[54] Carl Joachim Friedrich declared that "the decisive achievement of Grotius was to separate natural law from its Christian and theological basis as it had been understood in the Middle Ages." Carl Joachim Friedrich, *The Philosophy of Law in Historical Perspective*, 2nd ed. (Chicago: University of Chicago Press, 1963), 65.

[55] "Man of Science, Man of Faith," Lost 2006.

[56] "Live Together, Die Alone," Lost 2006.

[57] Knud Haakonssen, ed., *Hume: Political Essays* (Cambridge: Cambridge University Press, 1994), 69-70, 98; Mark Goldie and Robert Wokler, eds., *The Cambridge History of Eighteenth-Century Political Thought* (Cambridge: Cambridge University Press, 2006), 302-304; Frederick Copleston, SJ, *A History of Philosophy*, vol. V, part II: *Modern Philosophy: The British Philosophers: Berkeley to Hume* (Garden City, NY: Image Books, 1964), 115, 123, 128; Rodney W. Kilcup in David Hume, *The History of England from the Invasion of Julius Caesar to the Revolution in 1688*, abridged by Rodney W. Kilcup (Chicago: University of Chicago Press, 1975), xxv.

[58] Haakonssen, 140.

[59] Copleston, V:II, 147; see also Haakonssen, 73.

[60] "Not in Portland," Lost 2007. To Juliet belongs the best line yet heard on *Lost*: "It's very stressful being an Other." "The Other Woman," Lost 2008.

[61] Edmund Burke, *Reflections on the Revolution in France,* Thomas H.D. Mahoney, ed. (Indianapolis, IN: Bobbs-Merrill, 1955), 38.

[62] "The Other Woman," Lost 2008.

[63] "Not in Portland," Lost 2007.

[64] "One of Us," Lost 2007.

[65] "Exodus," Lost 2005.

[66] see Reill and Wilson, 319.

[67] Sander Lee in Kaye, 67-68. John uses the phrase "leap of faith" in "Orientation," Lost 2006.

[68] "The Moth," Lost 2005.

[69] "The Long Con," Lost 2006.

[70] "Everybody Hates Hugo," Lost 2006.

[71] "What Kate Did," Lost 2006; see Sander Lee in Kaye, 68.

[72] "Fire + Water," Lost 2006.

[73] In this connection I am indebted to an essay by Shai Biderman and William J. Devlin, "The Tao of John Locke" in Kaye, 193-203.

[74] "The Brig," Lost 2007.

[75] Jeremy Bentham, *A Fragment on Government and an Introduction to the Principles of Morals and Legislation*, Wilfrid Harrison, ed. (Oxford: Basil Blackwell, 1948), 3.

[76] Ibid., 49, 91.

[77] Waldron, *Nonsense upon Stilts*, 53.

[78] Jeremy Bentham, *Deontology; or, the Science of Morality*, John Bowring, ed. (London: Longman, Rees, Orme, Browne, Green, and Longman, 1834), 310. Google Books. http://books.google.com.

[79] Waldron, *Nonsense upon Stilts*, 73.

[80] "Raised By Another," Lost 2005.

[81] "Fire + Water," Lost 2006.

[82] "The Whole Truth," Lost 2006.

[83] Henry F. May, *The Enlightenment in America* (Oxford: Oxford University Press, 1976), 342. ACLS Humanities E-Book. http://quod.lib.umich.edu.

[84] William G. McLoughlin, *Revivals, Awakenings, and Reform* (Chicago: University of Chicago Press, 1978), 103.

[85] see Copleston, V:I, 157, 159, 165; Margaret Jacob, *The Radical Enlightenment: Pantheists, Freemasons and Republicans* (London: George Allen & Unwin, 1981), 70-71, 86; Mark Noll, *Princeton and the Republic, 1768-1822* (Princeton, NJ: Princeton University Press, 1989), 6 and passim; Perry Miller, *The Life of the Mind in America* (New York: Harcourt, Brace & World, 1965), 275.

[86] Kaye, 75.

A FAITH UNYIELDING:
CONSERVATIVE AND LIBERAL PHILOSOPHIES IN THE POST-9/11 WORLD, AS DEPICTED IN *BATTLESTAR GALACTICA* AND *24*

HUGO TORRES

In the years since the terrorist attacks of 9/11, two television programs have received wide recognition and critical attention for being heavily influenced by the post-9/11 environment—the Fox series *24* for its depiction of tough anti-terrorism agent Jack Bauer, and the NBC Universal program *Battlestar Galactica* ("*BSG*") with its nuanced depiction of flawed heroes and villains, where the line is often blurred between the "good guys" and the "bad guys." Though each program certainly draws fans from all areas of the political spectrum, these programs in many ways represent the two major strains of American political thought that have developed in response to the challenge of living in an age of terrorism. *24* offers a conservative outlook on confronting the challenge of terrorism, with its depiction of a single individual fighting terrorists by doing whatever it takes to stop threats to America. *BSG*, on the other hand, presents a liberal outlook on confronting terrorism, with its depiction of a society that experiences near annihilation, yet nonetheless grapples with a desire to maintain civil rights and democratic society.

Each program confronts its protagonists with nearly insurmountable threats. In *24*, Jack Bauer maintains his relentless pursuit of terrorists even as his faith in himself, his family, his friends, his colleagues, and his government is continually tested and shaken. The protagonists of *BSG* struggle to find ways to hold on to their democratic ideals, even as they are repeatedly tempted to lose faith in themselves, in their leaders, and in their mission. Yet a common thread that permeates both programs is a deep and unyielding faith in the value of democracy: Jack Bauer risks life and sanity to protect democratic America and its government, and *BSG*'s protagonists struggle valiantly to maintain a democratic post-apocalyptic government. Both programs understand that times of crisis often require compromising one's ideals—the rule of law and other democratic principles may, on occasion, need to be put aside in order to keep alive the very society that holds these ideals—but democratic civilization is always worth protecting.

The Conservatism of *24* and the Liberalism of *BSG*

Modern American conservatism is closely aligned with a belief in small government, individual self-reliance, and deference to authority. Since 9/11, it has also been infused with neo-conservative thought which promotes a hawkish foreign policy and a tough stance on national security. *24* certainly demonstrates a similar viewpoint on national security, with its tough and forceful outlook at fighting terrorism. Joel Surnow, the co-creator and executive producer of *24*, is quite open about his admiration for conservatism, offering the following praise for a conservative icon: "I just felt Ronald Reagan was the father that this country needed. . . . He made me feel good that I was in his family."[1] Surnow goes further in the same interview, offering up the viewpoint that America "is sort of the parent of the world, so we have to be stern but fair to people who are rebellious to us. We don't spoil them. That's not to say you abuse them, either. But you have to know who the adult in the room is."[2]

Perhaps unsurprisingly then, *24* is popular among those who share a conservative ideological outlook--many conservatives publicly praise the show, including radio host Rush Limbaugh and Senator John McCain. Indeed, Sen. McCain's support of the show runs so deep that he made a minor guest appearance on the show. The Heritage Foundation, a conservative think-tank, hosted a panel discussion on *24*, with Limbaugh as moderator and Michael Chertoff (Secretary of Homeland Security for the Bush administration at the time) as the featured speaker; Supreme Court Justice Clarence Thomas, a well-known conservative, was a special guest sitting in the front row of a packed auditorium. Indeed, the show's conservative leanings are accepted as an article of faith among conservatives: "Among other things, Limbaugh asked the show's creators and stars whether they're snubbed by "Hollywood liberals" for making a "pro-America show.""[3]

American liberalism is an ideology committed to a belief in civil liberties, empathy towards the welfare of individuals, and the importance of government action for the common good. *BSG* conveys a gritty depiction of the costs of war and explores the tension between civil liberties and security; the series conveys a liberal concern for maintaining civil rights in times of crises and portrays the role of government in a largely positive manner. This liberal outlook on the costs and challenges of fighting terrorism flows from the stated aims of Executive Producer Ron Moore, who has expressed a belief in empathy and debate:

> I want the show to provoke you into thinking about the times you live in and the choices that are being made all around you every day. In a time when the President of the United States actually asserts that he has the power to arrest without warrant and detain indefinitely without charge or appeal, any citizen (indeed any person on the face of the Earth) simply by designating them as an "illegal combatant," we should all be engaged in a vigorous and energetic debate about who we are as a people and as human beings and exactly how we do intend to respond to the very real threat posed to this nation and to the foundations of liberal democracy posed by people capable of, and willing to, fly airplanes into buildings.[4]

For Moore, there are no firm answers that can be derived from deferring to a "father" figure or having an "adult" in the room. Instead, challenging questions are to be debated and discussed communally, with no easy answers flowing from a single source.

Given that a show promoting such an outlook aired primarily during the presidency of George W. Bush, it follows that *BSG* draws a devoted following among liberals. Though the show originally drew praise from both sides of the political spectrum, its turn in the third season towards a nuanced examination of insurgent warfare alienated conservatives and reinforced the perception of a liberal outlook. Indeed, the show's liberal bona fides are so widely accepted now that the New York Times declared that *BSG* "upheld certain liberal pieties without the utmost subtlety."[5] While not having fans quite as prominent as a US Senator or a Supreme Court Justice, *BSG*'s more prominent liberal supporters include writers from the liberal Think Progress and Commonweal, as well as numerous liberal bloggers.

Prescriptions for an Age of Terror

In looking at the ideological forces presented on each program, one can also see traces of conservative and liberal values that are not related to terrorism. Conservatives, who generally oppose welfare and big-government, believe self-reliance to be a virtue and that government's role should be minimal as individuals should be able to care for themselves. Meanwhile, liberals emphasize community and social ties. They tend to believe in community responsibility, and that some problems can only be surmounted by collective/government action. An examination of each program reveals that each one does indeed largely reflect and confirm the values of its creators and respective ideological fan base. *24* promotes self-reliant toughness in the face of terrorism, while *BSG* depicts an empathetic communitarian ethos. Each program presents different ideas on how best to confront the various challenges and issues raised by the threat of terrorism, offering different ideas on the value of empathy, the portrayal of torture, the depiction of big government, and the role of religion.

The Value of Empathy

Terrorism is a foremost political concern in the United States ever since 9/11 and both television programs mirror the viewpoints of their respective ideological bases in presenting terrorists: *24* is unrepentant about their threat and villainy, while *BSG* explores what motivates those who would do us harm. *BSG*, true to its empathetic liberal leanings, on occasion invites the viewer into the mind of a "terrorist", both subtly and directly.

In the episode "Downloaded" the show focuses almost exclusively on two Cylons (the robotic villains or "terrorists" that the humans are fighting) and their life after having encountered the humans. We see these Cylons uncomfortable with the violence their people have wrought upon humanity and questioning whether further violence and genocide is truly God's will. The episode is clearly meant to flesh out these seemingly menacing beings and demonstrate that they are neither one-dimensional nor uniformly evil. Furthermore, the episode highlights how "terrorist" is often a term defined by the beholder as, in the same episode, we see a group of humans preparing a bomb to attack the Cylon occupiers. While in any other episode a viewer might unquestioningly regard the humans as freedom fighters, in this episode the moral lines become blurred when the viewer discovers that the target of the human bomb is a café full of Cylons, including the two Cylons to whom our sympathies have been drawn. At one point, a conversation ensues among the human fighters that illustrates the difficulty in deciding whether they are terrorists or freedom fighters:

> Woman: What military value does this café have?
> Man: None. But we have to make them feel as if they aren't safe anywhere.

This conversation chillingly echoes the goals of suicide bombers in Israel, Iraq, Sri Lanka, and elsewhere. Yet in *BSG* the viewer is inclined to support the humans about to plant the bomb, as they are the protagonists of the show. The scene is clearly meant to challenge the viewer into questioning the righteousness of the heroes and whether their tactics are noble or extreme; in doing so it places the viewer in the uncomfortable position of rooting for the "terrorists."

Part of the premise of *BSG* is that some of the Cylons look human and have blended into the human population. In many ways this alludes to the modern fear of terrorists infiltrating democratic societies and blending into the population until such time as they decide to strike. However, *BSG* again takes this notion and suggests that perhaps infiltration is not always frightening—though some of the Cylons do in fact commit violence from within the human community, one of them becomes romantically involved with a human officer and ends up becoming a great ally for the humans, having grown to prefer human society. As the series nears its conclusion, the humans begin to realize that their own salvation lies in understanding and accepting the Cylons. Winning over hearts and minds through empathy, not military force, is part of the key to defeating terrorists.

24, on the other hand, rarely offers much in the way of sympathy or empathy towards terrorists, following instead the stark black and white outlook of conservatism as reflected in President Bush's "Axis of Evil" rhetoric. Tortured into confessing his role in various murders, Graham Bauer, brother of protagonist Jack Bauer, pleads to Jack: "We're the same Jack!" He suggests they are both patriots, doing whatever it takes to protect the nation. Rather than allowing the character to elaborate further or drawing similarities to their motivations, the scene abruptly concludes with Jack shouting "We are not the same!" and nearly killing his brother. The show allows little room for sympathy towards its villains—this despite the fact that Bauer has himself committed similar horrific deeds during the course of the show, all in an attempt to protect the United States. (To name a few of Jack Bauer's more egregious actions: torturing innocents, beheading a federal witness, murdering a co-worker, shooting civilians deliberately...) According to *24*, actions in defense of America are almost always justified; actions *against* America never are.

The Portrayal of Torture

On *24,* torture is a tactic used by Jack Bauer frequently and effectively. The repeated use of torture by the heroic protagonist of a popular program has had an effect on American culture, making the use of torture palatable to some Americans, including military interrogators.[6] "Torture, presented with gusto and almost no moral compunction, is an increasingly popular way of gathering intelligence on "24." If anything, the new season seems even more intent on hammering home the message that torture is necessary in the war against terror, and that despite what some experts claim, torture works."[7] Interestingly, there is one sole recurring instance in the show where torture never works—when it is committed against Jack Bauer. Torture, such an effective tool on bad guys and weak-willed government agents, proves futile against the awesome willpower of Jack Bauer. Torture works on villainous "others" but it never works on tough heroic Americans.

In Season 7, the show appears to soften its stance a bit, shifting its tone if not the core message. Early on in the season, Jack Bauer acknowledges that there should be accountability for those who engage in extra-judicial acts like torture, and Season 7 also presents a newly elected President who takes a hard stance against the use of torture. But the show doesn't tread too far from its original stance on torture, as the talk of taking responsibility only goes so far, with Jack Bauer continuing his torturing ways as the season progress, much to the chagrin of the anti-torture president and Bauer's law abiding FBI colleagues. The anti-torture position gains a voice, but the torturing of suspects remains an essential tool in the *24* interrogation toolkit. *24* promotes the conservative belief that national security concerns trump all other issues, and exemplifies Goldwater's adage that "extremism in the defense of liberty is no vice."

On *BSG* meanwhile, torture is deployed on rare occasions, and its utility is doubtful. When the hotshot pilot Starbuck interrogates a Cylon, her harsh interrogation techniques elicit little in the way of useful information. It is only when she engages the Cylon as a thoughtful being that the Cylon opens up and talks to her. Similarly, when the main characters encounter another human ship, the Pegasus, they find a tortured Cylon aboard who is nearly catatonic. Attempts to elicit information through torture prove futile until Baltar, a morally ambiguous scientist, approaches the Cylon with compassion, feeding the Cylon and giving her space. Whereas *24* uses torture as a plot device, to get from one point to the next, *BSG* displays it as a gruesome act, one that damages the psyche and poisons society. The Pegasus crew that uses torture without remorse is shown as barbaric and violent, in stark contrast to the civil Galactica crew. The empathy and respect for individual rights on display in *BSG* leads to a concerned and cautious depiction of the consequences of torturing one's enemies.

Big Government

In addressing the challenges of terrorism, *24* adheres to conservative convictions through a continual distrust of government power and bureaucracy. Government power is viewed increasingly suspiciously as the series progress—the ethos that most predominates on *24* is a conservative self-reliant one. Many of the dramatic setbacks Jack Bauer faces arise not so much from cunning terrorists, but from the government questioning or meddling in his decisions. The common mistake by government officials is failing to trust Jack Bauer. As one television critic notes: "One thing never changes: the president and his aides keep making the critical blunder of not trusting Jack's instincts."[8] The old adage "that government is best which governs least" is shifted a little here, to being "that government is best which interferes with Jack Bauer least."

Government agencies are depicted as bureaucratic at best, and riddled with moles and corrupt officials at worst. Politicians constantly prove to be obstacles in the way of Jack Bauer's attempts to defend America, and the program constantly shows Jack Bauer saving the day despite government meddling. Jack Bauer begins the series as a government agent, but in later seasons strikes out on his own. The anti-government motif reaches its zenith in Season 5, when Jack Bauer has to take down the President of the United States himself, who has been behind many of the acts of terrorism of the day. This theme continues in season 7, where Jack Bauer teams up with former anti-terrorism colleagues who have formed a rogue non-governmental unit due to the presence of a mole with the government—the government simply cannot be counted on to protect America.

In prescribing caution towards overreaching government power, the show's conservative outlook diverges somewhat from recent beliefs espoused by Republican policy makers. Take Season 6, where the show displays praise for a restrained executive branch. In that season, the President's chief of staff advocates for an expansion of presidential power and the creation of camps to detain suspicious persons (mainly of Middle Eastern descent). When the president rejects the aide's idea, he speaks of not wishing to alienate the Muslim American community, whom he believes to be the "greatest asset" the U.S. has in finding terrorists. This scene is played as a moment of strength and conviction by the president. In critiquing executive overreach and praising executive restraint, *24* challenges the "unitary executive" theory that promotes wide powers as residing in the presidency, At least one critic has noted that *24* carries a warning about how fear pushes us towards the embrace of intrusive state power. "More engaging, though, is the way in which fear, not terrorism, proves to be the ultimate destructive device. It darkens the judgment of honorable men, poisons the sanctity of the Constitution, makes people turn on each other and pushes America to the verge of becoming a police state dotted with detention camps."[9] In this way, the show is more in line with historical conservatism and its skepticism of big government, than with the modern conservative fixation on a strong and powerful chief executive.

BSG, in stark contrast to *24*, offers up a largely positive view of the role of government in times of crises. Liberals believe that government is necessary to confront societal issues, and BSG exemplifies this message by displaying a strong and effective government apparatus. Though not without its flaws, the human government in BSG works to maintain democratic elections, provide hope and guidance to a desperate people, and is portrayed as working hard on behalf of society. BSG shows this to be a difficult task, but throughout the entire series the rule of law largely persists: elective government continues even as extinction looms near, trials are given to war criminals, and the military often shows deference to civilian leadership. The show therefore conveys a liberal belief in the necessity of preserving civil rights and the rule of law in the face of great security threats.

The Role of Religion

BSG presents a favorable look at the impact of religion, tackling the issue head on and challenging viewers to do the same. Religion is a potent force right from the beginning of *BSG*, with scripture and religious rituals constantly coming into play, and with religion being explored with as much nuance as the political elements, presented as both a positive and negative force. This may be initially surprising, given the prevalent meme that liberals and religion do not mix. However, 9/11 brought to the forefront the role that religion and spiritual beliefs often play in shaping political ideology, and the liberal desire to understand other cultures and to understand the root causes of terrorism means that *BSG* exploration of religion's role is well in line with a liberal outlook.

Perhaps more than any other dramatic television series in recent memory, *BSG* explores the importance of faith in shaping societies and in influencing individual and communal decisions. The Cylons are driven by a zealous monotheistic faith that drives them to destroy the humans at times but also challenges them to follow what they perceive to be god's will, showing mercy and compassion in unexpected ways. The polytheistic humans often times make risky decisions based on nothing more than faith, but at the same time it is their faith in prophecies and in a promised land that drives them forward amidst catastrophe and gives them hope for surviving in a post-apocalyptic age. A reluctant human president, initially skeptical of religion, gradually grows to accept the fact that she may be a religious leader foretold in prophecy. Decisions undertaken on the basis of faith oftentimes prove to be the correct course of action. Baltar, perhaps the most morally ambiguous character on the show, begins as a cynical scientist who scoffs at religion. Facing hardship, however, he begins to open himself up and grows to accept the Cylon perspective on a single god, eventually brining monotheism to the humans.

BSG stands out not just for being a liberal show with strong religious themes, but for having religious themes at all. When one examines the landscape of American television, one finds that televised works of fictions that address religion in any form are rare. *BSG*'s status as science-fiction gives it more leeway than most fictional programs to deal with religious issues, and *BSG* takes advantage of this in featuring religious issues prominently, giving full weight to the power of religion and spirituality to shape human decisions and human psychology. Indeed, the entire series concludes with an air of mystery that lends some weight to the prominence of the religious/spiritual side of the universe and seemingly suggests that not everything can be explained by science.

Such a strong and prominent depiction of the importance of religion serves as a reminder to liberalism that secularism does not mean the absence of religion. Religion can play a role in secular society, and it is such a powerful force that it often will regardless of efforts to stifle or ignore it. Moreover, the close examination of religious belief on *BSG* also serves the function of exploring religiously-motivated terrorism, with the Cylons often declaring religious motivations behind their actions. If understanding the roots of terrorism is part of the key to eliminating its threat, then *BSG* makes it absolutely clear that the role of religion cannot be ignored. For liberals who may have grown reluctant to discuss religious belief, *BSG* serves as a reminder that a force this powerful cannot be swept out of sight, either in domestic politics or in foreign policy.

This strong engagement with the subject of religion and spirituality is in stark contrast to 24, where characters are rarely depicted as displaying religious faith or any opinion on religion at all. Though perhaps not uncommon for a prime time television program, the show displays a marked lack of attention to Judeo-Christian faith in America. As for Islam, the series noticeably avoids centralizing the U.S. fight against Islamic terrorism as a centerpiece of the show, despite drawing heavily from other elements of the post-9/11 world. When religion is introduced in Season 2, it is as a feint, as the series toys with the prospect of Islamic terrorists only to reveal one of the terrorists to be a Caucasian American woman. In Season 4, Islamic terrorists are finally featured as villains, but religious talk is even then kept to a minimum. The discussion of interning Muslims in Season 6 is only briefly touched upon. Islam is therefore referenced in passing, but Christianity is never addressed and *24* does not to explore the religious motivations of its villains or its heroes, focusing instead on the need to defend the country no matter the cost. Understanding the motivations of one's enemies is simply not part of its agenda.

Faith in Democracy

Ultimately, although *24* and *BSG* often diverge in their approach to social/political issues due to their ideological tilts, the two shows remain securely rooted in American political ideals and seem to agree that, despite living in perilous times with enemies out to destroy us, the rights and ideals upon which America was founded are worth protecting. Despite a hero who is often Goldwater-esque in his extreme actions in defense of America, *24* remains suspicious of government attempts to strip away civil liberties and to impose martial law. In *BSG*, heroes commit villainous deeds and villains perform acts of heroism, showcasing moral ambiguity, but the importance of the rule of law is always at the forefront. Where both programs are similar, however, is in depicting the challenges and existential angst that come from living in an age of terror. While *24* and *BSG* may disagree on many things, they both agree on the darkness that terror delivers to democratic societies, a darkness that often requires a bargain to be struck between liberty and security. That both shows present this as a high price to pay, even in times of great crisis, makes them not only similarly relevant to this day and age, it also makes them part of a long-running conversation on the meaning of America and the challenges of democratic society.

Notes

[1] Mayer, Jane. "Whatever it Takes, The politics of the man behind '*24*'." *The New Yorker*. 19 Feb, 2007.

[2] Mayer.

[3] Farhi, Paul. "Calling On Hollywood's Terrorism 'Experts', Homeland Security Chief Compares Reality and '*24*.'" *Washington Post*, *24* June, 2006: C01

[4] Moore, Ronald D. *BSG Blog*. 1 April 2005. Scifi.com. 2 Feb. 2007. <http://blog.scifi.com/battlestar/archives/2005/04/> (Seems to no longer be accessible at that address: try

http://www.scifispace.com/members/forums/lofiversion/index.php/t2904.html for a reposting)

[5] Bellafante, Gina. "Show About the Universe Raises Questions on Earth." New York Times. 20 March 2009. NYTimes.com. 29 August 2009.

http://www.nytimes.com/2009/03/21/arts/television/21batt.html

[6] McFarland, Melanie. "As Day 6 of '*24*' unfolds, a new Jack Bauer steps into action." *Seattle Post-Intelligencer* 12 Jan. 2007. Seattlepi.com. 25 July 2009. <http://www.seattlepi.com/tv/299361_tv12.html>

[7] Stanley, Alessandra. "Bombers Strike, and America Is in Turmoil. It's Just Another Day for Jack Bauer." *New York Times*. 12 Jan. 2007: E1.

[8] Stanley.

[9] McFarland.

DEMOCRACY INDICTED:
THE CASE FOR POLITICAL JUDGMENT FOUND
IN *BATTLESTAR GALACTICA*

LEAH A. MURRAY

Many times in popular culture the entertainment media take us into a thought experiment along the lines of social contract theory. We ponder what would happen if there were no government, no rules to keep us accountable, no binding social contract. We explore how we would survive post-apocalypse or we invent other world cultures to explore how it could be different. We find this in movies like the Terminator and Matrix series and in television shows like Lost and Doctor Who. This thought experiment is very interesting to people, as evidenced by the vast popularity of shows that formulate the age old question of Locke, Hobbes and Rousseau. Often the culture is some kind of utopia, ala Star Trek, or some kind of primitive culture that is better, ala Avatar. When we explore post-apocalyptic moments in a linear history that is intended to be our own we fail, mostly. We are in civil war or we have destroyed our planet or some kind of tyranny governs. As though we could only imagine a life after apocalypse that is Hobbesian[1]. We have no faith in our ability to survive otherwise.

Enter the television series *Battlestar Galactica* (*BSG*), which generated much cult fandom for its rethinking of an old series. This show is compelling for many reasons, the acting is good, the writing is sharp, and series producer Ron Moore has created a fascinating universe. Many different types of people were attracted to the series: neo-conservatives because it took a tough stance on terrorism; liberals because it took a tough stance on the military; and religious people could find its devotion to religion playing an important role in decision making compelling. The show, however, is interesting to the political theorist because it tackles this social contract theory question using the limits of the human ability in another human species' linear existence. Instead of being *our* earth, post crisis, it is some other set of humans living in some other galaxy in some other time (we eventually come to learn it takes place during prehistorical times) dealing with what to do when civilization as we know it comes to a crashing halt. Instead of inventing some perfect people or some primitive people to show us the flaws in our human society, we get to see people just like us dealing with these questions. Furthermore, *BSG* makes the most compelling argument for what would happen post-apocalypse. Bureaucracy would survive. All else fails, leadership, democracy, relationships, but bureaucracies – the military organized religion, government – survive. While elections happen periodically throughout the series, which is seemingly due to Ron Moore's faith in democratic societies, these elections generally do not provide legitimate government. The state of nature that the humans are thrust into demonstrates the flaws in democratic leadership – the way that we choose is thrown into stark relief. Thus these elections exist only to hinder decision making; all decision making is made by elite actors and their decisions tend to be good ones. The show explores the different types of bureaucratic leaders that a social contract can call forth to deal with a crisis and makes a compelling case for Max Weber's vocational politician as the best leader.

Toward this end, I examine *BSG* to flesh out one piece of the social contract that is prominently developed – that of political judgment. Hobbes's political judgment entails the people being tyrannized because they are generally evil.[2] Locke's political judgment entails people only having the option to decide when the government is found to be in violation of the contract.[3] Rousseau has political judgment much more closely woven through his contract in that the general will of the people serves as the collective's political judgment.[4] I argue that Weber[5] has added a piece to the political judgment conversation by demonstrating the types of leaders that are necessary for a social contract to survive and that *BSG* exemplifies the validity of Weber's call. I explore Weber's four possible leadership models using four major characters of *BSG*, but first I will demonstrate how *BSG* demonstrates that democratic decision making fails. Thus, political judgment must be separated from democracy and given over to some kind of leader. Good political judgment happens when a leader is good, and *BSG* demonstrates that the best leader is the vocational politician: the perfect civil servant.

Democracy Fails

The Cylon War is long over, yet we must not forget the reasons why so many sacrificed so much in the cause of freedom. The cost of wearing the uniform can be high, but -- (long pause) sometimes it's too high. You know, when we fought the Cylons, we did it to save ourselves from

extinction. But we never answered the question, why? Why are we as a people worth saving? We still commit murder because of greed, spite, jealousy. And we still visit all of our sins upon our children. We refuse to accept the responsibility for anything that we've done. Like we did with the Cylons. We decided to play God, create life. When that life turned against us, we comforted ourselves in the knowledge that it really wasn't our fault, not really. You cannot play God, then wash your hands of the things that you've created. Sooner or later, the day comes when you can't hide from the things that you've done anymore.
—Adama (Pilot)

The series opens with the destruction and near genocide of the human race a generation after a tentative peace with the Cylons – a robotic "race" created by humans. Forty years earlier, humans and Cylons battled it out and left it at a truce. Cylons and humans are supposed to meet every year to make sure the truce holds. Every year the humans send someone and the Cylons send no one. The series begins when the Cylons change the decades-long convention by sending a new model (Cylons now look human) and then blowing up the station. Meanwhile, the Battlestar Galactica is being decommissioned and Adama is retiring. The Education Secretary, Laura Roslin, is present at the decommission as a representative of the president. Lee Adama, aka Apollo, is coming to fly his father's viper for the last time at the ceremony. Gaius Baltar, an eminent scientist, is being interviewed for his argument that networking, while dangerous during a war with Cylons, is no longer problematic. Thus the stage is set. The Cylons destroy life on the twelve human planets and the only people left are either scattered across the planets in pockets of resistance or on military vehicles traveling in space.

The arrogance inherent to humanity is the general thrust of the beginning. The Cylons come to attack because humans never questioned their attitude toward creating artificial intelligence. While the new series, Caprica, looks set to address these more general ethical questions, BSG did not do so. Adama's speech at the opening is a nod to the underlying problem that people make bad choices. BSG address the issues more specifically of political judgment.

Every time people are asked to make a decision they choose wrong, whether it is voting for Baltar, essentially a vote for landing on a planet and living which results in being oppressed within a year by Cylon forces (Lay Down Your Burdens); or when the media informs the people about humanoid Cylons which results in violence throughout the fleet (Litmus); or when the people vote for a radical prisoner for vice-president, Tom Zarek, which leads to problems down the line because he is not good at governing. Time and again political judgment runs askew when democracy is asked to play a role. Roslin is a good president, but she only gets to be president due to the line of succession after the genocide. Adama is a good leader, but he only gets to make decisions because he is the highest ranking officer in what is left in the military.

BSG appears to tell us that democracy simply is not a good way to make good political judgments. At one point in the series, the fleet comes upon a planet that could barely sustain human life – but it can sustain human life thus the people – exhausted after spending months in claustrophobic spaceships - beg to get time on the surface. Roslin argues that "this is a rest stop … we're not settling here, obviously" (Lay Down your Burdens Part 1). But to a democracy inclined toward short term political judgment, it is not obvious. Baltar wins the election because Roslin has the exact wrong response to this issue. In complex situations the people can be counted on to be passionate and unruly, generally they are not deliberate and they lack foresight. Leadership is needed to make decisions. We have an argument here for leadership playing a crucial role in social contract theory – we come together to be governed, but we will not all make decisions and we need leaders who will govern us. *BSG* demonstrates, which is the most realistic, that the bureaucracies will be called upon to survive and make decisions.

Leadership

In Weber's lecture given to students at Munich University in 1918, *Politics as Vocation*, he argues that there have been three pure types of legitimate leadership: traditional, charismatic, and legal.[6] The traditional leader is legitimate through the "mores sanctified through the unimaginably ancient recognition and habitual orientation to conform."[7] In this case, the leader can make a claim to time immemorial – the people follow him or her because lifetimes of habits lead us to do so. The charismatic leader has a gift of grace legitimation or "the absolutely personal devotion and personal confidence in revelation, heroism, or other qualities of individual leadership."[8] This type of a leadership is about people reacting to a person's innate ability to move them – a transformational leader. Third, the legal leader has legitimate authority because "obedience is expected in discharging statutory obligations."[9] Statute has made this person the leader so people follow due to the law. For Weber, these three types of leaders fail and he calls for a new type of leader, the vocational politician – the civil servant who always chooses to do the right thing. In *BSG*, four leaders emerge in the show as having legitimate decision making authority: Roslin, Baltar, Bill Adama (Adama) and Lee Adama (Apollo).

Roslin as Traditional Leader

Roslin begins her leadership on *BSG* as a result of the genocide. She is 43rd in line to the presidency and as they discover that the other 42 have been killed, she becomes president. Her first act is to organize a rescue mission and a power struggle ensues between her and Adama who will not deign to follow the lead of a mere "schoolteacher." Eventually, Adama acquiesces to her leadership, but only reluctantly and only conditionally. He is able to retain military leadership after Roslin catches him in the lie of knowing where earth is. Slowly, Adama allows her into the military decision making apparatus. To a certain extent, this beginning suggests that Roslin will be a legal leader, with her legitimacy only due to the statute of the line of succession, but over time Roslin builds a new base of leadership based on religion – thus taking on the mantle of traditional leader.

The *BSG* world has a polytheistic religious underpinning with ancient scrolls telling the narrative of the people. The story goes as follows, this has all happened before and this will all happen again, as though people merely played out a role in a predestined manner – there is much emphasis on the idea that everyone has a role to play in this world. Roslin has discovered she has terminal cancer and chooses to take hallucinogenic drugs to treat her condition. These drugs lead to her having hallucinations which turn out to be part of the narrative. A religious leader informs her that the ancient scrolls predict that a dying leader will lead the people to a new home during a time of crisis (The Hand of God). Roslin, assumes the mantle of that dying leader, develops a base of leadership based on ancient traditions. In The Farm, Roslin very clearly states that she will play the "religion card." She appeals to the people to follow her rather than Adama based on her being this religious leader.

In Home, Roslin leads a small band to find the path to Earth. Roslin is committed the entire series to finding Earth for the people, and most of this comes from her belief in the ancient scrolls. That Earth exists, that she is the leader to find it and that the people should follow her to Earth – this axiom guides all her political judgment. She decides to break from the fleet to ultimately find a cave that shows a constellation system that viewers would recognize as existing in view from earth. This is a path to earth. They find this path based on the ancient scrolls, thus lending legitimacy to her claim as traditional leader.

Roslin becomes the resistance leader when the Cylons take them over on New Caprica. She can so powerfully draw people in that she is able to persuade them to use terrorism in an effort to end the occupation. In the end – after a daring rescue mission led by Adama, the vice-presidential candidate who had previously beaten her in an election, defers to her rule and allows her to leave the planet in the president's flagship, Colonial One.

She is the archetypal traditional leader. Because ancient mores, and the ancient scrolls, say that a dying leader will take the people to earth and generally people believe, especially in a time of crisis, in ancient traditions, Roslin has a legitimate claim to leadership. This guides her political judgment as well. She believes that she is the prophesized leader and this belief sends her onto a planet to find the path to earth. Because she is the ancient leader she refuses to consider any compromise that halts the flight of the 40,000 humans before they reach earth. She makes decisions to send Starbuck back to find the arrow of Apollo which is not necessarily in the good of the people, but is in line with what the ancient scrolls tell her to do. Finally, her political judgment is affected by a religious vision in the Hub, in which Elosha, her original religious advisor, appears to her and causes her to not take out her chief rival for power.

Baltar as Charismatic Leader

We are introduced to Baltar as a scientific genius in the first episode. He is seen instantly as a leader who would invoke obedience and devotion due to his innate self-confidence and charisma. Baltar is pushing for progress in the technological world, to go into networking in a way that would have been unheard of a generation earlier. After the destruction of the Twelve Colonies, Baltar is allowed into the upper echelons of political leadership early because he is a scientist who develops a Cylon detector. First he joins the Quorum of Twelve as a representative and then he is asked to be vice-president by Roslin so that she can block Zarek's rise to power.

In Final Cut, Baltar is encouraged by a vision to try to take over leadership of the fleet. This is Baltar's claim to power – even though he does get elected president and is elected to the Quorum – he uses his personal persuasive abilities to get people to follow him, his claim to legitimate power is based entirely on his intelligence, charm and charisma. Although he is initially unsuccessful, Baltar will come back time and again to this type of leadership.

Baltar becomes increasingly a threat to Roslin's power base, as a charismatic leader would be to a traditional leader. Both are drawing on people's emotions and passions for a following, so people can be torn as they choose between them. Roslin tries to get Baltar out of the vice-presidency but Baltar refuses to leave. He then decides to run against Roslin for president. He takes on Roslin at the core of her leadership base, saying that they must land on a habitable planet rather than searching for earth. When the people choose Baltar, they indicate a shift away from religious leadership to a personal leader. This rocks the underpinning for Roslin which she cannot shore up until Baltar is shown to be a collaborator with the Cylons.

Interestingly, the show demonstrates the limits of the charismatic leader's political judgment. Obedience depends on the belief in the man or woman in the office – the people believe he was called. Once you have to govern, however, the flaws in any administration become evident and people begin to question the ability and thus the obedience falls off. As we see in Lay Down Your Burdens, Baltar is a cult of personality, but not a governor. These types of leaders are politicians because they are called – a great mobilizing force, good for mass movements, but not for making decisions.

Later, when Baltar is in detention about to go up for trial, he decides to try to sway his chances by appealing directly to the people. Again, as a charismatic leader he relies more on his charismatic connection to the people rather than trusting in the legal system to free him. In Dirty Hands, Baltar publishes his life story and reveals that he was raised as a farmer who trained himself to lose the accent of his simple, "salt of the eart" homeworld. The publication of his story results in a labor strike indicating Baltar's leadership abilities are intact –people believe in him. After his trial he is secreted off Galactica by a group of women who become a religious cult who ostensibly worship Baltar (Crossroads). Eventually Baltar will try to get representation for this group in the fleet government – again using his charisma to land him political power.

An interesting piece of Baltar's judgment in the show is the side story of Gaeta. Gaeta worshipped Baltar from the beginning of the series – trusting in his judgment time and again until Baltar fails so spectacularly on New Caprica. This outward worship, when its object fails, leads Gaeta to connect with Zarek, the next best charismatic leader, and try to initiate a coup. Gaeta is ultimately executed – demonstrating the failure of charismatic leadership. If your leadership base is centered on cult of personality status, your judgment depends on their following you, which can result in disastrous consequences.

Adama as Legal Leader

Adama is the archetypal legal leader – he discharges his statutory obligations in such a way that he commands respect. His leadership base is dependent on his always following the rules. In the series, Adama demonstrates a political judgment that is often superior to both Roslin and Baltar, which offers a Hamiltonian insight into bureaucrats offering a better type of leadership. Bureaucrats will always do a better job administrating than elected officials as they are more professional. Adama never wavers in his command – he protects his agency, as a bureaucrat would, prioritizing military needs, but also submits to the command of Roslin because the military is technically secondary to the elected leadership.

For the series, Adama is the most obvious choice of leader as he guides the fleet through its initial run away from the Cylons. In 33, all decision making happens within half an hour as the Cylons take that long to find them. In that expedited manner, the top bureaucrat in the military is the person in control. When Roslin breaks off from the fleet to find the Tomb of Athena, or the path to earth, it is Adama who apologizes first and works to mend the fleet. Because he is a statutory leader, he respects the law which places her in command. He is public about submitting to her.

We see this also in the arch of episodes that has the fleet coming back into contact with the Pegasus – another battlestar, which is commanded by Adama's superior officer Admiral Cain. Although it is clear that Adama is by far the better choice as leader, he accepts Cain's command. Even though he is encouraged to do so, he never attempts to overthrow his command, in the course of things she is murdered by a Cylon agent and Adama again takes command of both ships. It is important to note that the statutory leader would not grasp when the law clearly indicates other action is warranted. He submits to his superior officer because he obeys the law.

In Lay Down Your Burdens, we see Adama behaving in a legalistic manner again. Even though both he and Roslin know that Baltar will be a disaster as president, when he discovers the plot to steal the election by Roslin, he announces the misdeed. He protects the traditional leader in the process by covering up the conspiracy but he submits to the electoral results. Again, if the law says Baltar has won, even though Adama is highly suspicious that Baltar was responsible for terrorism in the fleet, he submits to Baltar's leadership. As this story arc plays itself out, we see Adama rescuing the people from New Caprica but then immediately submitting to Roslin as president.

Perhaps the most persuasive moment of Adama's legalistic leadership is at Baltar's trial, Crossroads, Adama votes for Baltar's acquittal even though he passionately hates him. Apollo makes an impassioned plea for justice, and the legalist is persuaded by the rightness of it.

Again and again Adama will save the fleet or make decisions to save the fleet, but always submits to the authority of the law once crisis is averted. Whether it is Roslin as president or Baltar as president, he respects the rule of law and never tries to subvert the process.

Apollo as Vocational Politician

While these three leaders are generally seen as the main sources of decisions and judgment in the show, *BSG* makes a pitch for what Weber calls the vocational politician in its character of Lee Adama (Apollo). Throughout the series, Apollo always makes the correct choices. He has a very refined sense of what is the principled position for the twelve colonies and we see him being the conscience throughout the series. He is the perfect civil servant.

> To take a stand, to be passionate – *ira et studium* – is the politician's element, and above all the element of the political leader. His conduct is subject to quite a different, indeed, exactly the opposite, principle of responsibility from that of the civil servant. The honor of the civil servant is vested in his ability to execute conscientiously the order of the superior authorities, exactly as if the order agreed with his own conviction. This holds even if the order appears wrong to him and if, despite the civil servant's remonstrances, the authority insists on the order. Without this moral discipline and self-denial, in the highest sense, the whole apparatus would fall to pieces. The honor of the political leader, of the leading statesman, however, lies precisely in an exclusive personal responsibility for what he does, a responsibility he cannot and must not reject or transfer.[10]

We see Roslin, Baltar and Adama as political leaders – everything they do manifests a personal responsibility. When Adama blames himself for everything toward the end of the series; when Roslin gives up on her faith toward the end of the series; when Baltar tells the cult that they have used him and refuses to escape with them – each of these times they are acknowledging a personal failure. Their political judgment has failed the people who follow them and they feel personally to blame. But not Apollo; his political judgment is based on his adherence to a set of principles that the colonies originally espouse. Imagine an American civil servant who defends the Bill of Rights, regardless of the consequences. Apollo defends the colonial equivalent throughout the series.

Since a young boy Apollo had clearly admired the legal career of his grandfather who was renowned for defending the worst of society. Therefore, he gets exposed early to the principles of the twelve colonies and he adheres to them. The way that Roslin makes her decisions based on anything that squares with religion and Baltar makes his decisions based on anything that supports his personal rise to power and Adama makes his decisions based on statutory rules – Apollo always makes decisions based on an adherence to the principles of the twelve worlds. He does not claim personal responsibility for what happens – his "moral discipline" means that he must execute conscientiously the principles – even if it means destroying a ship full of citizens or defending the greatest traitor to the twelve colonies, Baltar.

Apollo is the military advisor for Roslin and lead pilot of the Galactica viper squadron. In Kobol's Last Gleaming, he demonstrates his adherence to democratic principles by rescuing Roslin from Tigh's military coup. First, he draws his gun on Tigh to prevent the removal of power of Roslin and then when his father is shot, he secrets Roslin off Galactica to the planet to find the tomb of Athena (Resistance). In Bastille Day he insists on negotiating with radical Zarek so that the prisoners on the Astral Queen have control of their ship and forces Roslin to hold a special election for vice-president, which she does not want to do.

He is also committed to human ideals as well as political ideals. In Pegasus he is urged by the lead pilot of the other ship to force his pilots to keep kill counts but he insists on keeping his pilots alive. His judgment is in line with higher ideals. On Resurrection Ship, he is so despondent about Adama and Roslin's plan to assassinate Cain that he does not make an attempt to save himself. His adherence to higher ideals means he has problems seeing leaders not adhere to said ideals.

The only time we see Apollo behaving in a less than perfectly humane way is in A Measure of Salvation in which he is the person who suggests using the biological weapon of a Cylon virus to end the fight. But, in purely bureaucratic terms, Apollo is a human and the Cylons are the enemy. This is the most rational way to end the war and give his people latitude to find earth – to complete their journey. So in some sense, while this does not seem to adhere to the highest ideals, it is a problem case that demonstrates his commitment to serving his people.

We see Apollo at his best in the trial for Baltar's life. Roslin wants him put in charge of the trial but he initially refuses thinking he has too much work to do on Galactica. Adama then puts him in charge of security since

Baltar's first lawyer was killed. Drawn into the process by Baltar's lawyer (the Son Also Rises), Apollo embarrasses Tigh in court which leads to Tigh's resignation from the military (Crossroads). Apollo is the person who makes an impassioned plea for justice. His argument is that everyone has been forgiven mistakes – why should one person be made to pay for the entire genocide of humankind. His argument is the one that sways Adama to vote for an acquittal. Eventually Zarek nominates him to serve on the Quorum where his idealism again shows through. He refuses to allow the political rights of Baltar's cult to be restricted – again demonstrating his commitment to the right to exercise religion and to organize in groups. His political judgment is totally that of a loyal civil servant – loyal to the authority of the original colonies' political ideals. Although Roslin, Adama, and Baltar have problems with him, even Roslin has to acknowledge, and respect, his idealism (Escape Velocity).

As the end of the series, it is Apollo who reorganizes the political world for the refugees. He decides that the planetary representation makes no sense on the Quorum because people do not live on the colonies anymore – so they should be represented by ship. Roslin agrees and leaves most of the political judgment to Apollo as they get closer to earth. Finally, when they discover a habitable planet to live on, he makes the decision to leave all of their technology behind so that humanity can start again.

Again, Apollo makes a decision that is not necessarily the easiest for humanity, but probably the best decision to make for them to have a chance at living in adherence to the high ideals he manifests throughout the show. They will teach the primitive cultures they find language and culture but not technology. They will give the people the best of themselves and try to shield them from the worst of themselves. This political judgment is that of the truest vocational politician – it asks nothing of tradition, charisma or law. It makes a decision based on ideals – not on a person.

Conclusion

The interesting piece of *BSG* is that it allows us to take political leadership into a state of nature and it so beautifully demonstrates the three pure leadership types of Weber while also making a case for vocational politicians. We see that bureaucracy marches on through an apocalypse. We discover that democratic political judgment - whether it is elite or participatory – fails in apocalypse post-apocalyptic state of nature.

Political judgment is put to the test and we find that it is best from a civil servant.

Notes

[1] Hobbes, Thomas. 1968. *Leviathan*. New York: Penguin Books.

[2] *Ibid.*

[3] Locke, John. 1997. *Two Treatises of Government*. New York: Cambridge University Press.

[4] Rousseau, Jean-Jacques. 1987. *On the Social Contract*. Indianapolis: Hackett Publishing Company.

[5] Weber, Max. 1918 "Politics as a Vocation."
http://www.ne.jp/asahi/moriyuki/abukuma/weber/lecture/politics_vocation.html

[6] *Ibid.*

[7] *Ibid.*

[8] *Ibid.*

[9] *Ibid.*

[10] *Ibid.*

POPULAR CULTURE OF THE PRESIDENCY

Presidential Debates
in the Infotainment Era

Jeffrey Crouch and Richard Semiatin

"I think the presidency ought to be held at a higher level than having to answer questions from a snowman."[1] So said Republican presidential candidate Mitt Romney on his initial plan to skip the Republican CNN/YouTube debate because he felt the format was beneath the office of the presidency. Romney's view echoes wide-spread reservations about changes that have permeated all aspects of the campaign process, from rubber-chicken dinners to the formality of structured debates. To many candidates, recent campaigns are, regrettably, often more about entertainment than information. Indeed, American politics has moved from the party-driven elections of the early 1960s to the personality-centered elections of today, a time when politics and entertainment have become increasingly intertwined.[2] One result is that voters – and not parties – now select how they wish to learn about the candidates.[3] Increasingly, voters are deciding that entertainment value is as important as educational content. Nowhere has this been more apparent than with presidential debates.

The political science literature on presidential debates and candidate communications reflects the evolution of modern campaigns. While the entertainment aspect of debates is important, Thomas Holbrook points out that voters are information seekers and that the greater the exposure they have to debates, the more they learn about politics and issues, as well as personality. Holbrook's recent writing affirms Samuel Popkin's earlier work that voters parse information and act rationally. Popkin asserted that the volume of information was important but also that political symbols (*e.g.*, parades, debates, conventions) invest voters in the value of the process. Furthermore, Doris Graber points out that parsing information has become more specialized in an era where news coverage is narrowcasted beyond the traditional broadcast media into specialized media such as YouTube and Twitter, and where information is edited by a different source to highlight the punches, counterpunches and pratfalls of candidates. For those who seek to view or read about the highlights of major political events rather than view them in their entirety, the immediacy of such information can short-circuit the valuable substantive information.[4]

Thus, the purpose of this chapter is to examine the transition of presidential debates from formal political theater (*e.g.,* Kennedy-Nixon) to the emergence of debates as "must-see" television in the 1970s through the end of the twentieth century. The chapter then pursues a discussion of presidential debates in the multi-media era. Finally, it concludes with an exploration of the next frontier, such as on-line and Twitter debates.

The Emergence of Presidential Debates as Formal Theater

Television changed politics. Beginning with the 1952 campaign, candidates began to take advantage of a post-war bump in television ownership by advertising over the airwaves. The Eisenhower and Stevenson ads from 1952 seem primitive today, but back then, they represented cutting-edge technology. Not only have paid media become important, so too has the unpaid or "earned media" portion of the campaign. In 1956, the Democratic convention brought drama into living rooms across the nation as the party deliberated whether to select as Adlai Stevenson's running mate either Estes Kefauver, the reform-minded senator from Tennessee, or telegenic upstart John F. Kennedy, the young senator from Massachusetts. While Kefauver may have been the choice, a media star was born in Kennedy. The nomination fight was not the stuff of Greek drama, but it did help make television a theater event for politics, which fully culminated in the 1960 presidential debates between John F. Kennedy and Richard M. Nixon. The formal theater of the 1960 presidential debates changed politics, and how we view it, forever.

The Kennedy-Nixon Debates

The 1960 presidential race between Democrat John F. Kennedy and Republican Richard M. Nixon coincided with the continuing trend of mass availability and ownership of televisions to help permanently transform politics. Now, voters could see and hear live candidates debating political issues on a world stage. Performing well on camera became another unofficial, though key, presidential qualification. Indeed, historian Gary Donaldson writes that after the 1960 election, "Image, physical appearance, and presence before the camera became as important as issues, endorsements and political events."[5]

The Kennedy-Nixon debates certainly seemed to bear out this contention. The contrast between the candidates' appearance on the night of their first debate was stark: while Kennedy was "tall, thin, tanned, and wearing a well-tailored dark suit," Nixon was, in the words of reporter Theodore White, "tense, almost frightened, at turns glowering and, occasionally, haggard-looking to the point of sickness."[6] Nixon, who had been sick during the days leading up to the debate, was running a fever of 102 degrees, was tired, had lost weight, and was wearing an unflattering coat of "pancake make-up." White memorably noted "that famous shot of the camera on the Vice-President as he half slouched, his "Lazy Shave" powder faintly streaked with sweat, his eyes exaggerated hollows of blackness, his jaw, jowls, and face drooping with strain."[7]

The key point here is that Nixon's appearance was only an issue to the television audience, which rated Kennedy as the unquestioned winner of the debate. In contrast, those who followed the debate on the radio, according to a poll, decided that Kennedy and Nixon had tied.[8] To Donaldson, a candidate's image as beamed through television was now crucial, and thus "1960 set the stage for manufactured political candidates and manufactured images."[9] The debates also had a lasting effect on the loser, Richard Nixon, who never again would appear to debate on the national stage.

The Backlash from Kennedy-Nixon

Nixon was permanently scarred by his first debate with Kennedy. In *Six Crises*, he wrote, "one bad camera angle can have far more effect on the election outcome than a major mistake in writing a speech, which is then picked up and criticized by columnists and editorial writers."[10] While he did not concede that the debates cost him the election, they clearly played a substantial role in his refusal to participate in future ones: Nixon passed on debating his Democratic opposition in 1968 (Vice President Hubert Humphrey) and 1972 (Senator George McGovern).[11]

Lyndon Johnson, who succeeded Kennedy in 1963 following the latter's assassination, eschewed debates as well. Johnson refused to debate his Republican rival Barry Goldwater "so voters could avoid making direct comparisons between the two candidates' positions."[12] Furthermore, Johnson had been running ahead of Goldwater in the polls at a rate of more than two to one, so he had nothing to gain from a debate. Neither Johnson nor Nixon was as telegenic a candidate as Kennedy. Both men were painfully aware of their shortcomings as candidates on the stump. Nor were presidential debates yet a standard feature of presidential campaigns. There was no public expectation or clamor for debates since they had only been held once.

The Reemergence of Presidential Debates as Must-See TV

The turmoil of the Vietnam War and Watergate in the late 1960s and early 1970s helped renew public interest in presidential debates. President Gerald Ford's controversial pardon of his predecessor, Richard Nixon, contributed to a particularly hostile environment for Republicans seeking elective office.[13] At the same time, broadcast news coverage continued to grow in popularity. Both Vietnam and Watergate were featured most evenings on television news. In 1976, the Democrats nominated former Georgia governor Jimmy Carter, a reform-minded candidate, who promised to never "tell a lie." Thus, the institutionalization of presidential debates occurred not because of the Kennedy-Nixon precedent; rather, the public outcry for transparency in the wake of Vietnam and Watergate made the appearance of presidential debates an inevitable quadrennial event.

Debates became a regular feature of presidential campaigns, with tens of millions of people watching them every four years. For example, the lone Jimmy Carter-Ronald Reagan debate in 1980 generated a record audience of 80 million viewers—an audience only rivaled that year by the Super Bowl.[14] The largest viewing audience in 2008 was for the Joe Biden-Sarah Palin vice presidential debate, which drew an audience of 70 million viewers, about 7 million larger than any viewing audience for a presidential debate in 2008.[15] Like the Super Bowl, presidential debates are "must see" television events.

Debates as Earned Media

The institutionalization of debates has encouraged campaigns to use them to advertise their candidates. As such, a major purpose of holding debates is to increase the public's exposure to the candidates' parsed and planned answers. Candidates "earn" free advertising through debates, thus it is in their self-interest to prepare in terms of substance and appearance for the debate. Mike Duval and Foster Canock, who wrote a strategy memorandum on June 11, 1976 for the Ford campaign, articulated the importance of what could be gained from a debate. "In this situation, we can maximize the advantage of incumbency, since the President is far more knowledgeable, experienced and *balanced* (emphasis added) than Carter."[16] The implications were clear: show Carter to be a risk. You may not like Ford, but at least you know what you are going to get. Unfortunately for Ford, Carter had matters well in hand during all three of his debates with Ford, while it was the incumbent (as seen later in the chapter) who may have muffed his chance because of a verbal miscue.

How Debate Preparation Has Changed

Presidential elections are rare, high-stakes occurrences, and candidates spend millions on teams of political experts. Pre-debate preparation is one of the few times when these consultants can control what happens in a presidential debate.[17] In light of the lessons from the 1960 debates, presidential candidates have come to know that debate preparation is essential.

In 1960, John Kennedy and Richard Nixon had differing views of debate preparation. Kennedy's people had assembled a briefing book on Nixon, and the candidate agreed to be peppered with questions by his aides. Nixon had a briefing book on Kennedy, but was supremely confident both in his knowledge of the issues and his own debating skills. He did not even practice for the debate, according to his campaign manager.[18] Nixon's haggard appearance and his occasional hesitations in answering questions contrasted with Kennedy's handsome face, self-assured manner, and flawlessly delivered lines.

The lessons of 1960 have proven to be enormously valuable to presidential candidates in the nearly five decades since the Kennedy/Nixon encounters. Most presidential contenders have at least tried to prepare for their opponents. Jimmy Carter, for example, studied film of the 1960 debates with actor Robert Redford. Gerald Ford became the model for many presidential debaters with his "full-scale" debates featuring "lecterns, stand-in questioners, cameras, lights, and makeup."[19] Ronald Reagan, a former professional actor, was nevertheless lackluster in rehearsals. Still, he practiced until he hit his stride.[20]

Bill Clinton, who worked enormously hard at debate preparation, reportedly "ran drills on everything from physical posture to facial expressions." For his town hall performance, Clinton worked with Hollywood producer Harry Thomason to plan the candidate's movements so that George H.W. Bush and Ross Perot remained in the camera shot while Clinton spoke. By doing so, the Clinton team circumvented the debate's rule forbidding "cutaway" shots to other candidates, which might catch them in an unguarded moment. The infamous shot of Bush checking his watch resulted from this clever strategy.[21] In 2008, David Axelrod, Obama's chief strategist, described his candidate's substantive preparation for a third debate with John McCain as minimal. After having had at least two dozen prior experiences debating throughout the campaign, Obama had a firm grasp of the issues. "It's less about preparing for the substance…The candidates are sitting at a table tonight, sitting in close proximity. It sounds silly, but those are the things you've got to consider as you prepare."[22]

Not every modern presidential candidate uses elaborate sets with stand-ins, lighting, cameras, makeup, and the like. Still, those tools are all available today. The key is to present the best version of the candidate possible: confident, comfortable with the setting and the issues, and, if possible, warm and witty. An over prepared candidate can be just as bad as an underprepared one, so it is important for advisors to size up their clients and find a happy medium.

Debates as Car Crashes—Self-Inflicted or Not

The late Texas political columnist Molly Ivins once said, "political debates are sort of like stock-car races—no one really cares who wins, they just want to see the crashes." Without the crashes, Ivins states that viewers think the debates are "a complete bore."[23] While Ivins may have overstated her case, the fascination with human character and frailty is particularly important when making a presidential choice. Even though the event is infotainment, viewers know in the backs of their minds that the results do matter. Below we present several examples of debate "car crashes" and how they impacted particular presidential elections.

A. Gerald Ford and "Eastern Europe"

In 1976, incumbent president Gerald Ford answered a question in the second presidential debate on foreign policy that may have cost him the election. In a lengthy retort to a question from Max Frankel of *The New York Times* about whether the Soviet Union had gained an upper hand over the United States in influencing world politics, Ford ended with a perplexing statement: "There is no Soviet domination of Eastern Europe."[24] When asked for clarification by his questioner, Ford stood his ground. Initially, the mistake did not affect viewers' assessment of the debate's winner: Republicans believed Ford had won, and Democrats backed their candidate, former Georgia governor Jimmy Carter. However, after several days of media reports drawing attention to the gaffe, a new poll revealed that significantly more respondents believed that Carter had bested Ford in the debate, and, accordingly, Carter's public image received a boost.[25] While Ford had meant to say that the people of Eastern Europe did not see themselves as communists, he muddled his words both in the debate and through a later explanation. In the end, Carter went on to defeat Ford in the general election by a narrow majority of 1.7 million votes out of 80 million ballots cast.

B. Michael Dukakis and the Death Penalty

One of the most perplexing responses a presidential candidate has given to a reporter's question came in the second debate of 1988 from Massachusetts governor and Democratic nominee Michael Dukakis. Dukakis was facing Republican nominee and vice president George H.W. Bush in a very close election campaign. One of the problems that Dukakis faced was his failure to personally connect with audiences. Dukakis prided himself on being a technocrat: once, he even carried Swedish planning manuals along as fun reading while on vacation. His stoicism was often mistaken for indifference regarding the issues, and Dukakis's lack of passion hurt him with the voting public leading into this debate. A controversial question posed by CNN reporter Bernard Shaw offered a widely viewed opportunity for Dukakis to show the emotion that had been missing from his campaign. Instead, Dukakis muffed the chance.

> Shaw: Governor, if Kitty Dukakis were raped and murdered, would you favor an irrevocable death penalty for the killer?
> Dukakis: No, I don't, Bernard, and I think you know that I've opposed the death penalty during all of my life. I don't see any evidence that it's a deterrent, and I think there are better and more effective ways to deal with violent crime.

What was missing from Dukakis's response? Any mention of Kitty, his wife, and any sense that he found the question offensive, or at least inappropriate. With his flat delivery, Dukakis confirmed his negative public image as an "iceman," someone who was not especially warm or personable.[26] George H.W. Bush went on to defeat Dukakis in the general election by a comfortable margin, in part because Dukakis could not establish a personal connection with voters. If he could not show emotion about his wife, then how could he empathize with the problems facing ordinary Americans?

C. John McCain Shows Exasperation

In 2008, Republican presidential nominee John McCain displayed frequent frustration in his last debate with his Democratic counterpart, Barack Obama, through "copious eye-rolling" and "frequent and exaggerated wide-eyed 'I can't believe what he's saying' looks." Indeed, "McCain looked like the quintessential exasperated older brother who can't believe anyone is taking his kid brother seriously."[27] Perhaps McCain's most famous misfire occurred during the second debate. McCain, arguing that Obama had backed a particular Bush administration policy, said "You know who voted for it? You might never know. That one." "The One" was apparently the nickname McCain supporters had hung on the Democrat, a reference to Keanu Reeves's Messiah-like character Neo in the 1999 film *The Matrix*.[28] By contrast, Obama appeared cool, calm and collected; he seemed non-plussed by McCain's behavior, which came across as less than presidential. McCain's attitude may have contributed to a substantial Obama victory in 2008. The nation was facing the greatest economic crisis since the Great Depression, and Obama's steadiness was viewed as a valuable commodity for a potential chief executive to display.[29] In contrast, McCain's performance in the last debate eviscerated the underpinnings of his campaign—that experience provides wisdom and calmness in the face of a calamity.

Presidential Debates in the Multi-Media Era

With over 200 channels, three cable news networks, and instant blog reporting by citizens acting as journalists, media coverage of politics has become instantaneous. According to political consultant Tim Crawford: "You say something today, and it will be on the air in eight or nine minutes."[30] The news filter that sourced, analyzed and reviewed news coverage two decades ago is now gone forever. The emergence of a 24 hour news cycle demanding instant reaction has provided less time for reflection in this era of digital technology. Our media sea-change may have a profound effect on presidential debates.

Instantaneous Reaction—The YouTube Effect

In 2008, the video-sharing website YouTube, which did not exist during the last presidential race, introduced a new member to the usual cast of characters: you. That is, anyone with a computer could view video clips on the site, and anyone with a video camera could upload their own work to be viewed by potential millions worldwide. YouTube helped to spread the American presidential campaign instantaneously to the farthest corners of the globe, in the process contributing to fleeting fame for Samuel "Joe the Plumber" Wurzelbacher and Amber Lee "Obama Girl" Ettinger, among others.

YouTube is one manifestation of technological advances that are transforming American elections, including presidential debates. For the first time ever, CNN and YouTube teamed up to offer the Democratic and Republican parties a debate format in which average Americans sitting at home could submit prerecorded queries to the parties' aspiring presidential hopefuls. The video clips ranged from quirky – such as the infamous talking snowman – to downright uncomfortable: In their debate, Republicans were name-checked by an acoustic guitar-playing YouTube user named Chris Nandor,[31] while in the Democratic engagement, Senators Obama and Hillary Clinton were asked how they address accusations of not being considered "black" or "feminine" enough, respectively.[32]

The YouTube debate was the most significant innovation in presidential debate format since the town hall was first used in 1992 because average Americans who were not physically present in the hall were nonetheless asking questions of the candidates.[33] The positive side is that YouTube increases the democratization and input of the nation's citizens. On the other hand, YouTube's effect is immediate because it is uploaded by the user for a mass audience. There is no independent panel that reviews the fairness or bias of each video or live feed. Although nothing egregious happened in 2008, one has to wonder whether distortions might occur in the future.

24 Hour News Coverage

Round-the-clock coverage of news means that presidential debates are scrutinized instantaneously by broadcast news organizations around the world. Cable news stations will provide blanket coverage of debates into the next day's cycle. Media organizations such as CBS, CNN and ABC conduct instant surveys of preselected debate viewers. Coverage focuses on "who won" and "who lost" the debates. And, of course, the networks look for the ten to fifteen second exchange or sound bite that wins or loses the debate. Today, that moment will be available on YouTube within several minutes, and thousands of viewers may see it within 24 hours. Given the speed and intensity of response in today's media environment, it is possible that any debate gaffe may have an even more devastating effect on a candidate's chances than in the past. What would be the impact of the Ford comment on Eastern Europe, or Dukakis' response to the death penalty question, today?

The rapid response world of presidential debates is further impacted by the "debate after the debate." Following each encounter, surrogates for both candidates gather in the media room and "spin" their interpretation of the debate for slews of reporters. Many in the press love this opportunity for unfettered access to the campaigns. David Corn of the *Nation* magazine stated: "For a political reporter, it's paradise. Everybody who may not return your phone calls is in there with a big sign behind them. They have to take your questions, and you're under no obligation to accept their spin, and they have to be polite to you."[34] While the spin room provides great theater and quotes for reporters, it is certainly not a place for great substance. As one reporter has said, "it's also become a cheap alternative for cable news shows looking to cover some airtime."[35]

Today, there is a new spin room populated by citizens who respond directly via media blogs. CNN, MSNBC and FOX encourage viewer email responses to the debates. CNN, in particular, plays an active role in reading some of the blogs on air, or on their Internet simulcast. This appears to be the wave of the future as additional, often uninformed, commentary further overshadows the substance of a debate.

Conclusion: The Next Frontier?

Presidential debates have become a tradition of modern day politics. They symbolize the important democratic choices that voters face. And while they may often appear as little more than a side-by-side news conference, they do at least provide an opportunity to compare candidates together in the same room. Future debates may not even do that much: some day soon, debates may feature virtual candidate appearances, whereby the hopefuls debate online; Twitter debates, where the candidates answer questions in 140 characters or less; or remote site debates, where candidates debate from television studios located in different parts of the country.

Will these innovations increase the information conveyed, or merely the entertainment value? Certainly, the spontaneity of immediate response can be lost if we do not see the candidates' faces while they Twitter or debate online. On the other hand, perhaps greater attention could be paid to substance in non-Twittered online debates because there is less body language to show. This may actually yield positive consequences for political discourse and the country's choice for the preeminent job in the world. Whatever happens, Jaques's words from *As You Like It* still ring true: "All the world's a stage, And all the men and women merely players; They have their exits and their entrances, And one man in his time plays many parts…"[36]

Notes

[1] Amy Schatz, "Republicans Feud Over YouTube Debate," *Wall Street Journal*, July 27, 2007. http://www.blogs.wsj.com. Accessed June 29, 2009.

[2] Martin P. Wattenberg, *The Rise of Candidate-Centered Elections,* (Cambridge, MA: Harvard University Press) 1991; Sean Aday and James Devitt (2001), "Style over Substance:"Newspaper Coverage of Elizabeth Dole's Presidential Campaign," *Harvard International Journal of Press/Politics*, 6, (2, Spring), 52-73 for example.

[3] Richard J. Semiatin, "Introduction" in *Campaigns on the Cutting Edge*, ed., Richard J. Semiatin, (Washington, D.C.: CQ Press 2008) 1.

[4] Thomas M. Holbrook, "Cognitive Style and Political Learning in the 2000 U.S. Presidential Campaign," *Political Science Quarterly*, 59:3 (September 2006), p. 343. Samuel L. Popkin, *The Reasoning Voter,* 2nd ed., (Chicago: University of Chicago Press, 1994). Doris A. Graber, *Mass Media and American Politics*, 8th ed., (Washington, D.C.: CQ Press 2009).

[5] Gary A. Donaldson, *The First Modern Campaign: Kennedy, Nixon and the Election of 1960*, (Lanham, MD: Rowman & Littlefield, 2007) 112.

[6] *Ibid.*, 114-115; Theodore H. White, *The Making of the President 1960*, (New York: Antheneum, 1961) 289.

[7] See Donaldson, *The First Modern Campaign*, Chapter Eight; White, *The Making of the President 1960*, 286, 289; John W. Self, "The First Debate Over the Debates: How Kennedy and Nixon Negotiated the 1960 Presidential Debates," *Presidential Studies Quarterly* 35 (June 2005): 368.

[8] Donaldson, *The First Modern Campaign*, 118.

[9] Donaldson, *The First Modern Campaign*, 158.

[10] Richard Nixon, *Six Crises,* (New York: Doubleday 1962), pp. 501-502. Journalist Chris Matthews argues in his book, *Kennedy-Nixon*, that Nixon believed the Kennedy campaign stole the election from him, in particular, in Chicago, with the alleged graveyard vote. See Christopher Matthews, *Kennedy-Nixon: The Rivalry that Shaped Post-War America*, (New York: The Free Press 1997).

[11] Jessica Leval, "A Brief History of the Modern Presidential Debate," *The American* (Journal of the American Enterprise Institute), September 29, 2008. http://www.american.com. Accessed June 29, 2009.

[12] Maris A. Vinovskis, *The Birth of Head Start.*,(Chicago: University of Chicago Press, 2005), 58.

[13] Jeffrey Crouch, *The Presidential Pardon Power*, (Lawrence: University Press of Kansas, 2009), pp. 79-80, 84.

[14] "Bush-Gore debate draws big audience," *Associated Press*, October 4, 2000. Article contained data not only on the viewing audience of the first debate in 2000 between Bush and Gore, but data on previous debates including the Carter-Reagan debate of 1980.

[15] Leigh Holmwood, "Obama-McCain debate draws 63m US viewers," guardian.co.uk, October 9, 2008. Accessed on June 24, 2009.

[16] Martin Schram, *Running for President: A Journal of the Carter Campaign*, (New York: Pocket Books, 1977).

[17] Alan Schroeder, *Presidential Debates: Fifty Years of High-Risk TV, 2nd Ed.*, (New York: Columbia University Press, 2008) 80.

[18] *Ibid.*, 80-81.

[19] *Ibid.*, 81-82.

[20] *Ibid.*, 84.

[21] *Ibid.*, 89.

[22] Jeff Zeleny, "Obama Debate Prep: Style Over Substance, *The New York Times,* from nytimes.com, October 15, 2008. Accessed on June 24, 2009.

[23] From Richard J. Semiatin, *Campaigns in the 21st Century,*(New York: McGraw-Hill 2005), 202. Citing a quote from Sherrod Brown, *Congress from the Inside*, (Kent, OH: Kent University Press, 1999), 200 (quoting Molly Ivins).

[24] http://www.youtube.com/watch?v=w8rg9c4pUrg. Accessed June 29, 2009. Also, see Schram, op cit., 351.

[25] Stephen Ansolabehere, et al., *The Media Game: American Politics in the Television Age,* (New York: MacMillan Publishing, 1993) 178.

[26] *Ibid.*, 86; http://www.youtube.com/watch?v=DF9gSyku-fc. Accessed June 29, 2009.

[27] Liz Halloran, "McCain Fails to Trip Up Obama Over Joe the Plumber," *U.S. News & World Report*, October 16, 2008. http://www.usnews.com. Accessed June 29, 2009.

[28] Toby Harnden, "Barack Obama Ducks Blows from John McCain to Win Second Presidential Debate," *Daily Telegraph,* October 8, 2008. http://www.telegraph.co.uk. Accessed June 22, 2009; David Montgomery, "'The One'? Take a Number, Sen. Obama," *Washington Post,* July 31, 2008. http://www.washingtonpost.com. Accessed June 22, 2009.

[29] A CNN/Opinion Research survey from October 3-5, 2008 showed that 59 percent of the public believed that a depression similar to the one in the 1930s was somewhat or likely to occur at that time. Information obtained from http://polllingreport.com. Accessed on August 26, 2009.

[30] Tim Crawford, quoted in "Introduction," Semiatin, op.cit. *Campaigns on the Cutting Edge*, 1.

[31] "Republican Debate: Analyzing the Details," *New York Times*, November 28, 2007. http://www.newyorktimes.com. Accessed June 29, 2009.

[32] Associated Press, "Democrats Face Off in 'Youtube' Debate," MSNBC.com. July 23, 2007. http://www.msnbc.com. Accessed June 13, 2009.

[33] John W. Self, "The First Debate Over the Debates: How Kennedy and Nixon Negotiated the 1960 Presidential Debates," *Presidential Studies Quarterly.* 35: 2, (June 2005), p. 367.

[34] Ta-Nehisi Coates, "Talking Point," *The Village Voice,* from villagevoice.com, October 12, 2004. Accessed on June 24, 2009.

[35] *Ibid.*

[36] William Shakespeare, *As You Like It*, Act II Scene 7.

PROFITS AND PROTEST: THE CULTURAL COMMODIFICATION OF THE PRESIDENTIAL IMAGE

LILLY GOREN AND JUSTIN VAUGHN

On January 20, 2009, as the inauguration of Barack Obama as the nation's 44th president ushered in a fresh chapter in American history, the new chief executive enjoyed a visibility to a degree never before realized by any of his predecessors. Indeed, President Obama's visage was not limited to strained eyes peering toward the dais in front of the Capitol, but could be seen throughout the national mall and virtually the entirety of Washington, D.C. On placards and t-shirts and stocking caps, the already iconic image was everywhere, proudly sported by crowds of ecstatic supporters who found no shortage of shops and souvenir stands selling trinkets, tchotchkes, and thermoses – along with every other imaginable consumable good to which one could affix an Obama logo or image – to the eager throngs.

This plethora of memorabilia is nothing new to presidential politics, but rather a continuation of a long-standing practice of public consumption of the presidential image.

We contend that the production of these items is, at root, a rational act, and that entrepreneurs investing in the presidential image expect to receive significant return on their investment. Witness, for example, even the accidental profit windfalls that occur when the media spotlights the businesses that design George W. Bush's cowboy boots, John Kerry's pastel neckties, or Barack Obama's wristwatch, as well as the massive consumer response when presidential spouses wear J.Crew dresses, when vice-presidential candidates sport Kazuo Kawasaki glasses, or even when presidential mistresses wear Club Monaco Glaze Sheer lipsticks during national televised interviews with Barbara Walters.

Since the founding of the American republic, the presidential image has always been eminently visible and recognizable, and though occasional scandal and struggle have temporarily diminished the value of the presidential image (or, at least, of certain presidents), the visage of both current and key chief executives has frequently been the visual short-cut for the national identity. Whether taking the form of adoring throngs holding posters of visiting presidents or the burning of presidential likenesses in effigy in areas more hostile to the United States, the presidential image has become the most powerful symbolic national representation, rivaled perhaps only by the American flag.

The weight of this image is no less in the homeland, and indeed far greater, as the presidential image not only represents American leadership to its masses, but also becomes a market force. The presidential image is as powerful as a marketing slogan as it is anything else, and a long commercial history can be told of presidency-related merchandise. In this chapter, we unpack the various critical and commercial components of what we have dubbed the *commodification of the presidential image*. We base our discussion on the observation that the presidential image has taken on economic value, as evidenced by the frequency with which it is produced, bought, and sold. Involved in this basic transaction are numerous participants, each with disparate motivations. In the subsequent sections of this chapter, we evaluate the role and motivation of the producer (and seller) of the presidential image, the buyer, and the occupant of the presidency itself. As our essay develops, we also draw attention to key gender dynamics involved in this transaction.

Producing and Selling the Presidential Image

For the first actor in our discussion of the commodification transaction, we examine the role of the businessperson involved in producing and selling the presidential image. Clearly, production and sales are two very different aspects of a commercial transaction, and in any real-world transaction there are likely multiple individuals and/or institutions involved. However, what each of these individuals on the production/sales side of the relationship has in common is profit motive. Images are being produced and sold to make money, and for this reason we treat these individuals as a singular entity.

We contend that this actor is motivated primarily by economic self-interest; that is, profit. The producer and seller of a t-shirt commemorating Barack Obama's inauguration or a bobble-head with a humorous caricature of a president is not doing so as a political stance, but rather as a business venture. It is certainly possible that the vendor's political and profit interests coincide (perhaps the vendor selling the Obama inaugural t-shirt voted for the new president), just as it is possible that the vendor's personal political preference is at odds with his profit motive (perhaps the vendor voted for Senator McCain). In either event, the political motivation is secondary to the profit motivation, thus rendering the action a commodification. In the event the production or manipulation of an artifact that draws upon the presidential image is done for primarily political reasons, the process no longer qualifies as a fundamentally commercial act and, therefore, while the image of the president is culturally appropriated, that does not amount to commoditization. An excellent example would be the imposition of the cartoon and movie character Joker on a famous *Time* magazine cover image of Barack Obama[1]. The creation of this presidency-related image was not financially motivated and thus would not be considered commodification. However, when vendors began to sell t-shirts and other products with that image emblazoned upon them, the appropriation became commodification.

The history of corporate and commercial exploitation of the presidential image is long and varied, and while the strength of the symbol is not necessarily powerful enough so as to ensure financial success for even the flimsiest of business plans, the entrepreneur considering presidential image-related commerce has a surplus of previous examples to study, both direct and indirect. Since the election of Barack Obama, in addition to all the celebratory inauguration and election-related merchandise, there have been numerous attempts to affix the personally popular chief executive's image to products. From coffee roasters selling a mix of Hawaiian, Kenyan, and Indonesian beans dubbed "Barack O Blend"[2] to Kentucky-based novelty hot sauce bottlers producing official inaugural editions of their product[3], small businesses have attempted to survive the "Great Recession of 2008-2009" by capitalizing on the one item that seems to keep selling, regardless of the market's condition.

Small business owners are not alone, either. Pepsi, one of the world's leading soft drink companies, is alleged to have changed its corporate logo and slogan to reflect Obama's own campaign logo and rhetoric,[4] while the *New York Times* identified tote bags by leading fashion designers Diane von Furstenberg and Tory Burch among the products available for purchase during the inaugural festivities.[5] Jones Soda Company released a special inauguration soda (the Orange You Glad For Change Cola) with the president's image on the label, Southwest Airlines ran a "Yes You Can" ticket sale, Jailbreak Toys released several different versions of a Barack Obama action figure (with articulated limbs), and Vermont-based ice cream manufacturers Ben & Jerry's introduced a new *Yes Pecan!* flavor, playing on the Obama campaign's "Yes We Can!" slogan. Ty Incorporated, makers of collectible Beanie Baby toys, started a firestorm in the White House itself with a short-lived run of dolls apparently named after the new president's daughters (although the company asserted the naming was a coincidence), Marvelous Malia and Sweet Sasha. The marketing move caught the ire of the First Family and allegedly prompted White House legal advisers to begin investigating options for controlling access to and usage of the presidential image.[6] Even businesses overseas got into the act, with examples from Turkey alone including a bank advertising its new "interest supported credit" with an advertising campaign that borrowed liberally from Shepard Fairey's famous campaign posters during the 2008 election[7] and a bakery that created an image of the president's face composed of pieces of baklava pastry, which the baker dubbed Baracklava.[8]

In each of these cases and countless others, the creation of Obama-related products and the marketing of pre-existing products with Obama-related slogans and images was done for one simple and strategic reason: profit. As noted previously, the individuals responsible for these production and marketing decisions had good reason to believe that the strategy would pay off – previous items associated with the president and his family had sold incredibly well, even without direct marketing efforts to tie the Obamas to the products. For example, after it was announced that the Obama daughters had worn coats sold by J. Crew to their father's frigid inauguration, the chain's stock shares jumped in price 10.6%..[9] This phenomenon was only the latest in a string of profit increases related to fashion decisions made by key figures in the 2008 election, including the increase in popularity of the designer eye-glasses frames worn by Republican Vice-Presidential nominee and Alaska Governor Sarah Palin, a $148 dress from boutique chain White House/Black Market worn by Michelle Obama on a much-publicized interview on day-time television program *The View*, while a $126 dress from Talbots the First Lady wore on the cover of *Essence* became an instant best seller and prompted the company to place immediate orders for production of thousands more..[10] Barack Obama's wristwatch selection created change in *two* markets: the vintage resale market concerning rising prices for the commercially retired style of Tag Heuer 1500 wristwatch he wore early in his campaign and then a special replica watch made by Jorg Gray, who had designed a custom watch for Obama's secret service detail to give to the then-candidate as a gift. Indeed, the website (http://www.jorggray.com) that officially sells this watch currently markets it by drawing attention to key moments during the Obama administration when the president was seen to be wearing it, including the inauguration and the signing of his first executive proclamation.

Examples like these make efforts to capitalize on the presidential image rationale, and further cement the notion that the considerations made by those on the production and sales side of image-based transactions are rooted primarily and essentially in market dynamics and profit expectations. Even companies that play both side of the partisan fence have done quite well in treading on the presidential image and products that would appeal to politically opposite consumers. CafePress.com is a fascinating example of this idea, since they describe their company as a "leader in user-generated commerce" and they really came on to the marketing scene with tee-shirts that read "1/20/09: The End of an Error" that sold incredibly well. These shirts were selling long before either major party had nominated their candidates for president. During the election season, CafePress.com had options for Democrats and for Republicans; now their site has options for "Obama Shirts" and for "anti-Obama Shirts" among many other, non-political categories.

The consumers buying the products marketed by and festooned with presidential connotations or political slogans are not often making those purchases for reasons of market dynamics or profit expectations. In the next section of this chapter, we argue that these consumers are motivated primarily and essentially by political considerations, unlike the bottom-line focused businesses they patronize.

Purchasing the Presidential Image

Clearly, producers would not produce and sellers could not sell if a market did not exist for their product. This is where the second component of the commodification transaction, the buyers, comes into play. Unlike producers and sellers, who have a profit motive that explains their decision to exploit the presidential image, consumers of the image have no such rational economic consideration at work. Instead, we argue that individuals who buy the presidential image are doing so as a form of political statement. For example, while the producers and sellers of poster reproductions of Shepard Fairey's now-famous *Obama Hope* image are producing and selling these posters to make a profit, the individuals buying the posters are doing so as a political statement, spending their money on items in a way that amounts to public speech. Money being spent, thus, is the political act, as opposed to the money earned by the producer of the item.

Depending on the context of the purchase, the political statement made can be either one of solidarity or protest. For example, the aforementioned example of a consumer purchasing an Obama poster to hang in their home or office would almost certainly be a statement of solidarity and support. However, if an individual purchased instead a poster print of the previously discussed *Obama as Joker* image, with words like "Socialism" or "Nobama" underneath, the statement would almost certainly be negative. Examples of both solidarity and protest-oriented consumption are widespread, with the protest-oriented products often being quite witty, if not tasteful (e.g., toilet paper with reviled politicians portraits on each sheet; watches with the president's likeness on the face, but with hands that "run backwards;" dartboards with the president's face in the bulls eye; Halloween masks in the president's likeness; etc.).

Regardless of whether such purchases are positive or negative, most are motivated by political preference and allegiance. Of course, it is possible that market interests enter into the purchasing decision. For example, collectors of official presidential coins or individuals who buy limited-run merchandise with the intention of purchasing items with value that will increase over time. We reconcile these exceptions to our parsimonious "producer/seller as profit-oriented, consumer as politics-oriented" model by arguing that such purchases are actually only a continuation of the producer/buyer side of the commodification equation, since their motives are profit-oriented but with an added time lag.

Other than these long-term investors, the buyers of presidential-themed ephemera are acting as political entities, using their dollars to support images and perspectives they agree with, whether that is a favorable or unfavorable view of a particular president, party, or the nation. Without these consumers, the producers and sellers of the presidential image would have no natural customer base, and without these producers and sellers, the individuals wishing to exploit their freedom of expression through spending would have fewer options from which to choose. These buyers and sellers and producers, however, are not the only interested parties in the model. We also contend that presidents themselves – both as individuals and as members of administrative institutions – have an incentive to track usage of the presidential image, as well as exploit the powerful symbol themselves. In the next section of this chapter, we discuss the presidential incentives to enter the image market, both in terms of exploiting the image and controlling outside access to it.

White House Exploitation of the Presidential Image

Administrations devote a substantial amount of time, energy and employees to the task of "managing" the presidential image. This is also not a new or recent phenomenon; rather, it goes all the way back to our first president and the particulars that George Washington wanted in terms of the way that he was treated and "positioned." The presidential image has long been a "contested" area because, unlike all the rules and regulations that have been in place for centuries with regard to most members of royal ruling families, the president was specifically not supposed to be a monarch. Thus, from Washington on, the presidential image is both something that holders of the office have sought to protect from crude commercialization while still trying to portray themselves as connected to the "common citizen" and, on some level, one of us. This negotiation has become even more complex since the assassination of John Kennedy and the events of 9/11, as presidents have become more and more insulated by the Secret Service and the security requirements.

Political Scientist Karen Hoffman has studied the way that presidents communicate through visual presentations and her analysis of George Washington highlights this distinct negotiation that presidents in the United States must undertake because of the peculiarly fused position as head of state and political leader. Hoffman explains a particularly useful example by George Washington of this understanding of the president's role:

> [A]t the first public ball after his inauguration Washington arranged that he and his wife would sit on a sofa that was raised several steps above everyone's seat.[11] He did not want to appear as a monarch and sit in a throne, but he also wanted to establish a respected position for the president. In his view, the raised sofa struck the right balance. In observing Washington on the sofa people were supposed to understand that Washington could be distinguished as a leader, but he was not far removed from the rest of the group.[12]

Washington may have been the first but every president since Washington has had to try to appropriately negotiate this conundrum because it bears directly on each president's success and potential for re-election. And the public expectation also changes with time, so the cultural context does not lend itself, necessarily, to setting out parameters and having each president follow similar guidelines. There are often excesses in one direction: the common man as president as exemplified by Jimmy Carter's Administration, which brought us, famously, Billy Beer as a commodity, and Jimmy and Roslyn carrying their own luggage to the White House. Followed by excesses in the other direction: Carter was bracketed by the "imperialism" of Richard Nixon's presidency and presidential excesses in the use of power on one side; and on the other, by the grandiosity of Ronald Reagan's presidency, where Nancy Reagan and many of Reagan's presidential advisors sought to "re-elevate" the president through

traditionally aristocratic tropes, like the new and elegant décor in the
White House, purchasing sophisticated (and expensive) china, and hosting
highly publicized and formal dinners for visiting dignitaries. Thus, one
president's attempt to be a *man of the people* may lead the next president
to present an image that is more regal in disposition. In any of these cases,
the president and his advisors are seeking to protect the way in which the
president himself is "consumed" by the public and to control the use of
that image to the president's best advantage.

Obama is no different in this regard. He and his advisors would like to
position him in the best possible light during this first term as president
and clearly with an eye to mid-term elections in 2010 and to his potential
re-election in 2012. And the very success of the Obama campaign for
president in 2008 has made protecting the president's image all that much
more complicated; Obama and his advisors have sought to present the
president with a new kind of stature and gravitas, somewhat different from
the stature and image projected by candidate Obama. Once elected to
office, Obama became the most famous person in the world. This is a
difficult image to protect, and the image itself needs to be projected
differently to different audiences and different consumers of the presidential
image.

In the United States, Obama and his team have gone to great lengths to
groom the image as one of a serious and engaged president—continuing to
overcome the campaign attacks that he might not be serious enough or
experienced enough to be president during such fraught times. Obama also
entered office during a period when any image is instantly available
around the globe and can instantly become a problem, depending on what
is being said or projected. Thus, the efforts at tight controls over this
image are almost herculean as an undertaking. And this being the "No
Drama" White House, there is a very clear imperative, coming from those
working for the president, that the images projected publically (whether
officially or unofficially) need to express the gravitas and stature of this
president. The Obama White House has specific staff completely
allocated for "new media."[13] By regularly uploading videos of the
president that were specifically made by the White House and the Office
of the President, the administration is better able to control some of the
images that are regularly consumed by the public. This is only one avenue
of control of the presidential image, but it is one of the more recently
developed approaches to trying to keep a certain view of the president
front and center in the U.S. public's mind. (This is in contrast to the W.
Bush Administration, which did not have a similar allocation of staff to
producing this kind of extensive library of video images of the president—

though they did devote considerable time and effort to the photographs and the still images of President George W. Bush. This video technology came online during the course of the Bush Administration, which did not necessarily adapt its public relations to encompass video, especially in regard to YouTube.)

The Obama administration has also been drafting legal regulations for the use of the presidential image, in an effort to again rein in the way in which the president may be commodified—especially in ways that undercut the image that campaign strategists would prefer to project. Most presidents have often been wary of excessive commercialization of themselves and the office, and this presidency is particularly concerned, on a global scale, about the potential of others to "trade" on the fame and celebrity of Obama—this is, in part, because of the way in which the Obama campaign cooperated with the fluidity of use with regard to the Obama "brand" and image. "As someone with a fresh face and broad international and domestic appeal as the first black president, Obama's celebrity status is unusually susceptible to marketing pitches" according to experts in the marketing field.[14] Thus, Obama's White House attorneys have been working on legal regulations for the use of Obama and the presidency while also trying quite hard not to tread into free speech rights protected by the First Amendment.[15] This is a difficult balancing act, and, as noted previously, it comes after the 2008 campaign when the Obama team was much more willing or open with the use of both the candidate's image and his words. The will.i.am collaborative "Yes We Can" video that used an Obama speech, overlaid with celebrities singing and reciting his words became a huge internet phenomenon during the primary season and the campaign was more than happy to have this kind of "appropriation" of the candidate and his words. But what works and is "celebrated" during a campaign can be undermining of the presidential office and the way that individual in that office wants to be seen and heard.

This balancing act, between campaigning and governing, and especially with respect to efforts geared toward protecting the presidential image, can be even more complex when a sitting president is running for re-election. Going out on the hustings brings the president to the people in a way that is not always pursued by the person holding that office—thus during a re-election season, the president and his advisors must once again renegotiate the position of the individual who is holding the office, at once projecting an image that is presidential (since this is how the president wants the voters to see him and to consider him) at the same time that the presidential candidate must go to the people and campaign among them, as one of them. This is easier for some presidents and more difficult for others, in some part it is also dependent on the image that has been projected (perhaps even exploited) during the initial term in office. If one is projecting an image of "man of the people," then going out on the stump and shaking hands and hanging out at state fairs is part of that general image. If the presentation is more imperial, then this kind of retail campaigning can almost undermine the image that had been cultivated for the first four years in office. Reagan, even with the trappings of a more aristocratic presidency, was quite adept at negotiating this back and forth between images. His successor, George H. W. Bush, was not as able to negotiate these two roles and projected images, in large part because of H.W. Bush's own background and experiences, which were, in fact, aristocratic and more elite. Thus while H. W. Bush projected the image as an expert and capable during his presidency, his efforts to project his image as a common man during the campaign often came off as artificial. The White House makes great efforts to control the way in which we think about the occupant therein, but it has always been a difficult negotiation because of complex nature of the position of the president within our democratic system. This will be interesting to observe as Obama comes up for re-election, since his background and his own demeanor are cerebral—and yet his personal history is neither elite nor aristocratic but quite "common." He was able to marry these images and ideas during his campaign in 2008, especially since the cerebral and cautious demeanor appealed to many voters during turbulent economic times. But 2012 may produce a different climate and Obama will have to test his abilities to move between being president and being a candidate in a different way than he and his strategists did in 2008.

The Obama Administration (and previously the Obama campaign) had one more dynamic that they wanted to control and that they continue to want to control with regard to the president's image and, on some level, exploitation of that image: Barack Obama's race. Clearly distinct from any other individual elected to the presidency, Obama first had to negotiate the way that race came into the conversation during the campaign—and, at a certain point, he could no longer avoid the discussion when, in the late winter of 2008, the Reverend Jeremiah Wright became the racial controversy that the campaign had, up until that point, mostly avoided. This was a very interesting negotiation of image projection because Obama himself is bi-racial in fact and in, on some level, in disposition, and thus he straddled the issue of race throughout his campaign. With degrees from Columbia and Harvard, an appointment at the Law School at the University of Chicago, with conservative choices in clothing and in his manner of speaking (in some settings), Obama projected an image that was, in many ways, conventionally presidential—except for the color of his skin. At the same time, Obama's choice of sport for relaxation (basketball), his inflection and manner of speaking and word choice in some settings, his experience in community organizing and his life on the African-American South Side of Chicago all can be seen as hallmarks of his position as an African-American in U.S. society. One of the unprecedented aspects of Obama's campaign was the way in which he, as well as his opponents (in the primaries and the general election), had to work with the issue of his race. He and his advisors continue to negotiate this issue—which has become, on some level, even more controversial since he was elected president. Again, this is a unique situation that no other president has had to wrestle with in terms of the projection and protection of the presidential image.

Presidents, unlike celebrities, writers or others within a public spotlight, seek to exploit the power of their image for exclusively political reasons. They do not run for office because of the monetary rewards, thus the control and shaping of the presidential image is aiming at a distinct and clearly political end: how the public, especially the voting public, thinks about the person inhabiting that position. This is why the negotiation of images during an election campaign is so complex.

Commerce, Gender, and the Presidential Image

In Shakespeare's play *Henry V*, King Henry, in his discussions with Catherine, daughter of the King of France, whom Henry has just won as part of the peace negotiations, explains that "nice customs curtsy to great kings....you and I cannot be confined within the weak list of a country's fashions. We are the makers of manners." (*Henry V*, Act V, scene ii, lines 260-263).   This, of course, is how royalty has often thought and behaved—they are the makers of fashion, determiners of manners, arbiters of taste and appropriate conduct.   Once again, the absence of a royal family or monarchy leaves the citizens of the United States often casting about for ideas of how best to act, what fashions to follow, how to comport one's self. This is the beauty of democracy—we make our own manners, determine our own style. At the same time, we like to look to often unanticipated individuals to, perhaps, blaze a trail that many of us might choose to follow, because we like what we see, or consciously reject because it is not in keeping with our particular tastes or traditions. Into this democratic whirlwind of fashion and manners, we often examine celebrities, often exceptionally attractive, to see what they are wearing, and we turn to the first lady and, now, many of the women who are pursuing elected office, to see what kind of choices they make in all these areas.

Thus, the presidential image that is most open to commodification, in part because it is the least defined and because of the place that it occupies, tends to be the image that the first lady and the first family project. Presidents generally come with wives and children (of varying ages) and the role of the First Lady has, like the image of the president and the presidency, changed with time, with circumstances, and often in response to the previous occupant in that position. For much of our history, the First Lady occupied her time with supporting her husband, the president, and projecting an image as an arbiter of taste and culture in some measure. Some first ladies had more of a hand in advising their husbands in matters of state – going all the way back to Abigail Adams. If first ladies did this kind of advising, it was decidedly behind the scenes. In recent decades, this role has become more prominent and, as a result, more publically contested. The first lady (and the first family if there is one) has a prominent position within our culture in her role as mother and wife, but in a public arena, which is generally not where mothers and wives spend their time (or not until recently that is). Thus, in terms of her role, the first lady occupies a rather odd hybrid of a position, often doing the work of raising a family and "keeping a home," private undertakings for the most part, in the public sphere, where her decisions with regard to her family and her home (and how she comports herself) are publically inspected, commented on, often adopted by the citizens themselves, especially other wives and mothers.

In many ways, the role of the first lady has the potential for the most involvement in commercial enterprises, especially in the modern period when the choices made by this mother and wife are immediately communicated to others and, as a result, may prompt others to follow in her consumer choices, thus spiking sales of products, goods, clothing, hair styles, etc. A recent cover of the *Toronto Globe and Mail* highlights this commercial trajectory; the headline of September 4, 2009 edition of the *Globe and Mail* notes: "Michelle Obama's style secret sets its sights on Canada; She put J. Crew on the retail map. As the brand looks to expand, Canadians will soon get to steal the fashion-forward first lady's look."[16] The confluence of dimensions of the role of the first lady as connected to commodification are delineated within those two headlines (which was accompanied by a picture of Michelle Obama, outfitted in J. Crew, from her meeting with Prime Minister Gordon Brown at 10 Downing Street in the spring.) Michelle Obama, like many of the modern first ladies, is contextualized by her fashion choices—her own *style*—and the retailers and/or couture houses that benefit from her choices. The first lady is also critiqued (positively and negatively) with regard to her style choices, or, at times, her lack thereof or inconsistency with those choices.

Michelle Obama, a six-foot tall African-American woman, has distinct taste in clothing for herself (the majority of American women are not six feet tall) and her daughters. In many ways, she is following in the footsteps of previous first ladies: Nancy Reagan and "Reagan Red," Barbara Bush with her string of giant (fake) pearls, Hillary Clinton's famous headbands, and, perhaps mostly memorably, Jackie Kennedy and her Chanel jackets, sleeveless sheaths, and pillbox hats. Obama also negotiates the peculiar arena of being first lady with a graduate degree (only our second first lady with such a credential), as well as a clear profession and career that she pursued until she took a leave of absence to work with her husband as he ran for the presidency. Hillary Clinton, as first lady, was the first to try to negotiate some of these contested perceptions (career woman vs. homemaker; supportive wife vs. policy advisor, etc.) that make "first lady-hood" even more complex than in the past because of the advances of Second Wave and Third Wave feminism. Even with some of these more contested questions still being debated, a new first lady generally gets a honeymoon, like her husband, where her style, her ideas (of a particular kind) receive a great deal of attention and tend to be commodified in a straight forward commercial manner. The clothing she wears is often adopted by at least a sector of the population who like the first lady and want to emulate her style. Choices she may make for school-age first family children are discussed and debated and, again, imitated by portions of the population.

These discussions are written about extensively in "women's magazines," fashion magazines, and even mainstream media outlets that follow trends and popular culture. And these days, blogs and websites throughout the world follow the same discussions and trend reports. Designers whom Michelle Obama (Jason Wu, Isabel Toledo, J. Crew) or, in previous administrations, that Nancy Reagan (Bill Blass, Oscar de la Renta, Adolfo, etc.), or Hillary Clinton (Sara Phillips, Oscar de la Renta, etc.) chose to wear to the Inauguration and other state occasions receive extensive attention and often great commercial success, especially if they are less well known to the general public. Designers, stylists, interior decorators all make pitches to incoming first ladies so that they may highlight particular styles—in fashion, in home décor, in makeup or hairstyles, or even eye glasses. First ladies do not often choose a particular style or highlight a particular designer because they want to improve that designer's or that company's business, but their choice to wear a certain outfit or pair of shoes will often have that effect.

There is, generally, a significant market for imitation of what the first lady or the first family is wearing or even eating because these choices are highlighted and discussed by the media. There were days of discussion about what President Obama, Professor Henry Louis Gates, Police Officer Sergeant James Crowley and Vice President Joe Biden chose to drink when Obama invited them all to the White House to have a beer. This is the kind of market that swirls around the White House occupants, but it is often much more the domain of the first lady and the first family – who are making these kinds of domestic decisions – than it is the president's domain, since he is generally seen as occupied with much more weighty decisions.

Conclusion

Given the importance of the image of the American president in American political society, it is not surprising that the image has become a powerful one in American popular culture. Moreover, in a nation with a reputation for consumption, the rise of presidential image commodification is a phenomenon that should seem far more predictable than shocking to anyone who observes this trend. Like any other image with potent sales potential, entrepreneurs from the grassroots level to corporate high-rises have consistently received positive returns on investment by betting their business plan, at least in the short-term, on the presidential image.

What makes the commodification of the presidential image unique and attention-worthy, however, is that unlike most of the other commercially potent images traded and sold with such economic fervor, from sports franchise jerseys to athletic shoes to designer handbags, consumption of the presidential image is a political statement on the part of the individual purchasing the image that speaks volumes about that individual's partisan proclivities on an individual level and, when considered at an aggregate level, about the condition of American politics more generally. From election year cookie purchasing contests at bakeries to Halloween mask and costume sales, pundits look to idiosyncratic consumption trends as mock electoral tea leaves while the proprietors of the bakeries and costume shops remain agnostic, more concerned with sales volume than the predictions such data can generate.

In this essay, we have argued that the individuals involved in this commercial exchange come to it motivated by different interests; namely that those selling the presidential image do so in search of profit while those purchasing do so with the intent to make a political statement. That onlookers of the exchange - from objective scholars to horse-race journalists to those seeking to become president to those entrusted with the task of protecting the image so that the president himself may make best use of it when doing so is in his political interest – find importance in the dynamics of it only further cements the importance of understanding the forces (market as well as cultural) at work when trading on the presidential image.

Notes

[1] Kennicott, Philip. "Obama as the Joker: Racial Fear's Ugly Face." *Washington Post*. August 6, 2009.

[2] "Hawaii Coffee Traces Obama's Roots." *Pacific Business News*. December 30, 2008.

[3] Levine, Brittany. "Souvenir Watch: Obama Hot Sauce." *Washington Post*. December 28, 2008.

[4] Scherer, Michael. "The Obama Team's Drink of Choice? Coke, not Pepsi." *Time*. February 27, 2009.

[5] Macur, Juliet. "Inspired by Obama's Message? Pull Out Your Wallet." *New York Times*. January 13, 2009.

[6] Reid, Tim. "White House Moves to Protect Barack Obama Brand from Exploiters." *London Times*. February 3, 2009.

[7] Mondello, Bob. "Banking on Faux-Bama in Istanbul." *NPR.org*. April 5, 2009.

[8] Tuysuz, Gul. "Baker's Tasty Tribute to Obama: Baracklava." *NPR.org*. April 5, 2009.

[9] Donohue, Wendy. "J. Crew Reveals How Sasha and Malia Got Those Special Coats." *Chicago Tribune*. January 29, 2009.

[10] Malkin, Marc. "Another Michelle Obama Fashion Stimulus Package." *E Online*. April 7, 2009.

[11] James Hart, *The American Presidency in Action, 1789*, New York: MacMillan, 1948, 33.

[12] Hoffman, Karen. "Visual Rhetoric in the Early Presidency," presented at the American Political Science Association Annual Conference, Toronto, Canada, September 2009.

[13] Heffernan, Virginia. "The YouTube Presidency: Why the Obama administration uploads so much video." *New York Times Magazine*. April 12, 2009.

[14] Goldman, Julianna. "White House Lawyers Look to Limit Commercial use of President." *Bloomberg.com*. January 30, 2009.

[15] *Ibid.*

[16] Strauss, Marina. "Michelle Obama's Style Secret Sets Its Sights on Canada." *The Globe and Mail*. September 4, 2009.

ENTERTAINMENT MEDIA
AND THE YOUTH VOTE

GWENDELYN NISBETT
AND LINDSEY HARVELL

Election 2008 was in many ways the year of the youth voter. Young people across the nation were excited and mobilized for the presidential election, with more young people voting in 2008 than voted in 2004[1]. Along with a rise in youth participation, arises interest in the media they consume.

The academic community is uncertain about the impact of entertainment media's influence on politics. Recently, political entertainment media has become an increasingly relevant topic in terms of political knowledge[2], political participation[3], media impact[4], cultural relevance[5], and their impact on young voters[6].

Entertainment media personalities and celebrities have arguably increased their influence on politics, especially during presidential campaigns[7]. Politicians have become celebrities in their own right, with carefully crafted images and public relations efforts[8]. It is not surprising that entertainment media and politics have collided, with relatively unknown effects. One of the most talked about issues of entertainment politics is the impact of young voters. The 2008 election season carried a growing trend for entertainment media as an integral part of America's participatory democracy.

Using current research on the impact of entertainment media on audience political information consumption, we conducted focus groups during the final months of the 2008 presidential election with young voters as participants. Participants discussed media use, popular culture use and interpersonal influences.

We argue that interpersonal influence is still the most important factor in political attitudes of young voters. However, non-traditional political media are having an impact. The most interesting theme to emerge from our focus groups was the intersection of media bias, information source (news and entertainment), and interpersonal influence.

Impact of Political Entertainment Media

The appeal of shows like *The Colbert Report* and *The Daily Show* for young voters is evident in recent research on the genre. Entertainment media may present a more digestible form of political information than traditional news sources to people apt to be less engaged with the political process[10]. Moreover, research has shown that people who have less partisan attitudes tend to drift to more entertainment media, while people with strong partisan attitudes tend to consume partisan political information[11].

Politicians use entertainment formats like talk shows to carefully craft their images as credible and likeable candidates, while shying away from revealing too much about issues or their records[12]. Shows like *The Colbert Report* offer a venue to connect with an audience that is not usually offered by traditional news programming[13]. Entertainment media shows allow candidates and surrogates to show a lighter, more humorous side.

In some cases, news remains a stronger predictor of political issue salience when compared to entertainment shows[14]. The impact of political entertainment media is often overlooked even though it may be important in framing the way an audience understands real-world politicians and issues[15]. Entertainment media can even override government programs and officials in shaping and constructing perceptions of reality[16].

Perhaps one of the most memorable moments in 2008 was the gaffe committed by John McCain when he cancelled his appearance on *The Late Show* with David Letterman. Late night television is the place of comedy and satire, not usually the place of breaking news. However, when McCain skipped Letterman and showed up on the *CBS* nightly news, it arguably cemented McCain's down-swing in political momentum and reinforced his image of being erratic. Letterman angrily complained about McCain for the entire episode and weeks after. Images and video from the show circulated on the internet and even in the news media.

Implications on political participation, political knowledge, and voter efficacy are of interest in this study. Arguments lauding entertainment media suggests that political information presented in the context of entertainment may make it more approachable or understandable. However, research is mixed on the impacts. Entertainment media is decreasing the desire to engage in political participation, perhaps because late night talk shows, like the *Late Show*, tend to focus on presidential politics, with particular interest in the personal peccadilloes and positions of political players in lieu of presenting issue information[17].

Still other research has found that entertainment media consumption along with news consumption increases tendencies for young people to engage in civic activities and have increased salience of politics[18]. Hollander argues that "late-night television viewing increases what young people think they know about a political campaign but provides at best modest improvements to actual recall of events associated with the campaign"[19].

Previous research has shown that entertainment talk shows had a greater impact on less politically knowledgeable people compared to people classified as having higher political knowledge[20]. And watching shows like *Saturday Night Live* and *The Daily Show* may increase political knowledge among young people in particular (however, these results may be linked to young people with higher levels of education)[21].

Case Study: Youth Voters, Entertainment Media, and Election 2008

In a political season that was arguably one of the most dynamic and fascinating, perhaps one of the most interesting stories was the impact of entertainment media on the youth vote. Research on political discussion continues to suggest that the media does not have a greater influence than interpersonal connections on political attitudes. Yet, it is hard to ignore the popularity of Jon Stewart, Stephen Colbert, Tina Fey as Sarah Palin, and the other performers that intertwine politics and entertainment media.

For this project, we examined how participants interpret political entertainment media and how political information may be incorporated into personal dialogues within their community and families. Even though political discussions may be inspired by media consumption, it is unclear whether the content is directly linked to media content or how it subsequently impacts political attitudes[22]. We utilized focus groups to examine how individuals interpret political information received through media and interpersonal discussions of political campaigns.

By examining the impact of entertainment media on the way people use and discuss information on an interpersonal level, we can understand this phenomenon better. People do not make political decisions in a vacuum - they take into consideration their roles and standing within a wider framework of family and community.

Past research used focus groups to simulate interpersonal campaign discussions[23]. We invited students from a large Southern university to participate in small focus groups about the election, discussing politics and the impact of entertainment media. Our focus groups were conducted during the last 3 months of the 2008 election season. Each group consisted of 5-7 individuals that discussed a set of themes including political news, media use, entertainment media use, interpersonal discussions of politics, and interpersonal influence in politics. Media bias emerged as an important theme as well.

Relevant demographic information includes gender (males 42%, females 58%), political party identification (Democrat 42%, Republican 42%, other 16%), ideological identification (25% conservative, 42% moderate, 33% liberal), and presidential preference (33% for Obama, 33% for McCain, and 33% undecided/no opinion). Types of media used to gain political information was also gathered: watch news (25 % not often, 42% sometimes, 33% often), read newspapers (33% not often, 50% sometimes, 17% often), watch entertainment media (33.3% not often, 33.3% sometimes, 33.3% often), and use internet (25% not often, 17% sometimes, 58% often).

Analysis of the data suggests that the presence of political content in traditional entertainment forms was noteworthy; however findings suggest that young people continue to rely on traditional interpersonal influences more than mass media influences. Participants incorporated what they saw in the media into their interpersonal discussions. Based on the focus group data, many participants suggested this is inevitable because most of their news is gathered from the media. The majority of participants said they paid some attention to politics during the election.

The participants gravitated towards online sources for their main source of political news. In regards to media, the internet seemed to be the source used for factual information. Television seemed to be a source for a quick and up-to-date resource for political information. And with almost constant availability of the internet on home and work computers as well as PDA's, news that is found on the internet is most likely to come up in interpersonal communication. Sources used are mostly CNN or an online news source such as the BBC. For instance one student stated:

> For me personally, I tend to use the internet because I have a very full schedule between school and my job. And I volunteer in activities and in other things, so I log onto the net for ten or fifteen minutes to scan websites like the BBC or CNN.com or a couple of others that I look at to try and get an overall feel. I don't have time to sit down and listen for an hour or two hours or three hours to the radio or television. I don't have time!

If participants want politics, they choose either television news (mostly CNN) or an online news source. One student explains their view on gaining political information from the media:

Uh, I would say probably television just because you can just turn on CNN and just get the quick update about like what's going on in the, you know, the debates or whatever...and you know between different candidates or what not. So I guess that's me.

Some research suggests that young voters do tend to gravitate to entertainment shows like *The Daily Show* for political information[24]. Participants use entertainment shows such as *The Daily Show* for what they perceived as entertainment. There seems to be a source credibility gap between news and entertainment media. Young voters use entertainment widely, but reify the notion that news is a more suitable source for political information than entertainment shows. However, they do not necessarily trust or watch news programming. When asked about viewing cable news networks, one young voter commented that they were "much more into comedy like Conan O'Brien and things like that". Another participant offered, "I mean like I like to watch Jay Leno 'cause it's kind of funny and he usually makes fun of like the cool stuff and it takes about fifteen minutes".

Facebook appears to be a natural collision of entertainment media and interpersonal discussion. Barack Obama in particular was lauded for his clever use of the online networking site. Obama was seen as using the internet to a greater degree in order to garner the youth vote. One participant commented about Facebook that "if Obama is doing a thing, I look." However, the focus groups suggest that most of the time, students feel they are only on social network sites for entertainment purposes. For instance one student discusses the presence of politics on Facebook:

I have a Facebook page but about as political as my page tends to get is somebody sending me an invite saying do you want to come watch the countdown to George Bush getting out of office. We're gonna have popcorn and throw things. It's more for inviting somebody to a party.

Mitigating Media Bias

Most of the media reporting was judged to be highly biased, somewhat manipulative, distorted, and even as outright lies. One participant noted, "You can't be spoon-fed by what the media says. You have to go out and research a subject you know is a hot debate issue and see how it's affecting you personally." One of the major and more interesting themes among the participants was concern over bias – both from the media and their peers. One participant explained:

It sort of depends on the media source, I mean, like tabloids. I'll see the headlines at a grocery store and I'll ignore it, I see them but I don't let them influence my decisions, um, a discussion that may appear on PBS or OETA, you know might have more of an impact. The hate mail, smear campaigns that I get in my mailbox--this politician committed fraud thirty years ago and this politician had 15 divorces, uh you shouldn't vote for this politician for all these reasons. Those I tend to shred and I don't like watching the political ads, you know this person is a bad person because...because...because. I think they present, from what I interpret, a very biased view. I'd rather ignore those and go look up my own research and try to find a few different sources. So it kind of depends on where it's coming from.

Does this mean that young voters are seeking out entertainment media and the internet because they find more traditional media to be biased? Many participants preferred using the internet over television because they felt they had more control over the content on the internet and thus perceived it as less biased. One participant noted "with the net you can control what you see, what you think is credible and what you don't … you can go to the specific sites or go to a bias page." However, they did not mention the possibility of consuming news that had a self-selection bias (in other words, only consuming news that fit their political perspective). It seemed natural to one participant who noted that "you choose a news source that aligns with your views." Television news was viewed as more biased because participants had no control over content. Participants thought *Fox News* was very biased and only people who were conservative would agree. This was interesting given that the participants were not particularly skewed toward a liberal ideological identification. (Participants demographics were fairly evenly split between Republicans and Democrats, and support for Obama and McCain). *Fox News* was cited as a source for the ambiguity of Obama's religion.

Entertainment news was generally viewed as less serious and therefore less prone to bias. Participants also felt better equipped to discern the satirical messages and biases used. For instance, some participants thought political satire shows were entertaining but that "you take it with a grain of salt." Sarah Palin was seen as a subject that the media used to stir things up and comics used her as fodder for their comedy. Some of the groups were not sure what was true and what was distorted.

Interpersonal Discussion and Media Bias

From existing research on interpersonal discussion of campaign politics, media is just one of a number of influences that impacts the process and amount people discuss politics. Other factors include personal need to discuss, individual involvement levels, access to social networks, and demographic variables such as education, employment and marital status[25].

From a media standpoint, interpersonal discussion filters both campaign and media frames through guidance from community leaders and social relationships. Interpersonal influence has a greater impact than media influence on choosing a presidential candidate[26.] Moreover, interpersonal influence can limit the impact of media priming[27]. For those who discuss politics with ideologically similar others, the perception of media bias is higher[28] impacting the believability of media frames. Not surprisingly, community leaders and surrogates regulate the impact of media and candidate frames. Political discussion within social network groups can alter and even lower the impact of partisan allegiance[29]. Moreover, lower involved voters tend to be persuaded by social context (party identification and community leaders).

A common theme was the use of interpersonal networks to mitigate media bias. The participants said they discussed news and information they heard from entertainment media with their parents. A participant offered:

> Oh my dad was talking about an article in a newspaper and he said, I think it was about a quote, that Obama said and it ended up coming out the wrong way. I think it was about people in the Midwest are better, and I read or heard about it. I was shocked and just kind of uh and he kind of explained the position of what he said.

In general, the participants acquired their political views from family and friends. However, family seemed to have a higher degree of influence than friends. The family seemed to instill their values, culture, biases and political views. "I discuss politics with people who have the most influence on personal decisions, I respect my family". Participants felt that family discussions were easier because they shared values.

Gender differences were not a focus of this case study but were a rather apparent theme. Many participants cued into what their fathers had to say but not really their mothers. And many relied on their fathers for political information. "I just talk to my dad to understand what I hear". Indeed, many expressed the view that their mothers lacked credible opinions about political issues. One participant stated "for me if it's my Dad saying it, but my Mom no way". Resounding laughter and agreement followed from the group. Women were more likely to listen to their parents than men. And while party information was not gathered about participant families, many said they tended to adopt political party identification from their parents.

For the most part, participants are highly influenced by their parents and rather ambivalent about political discussions with friends. If they do engage in discussion with their friends, it is for the sake of arguing. They do not try to persuade their friends, and they do not want to be persuaded by their friends. The participants are not looking to persuade. They either desire to debate to a certain point and then stop, or they choose to debate with those that hold their views. This suggests that they preferred reinforcing their own political viewpoints. One student describes this view:

> Yeah, I talk to my family a lot about it because they're the people you aren't going to argue with as much and have the closest to what you believe I guess. If it comes up with my friends I talk about it but I'm not going to push it if they don't want to. I'm not going to force my opinions; that's not going to get you anywhere not if you're just talking about it.

Participants expressed that their knowledge of politics was limited so they refrained from discussions with friends. Moreover, many were hesitant to freely discuss politics with their friends lest they be judged or to avoid an argumentative exchange. Many participants believed friends "are going to think what they think." The male participants thought that friends "all put a spin on their opinions." The females saw discussions as a way to "understand all sides" while males thought their personal opinions were correct and could not be persuaded by their peers. In regard to the degree of discussion females were apt to argue more extensively and agree to disagree. Males thought it more prudent to "back off because it wasn't worth getting angry." They also believed that people in high school were likely to be persuaded because they typically are easily influenced by peers. One participant noted boldly that by the time "you enter college your opinions are formed."

Political Knowledge, Participation and Efficacy

Deliberation is used to increase political efficacy, issue knowledge, issue involvement, and political participation[30]. Specifically, information is exchanged by all involved in deliberation therefore deliberation exposes others to views[31]. Deliberation can also advance positions by making arguments that others can accept or by appealing to common interest[32]. Individuals who engage in political deliberation understand what they want and need in regards to political decisions[33]. In fact, some argue that deliberation can only occur in small, face-to-face groups of people and that it is an essential component of opinion formation[34].

While disagreements typically occur when deliberating about politics, it can have positive effects. First, these disagreements can lead to more political engagement[35]. Citizens also become more confident in their views and often learn new perspectives[36]. In fact, research has shown that deliberation produces positive effects on intentions of political participation[37].

A theme that emerged from the groups suggests that political discourse was rare and that political engagement was even rarer. Participants overwhelmingly relied on family opinions to shape their own. Deliberative discourse is rare among young peers. It is often seen as rude or a source of unwanted conflict. That being said, Facebook and other internet networking and entertainment sites were used for moderate levels of political participation. One participant noted "I noticed on Facebook whether there will be a picture of someone who supports a candidate. A lot of the debate stirs up on Facebook so it is a place to voice your opinion."

Levels of political knowledge were unclear. For many, politics and political issues had no salience. It was not as though they had a desire to avoid politically biased information, they simply had no interest. Many participants admitted that they stumbled upon information from entertainment sources. If they desired information about the election, most sought out internet sources or interpersonal sources.

Conclusion

When compared with media impact, interpersonal still dominates in opinion formation. However, the variety of political information available through entertainment media and the internet suggests that young people are perhaps becoming more skeptical about traditional media sources. Indeed, participants gravitated toward political information that they perceived they had control over (like internet news) and entertainment political information that was perceived as being so lacking in seriousness that media bias was not a concern. Future research should examine young voter's sophistication in their dissection of media bias.

Some aspects of entertainment media, like *The Daily Show*, are not subservient to more traditional political news sources[38]. Quite differently, Jon Stewart manages to weave entertainment and political news from a critical perspective is important to a deliberative political discourse process. Perhaps a continued political presence in entertainment media may inspire more discourse among young people[39].

Given that the participant population was drawn from college students, future research into a more diverse group of young voters would be useful. First, college students are more likely to have higher education level and perhaps higher political knowledge than peers that are not in college. Secondly, the discussion themes suggest that the participants had rather solid rapports with their families. Future research could look at how much entertainment media may influence young voters in different life situations.

Gender differences would be a worthy issue addressed in future research. This is particularly interesting because most political actors are men and most of the most popular political media entertainers (i.e. Stewart, Letterman, Leno, Maher and Colbert) are men. Future research could parse out the reasons behind the dependence of dominant male opinions. Also, as female political voices become more prevalent (i.e. Tina Fey in 2008), research could explore the impact of more diverse political sources.

Notes

[1] US Census Bureau Press Release. http://www.census.gov/Press-Release/www/releases/archives/voting/013995.html

[2] M.A. Baum, "Talking the vote: Why presidential candidates hit the talk show circuit," *American Journal of Political Science* 49 (2005): 213-234; M. Prior, "News v. entertainment: How increasing media choice widens gaps in political knowledge and turnout," *American Journal of Political Science* 49 (2005): 577-592.

[3] J. Pasek, et al., "American's Youth and Community Engagement: How Use of Mass Media is Related to Civic Activity and Political Awareness in 14- to 22-Year olds," *Communication Research* 33 (2006): 115-135.

[4] R.L. Holbert, N. Kwak, and D.V. Shah, "Environmental concern, patterns of television viewing, and pro-environmental behaviors: integrating models of media consumption and effects," *Journal of Broadcasting and Electronic Media* 47 (2003): 177-196.

[5] G. Baym, "Representations and the politics of play: Stephen Colbert's *Better Know a District,*" *Political Communication* 24 (2007): 359-376.

[6] B.A. Hollander, "Late-night learning: Do entertainment programs increase political campaign knowledge for young viewers?" *Journal of Broadcasting and Electronic Media* 49 (2005): 402-415.

[7] W. Babcock and V. Whitehouse, "Celebrity as a postmodern phenomenon, ethical crisis, for democracy, and media nightmare," *Journal of Mass Media Ethics* 20 (2005): 176-191; J.G. Payne, J.P. Hanlon, and D.P. Twomey III, "Celebrity spectacle influence on young voters in the 2004 presidential campaign: what to expect in 2008," *American Behavioral Scientist* 50 (2007): 1239-1246.

[8] T.C. Weiskel, "From sidekick to sideshow – celebrity, entertainment, and the politics of distraction: why Americans are 'sleepwalking toward the end of the earth,'" *American Behavioral Scientist* 49 (2005): 393-409.

[9] M.A. Baum and A.S. Jamison, "The Oprah effect: how soft news helps inattentive citizens vote consistently," *The Journal of Politics* 68 (2006): 946-959.

[10] A. Hollander, "Turning out or turning elsewhere? Partisanship, polarization, and media migration from 1996 to 2006," *Journalism and Mass Communication Quarterly* 85 (2008): 23-40.

[11] Schutz, "Entertainers, experts, or public servants? Politicians' self-presentation on television talk shows," *Political Communication* 12 (1995): 211-221.

[12] Baym, "Representations and the politics of play: Stephen Colbert's *Better Know a District,*" *Political Communication* 24 (2007): 359-376.

[13] L. Holbert, N. Kwak, and D.V. Shah, "Environmental concern, patterns of television viewing, and pro-environmental behaviors: integrating models of media consumption and effects," *Journal of Broadcasting and Electronic Media* 47 (2003): 177-196.

[14] L. Holbert et al., "The West Wing and depictions of the American presidency: Expanding the domains of framing in political communication," *Communication Quarterly* 53 (2005): 505-522.

[15] A. Graber, "Looking at the United States through distorted lenses: entertainment television versus public diplomacy themes," *American Behavioral Scientist* 52 (2009): 735-754.

[16] C. Besley, "The role of entertainment television and its interactions with individual values in explaining political participation," *The Harvard International Journal of Press/Politics* 11 (2006): 41-63; D.S. Niven, S.R. Lichter, and D. Amundson, "The political content of late night comedy," *The Harvard International Journal of Press/Politics* 8 (2003): 118-133.

[17] J. Pasek, et al., "American's Youth and Community Engagement: How Use of Mass Media is Related to Civic Activity and Political Awareness in 14- to 22-Year olds," *Communication Research* 33 (2006): 115-135

[18] B.A. Hollander, "Late-night learning: Do entertainment programs increase political campaign knowledge for young viewers?" *Journal of Broadcasting and Electronic Media* 49 (2005): 402-415.

[19] M.A. Baum, "Sex, lies, and war: how soft news brings foreign policy to the inattentive public," *American Political Science Review* 96 (2002): 91-110.

[20] X. Cao, "Political comedy shows and knowledge about primary campaigns: the moderating effects of age and education," *Mass Communication and Society* 11 (2008): 43-61.

[21] J.J. Mondak, "Media exposure and political discussion in U.S. elections," *The Journal of Politics* 57 (1995): 62-85.

[22] M.X. Delli Carpini and B.A. Williams, "Methods, metaphors, and media research: the uses of television in political conversation," *Communication Research* 21 (1994): 782-812; M. Kern and M. Just, "The focus group method, political advertising, campaign news, and the construction of candidate images," *Political Communication* 12 (1995): 127-145.

[23] B.A. Hollander, "Late-night learning: Do entertainment programs increase political campaign knowledge for young viewers?" *Journal of Broadcasting and Electronic Media* 49 (2005): 402-415.

[24] B.C. Straits, "Bringing strong ties back in interpersonal gateways to political information and influence," *The Public Opinion Quarterly* 55 (1991): 432-448.

[25] P.A. Beck, "Encouraging political defection: the role of personal discussion networks in partisan desertions to the opposition party and Perot votes in 1992," *Political Behavior* 24 (2002): 309-337.

[26] M. Mendelsohn, "The media and interpersonal communications: the priming of issues, leaders, and party identification," *The Journal of Politics* 58 (1996): 112-125; J.J. Mondak, "Media exposure and political discussion in U.S. elections," *The Journal of Politics* 57 (1995): 62-85.

[27] W.P. Eveland Jr. and D.V. Shah, "The impact of individual and interpersonal factors on perceived news media bias," *Political Psychology* 24 (2003): 101-117.

[28] P.A. Beck et al., "The social calculus of voting: interpersonal, media, and organizational influences on presidential choices," *American Political Science Review* 96 (2002): 57-73.

[29] P.J. Conover, I.M. Crewe, and D.D. Searing, "The deliberative potential of political discussion," *British Journal of Political Science* 32 (2002): 21-62.

[30] D.M. Curtin, *Postnational Democracy: The European Union in Search of a Political Philosophy* (The Hague, The Netherlands: Kluwer Law International, 1997); A. Gutman and D. Thompson, *Democracy and Disagreement* (Cambridge, MA: The Belknap Press of Harvard University Press, 1996); J. Habermas, *The Structural Transformation of the Public Sphere: An Inquiry into a Cateogry of Bourgeois Society* (Cambridge, MA: Beacon, 1962/1989).

[31] J. Cohen, *Contemporary Political Philosophy: An Anthology,* ed. R.E. Goodin and P. Pettit (Oxford: Blackwell, 1997); P.M. Shane, *Democracy Online: The Prospects for Political Renewal Through the Internet* (New York: Routledge, 2004).

[32] T. Christiano, *The Rule of the Many: Fundamental Issues in Democratic Theory* (Boulder, CO: Westview, 1996).

[33] V. Price, L. Nir, and J.N. Cappella, "Does disagreement contribute to more deliberative opinion?" *Political Communication* 19 (2002): 95-112.

[34] B. Barber, *Strong Democracy: Participatory Politics for a New Age* (Los Angeles: University of California Press, 1984).

[35] C.J. Nemeth, "Differential contributions of majority and minority influence," *Psychological Review* 93 (1986): 23-32; J.C. Turner, *Social Influence* (Pacific Grove, CA: Brooks/Cole, 1991).

[36] W.P. Eveland, "The effect of political discussion in producing informed citizens: the roles of information, motivation, and elaboration," *Political Communication* 21 (2004): 177-193; J.S. Fishkin, "Toward deliberative democracy: experimenting with an ideal," in *Citizen Competence and Democratic Institutions* (University Park: The Pennsylvania State University Press, 1999). 279-290; J. Gastitl and J.P. Dillard, "Increasing political sophistication through public deliberation," *Political Communication* 16 (1999): 3-23; M.E. Loycano, *National Issue Forums Literacy*

Program: Linking Literacy and Citizenship, 1988-1991 (Dayton, OH: Kettering Foundation, 1992); S.J. Min, "Online vs. face-to-face deliberation: effects on civic engatement," *Journal of Computer-Mediated Communication* 12 (2007): 1369-1387.

[37] G. Baym, "The Daily Show: discursive integration and the reinvention of political journalism," *Political Communication* 22 (2005): 259-276.

[38] G. Baym, "The Daily Show: discursive integration and the reinvention of political journalism," *Political Communication* 22 (2005): 259-276.

POLITICALTUBE:
THE IMPACT OF YOUTUBE ON POLITICS

LACHRYSTAL RICKE

During the 2008 campaign season, I heard someone say, in jest, that if you looked hard enough, you could probably find a video of then Senator Barack Obama brushing his teeth on YouTube. Although no such video was ever located, the context of the joke, that the Obama camp posted videos of nearly every facet of its campaign on YouTube, was not too far from the truth. While YouTube was a significant factor in some campaigns in 2006, most notably in George Allen's "macaca moment," the politically socializing power of YouTube was not tapped until the 2008 presidential election. In 2008, the use of YouTube emerged as one of the dominant Internet-based campaign strategies and fostered, perhaps for the first time in American history, a truly dynamic political conversation. As a video-based social networking site, YouTube's ability to provide political visibility and accessibility, to encourage the participatory class, and to alter the dynamics of control typically associated with political communication, has the potential to both disseminate political information and engage the public in democratic dialogue.

According to the study, *The Internet's Role in Campaign 2008,* released by the Pew Internet and American Life Project, television is still the primary source of political information for a majority of Americans. The study indicated that 80% of respondents reported receiving most of their information regarding the 2008 presidential race from television, with politically slanted cable news shows (e.g., MSNBC and FOX News) being viewed slightly more frequently than network news and CNN.[1] However, despite public reliance on television, Pew results show that nearly three-quarters of Internet users engaged in either online political information gathering or participation in 2008; this number represents 55% of the entire adult population and is the first time that reports have indicated political Internet usage this high.[2]

Reports from Pew[3] also indicated that during the 2008 election, 33% of wired Americans reported sharing digital political content with others,

18% of Internet users posted comments about the campaign on a blog or social networking site, 33% of online news consumers reported typically seeking out political information, and 52% of respondents said that they used their personal social network profile for political means.[4] These statistics indicate that although television continues to play an important role in the dissemination of political information, the Internet has indeed changed the ways in which the public engages in political communication.

Politics and Social Media

The use of social media in political campaigns has its roots as far back as Jesse Ventura's 1998 gubernatorial bid where the campaign organized and coordinated the campaign's single biggest event, a 72-hour final drive through the state, entirely via email.[5] Although social media has evolved considerably since then, the effort is indicative of a candidate understanding that the power of the Internet was in the social solicitation of support and no longer just simply in the dissemination of information. Through the creation of dynamic communication spaces, information in online social media spaces, much of which is initiated by users, is continually refined, and redefined, through social interactions.[6] These communication spaces have revolutionized the ways in which the public receives political information and has signaled an irreversible shift from the one-to-many political campaigning of the past to a two-way system of communication that voters have grown to expect.[7] The proliferation of online communication environments has not just affected the ways that people consume political information, but has also impacted the ways that the public interacts with political processes and has signaled the emergence of what has been dubbed the "participatory class" – individuals that use blogs, social networking sites, video clips, and email to gather and share political information.[8]

The explosive use of social media has allowed Americans to sift through more political information than ever before[9] and has empowered users, who are interested in obtaining timely and often customized information,[10] to participate in politics in ways never before possible. For example, Obama supporters could use MyBarackObama.com, the Obama campaign's own social networking site, to register for information updates, plan events, become part of local groups, make canvassing calls by participating in the campaign's virtual phone bank, and create individual fundraising pages.[11] Social media has emerged as a catalyst for transforming how the American public engages in politics, transforming the political landscape and ushering in a new era of political communication where the Internet is not only a dominant source of political information, but is in fact, a political tool.[12]

YouTube and Politics

YouTube emerged as one of the most significant social mediums used in, and incorporated into, campaign strategies during the 2008 presidential election. Through sharing a high degree of community formation and user-level content creation, YouTube's applications and services have helped to facilitate collective action through the exchange of multimedia information and the creation of aggregate knowledge, factors which have begun to dominate the Internet[13] and that help to create not only fundamental shifts in political communication, but also growth and excitement. YouTube has also changed the ways that individuals think about their ability to access information[14] and its free and user-driven communication environment allows for a greater sense of connection with the political world.

YouTube has been very successful in capturing the online digital video market. YouTube gets 60% of all online video traffic and has earned 54% of page views, receiving roughly 50% more traffic than 64 other video sites combined; this means that YouTube viewers stay on the site and watch more videos than people who browse on competing sites.[15] YouTube streams roughly 100 million videos each day and as of May 2008 had 81 million unique visitors.[16] YouTube uploads increased from an average of 6 hours of video per minute in 2007 to 15 hours of video per minute in January 2009, and by May 2009 uploads had jumped to 20 hours of video per minute; that equals, 28,800 hours of video uploaded every day, or the equivalent of 86,000 full-length movies each week.[17]

During the 2008 election cycle, YouTube users demonstrated a significant level of engagement with political advertisements and messages. YouTube was named by 2% of individuals as the site they went to for campaign news and information[18] and reportedly used YouTube for political information more than they used candidate Web sites, political blogs, or social networking.[19] Forty one percent of individuals under 30 years old, and 20% of those over 30, reported viewing campaign related videos on YouTube, contributing to candidates' videos being viewed between 3 and 27 million times each day.[20] Collectively, Barack Obama's and John McCain's YouTube videos were viewed 3 billion times (1.9 billion for Obama and 1.1 billion for McCain), leading many to believe that "if it was political and it was important, there was probably a video of it on YouTube."[21]

When YouTube initially emerged onto the political spectrum there was the assumption amongst politicians, promulgated most likely by Allen's and other's political missteps caught on camera, that YouTube was going to emerge as a "gotcha medium," according to Steve Groves, YouTube's news and politics editor.[22] There was fear that because of how easy it had become to locate, potentially mash up, and distribute video footage through YouTube, that politicians were going to be steamrolled by the medium; that an unscripted moment would take on new life online and result in serious, potentially career ending, repercussions for those in the political arena.[23] While there is little doubt that videos circulated on YouTube indeed forced some politicians to qualify previous political statements or explain conflicting positions, YouTube has moreover emerged as an environment where traditional barriers preventing individuals from engaging in national political conversation have begun to be eliminated. YouTube has made it easy for politicians to spread political messages, both in terms of financial and technological resources, and provides lesser known, or marginally funded, politicians a viable method for communicating with constituents.[24] Through encouraging and empowering users with relatively low technological sophistication by making it easy to create, upload and transcode video files, email video links, and post videos to any social networking site or other Website, YouTube has made it possible for the public to become integral participants of political discourse, making it feel as if the public is part of the political conversation and not longer simply political supporters.

YouTube, possibly more than any other medium, has been successful in gaining cross-demographic appeal and has been able to bridge demographic divides where other, more traditional, forms of political communication have been unsuccessful. Although precise user demographics are difficult to obtain because user information is only as complete and accurate as the users want it to be,[25] the 2007 CNN– YouTube Presidential Candidate Debates provide a clear case that YouTube, as a political medium, has the ability to appeal across demographic lines. A demographic analysis of debate participants found that just over 41% of participants were under the age of 30 [26] and that individuals over 55 accounted for roughly 11% of participants.[27] These results indicate that the YouTube debate format was successful in reaching younger participations and minorities, both populations that have been known for limited political engagement and populations that have historically demonstrated consistent political interaction. The analysis also indicated that the YouTube format successfully bridged racial lines, with minorities, across all racial categories, participating at a rate higher than in the 2004 presidential election.[28]

YouTube is a driving force in both the evolution of the Internet and online politics. The public expects to see digital video take center stage in campaigns and elections[29] and it is important for politicians to actively seek out ways to infuse videos into their political agendas. YouTube's rapid dissemination of popular videos and ability to reach all demographic populations provides a level of visibility and accessibility that the public has come to expect of its politicians. YouTube has also enabled the rise of the participatory class and has altered the political locus of control, both elements which could be instrumental in the development of a more transparent democracy and more vigorous national political discourse.

Visibility

As online democracy has grown, so has the expectation that because of technological developments, politicians should be more visible and more accessible. YouTube is the perfect vehicle for increasing both perceptions of visibility and accessibility because it simultaneously provides a viable outlet for the divulgence of political messages and also for the enhancement of political images, personalities, and character. YouTube videos, such as Obama's *A More Perfect Union* speech, which has been viewed over 6 million times, have the power to exponentially increase the exposure of politicians, and their messages, with little to no cost. These videos also visually connect politicians with the public in ways not possible through other mediums and in a manner that is either much more cumbersome, or not even possible, through other social media outlets.

Nearly 100 politicians, ranging from local politicians, to those in state, national, and international offices and races, have established YouTube channels where constituents can "tune in" to see politicians explain political stances or simply to see what the politicians are doing.[30] Collectively, as of July 2009, these politicians have posted 9,421 videos, amassing 217,533,659 user views, and given themselves not only unprecedented visibility, but also the public unprecedented access to the world's political conversation. Focusing specifically on the 2008 presidential election, Senators John McCain and Barack Obama uploaded 2,158 videos to their YouTube channels – 329 from McCain and 1,856 from Obama. Viewers watched the equivalent of 488,152 hours worth of video on McCain's channel and 14.5 million on Obama's channel; had the candidates paid for this amount of televised broadcast time, the visibility they achieved through YouTube would have cost a collective $47.5 million.[31]

YouTube also increased the visibility of campaigns in 2008 by highlighting one campaign per week beginning in April 2008. It was through this function that Hilary Clinton broadcast the request for viewers to select a campaign song and announced the winning song's selection in a video spoof of the final dramatic scene from the Sopranos. By encouraging viewership through making campaign information easily accessible, YouTube helped to elevate the visibility of all of the early presidential candidates.

Not only does YouTube allow politicians an alternate way of addressing the public, the medium allows them an alternate way of responding to the criticisms and challenges of other politicians. YouTube makes it easy for politicians to quickly, and affordably, clarify key messages and offer retorts, an option that is as easy through traditional media channels. Candidates can also respond to the public's questions regularly by posting video responses to frequently asked questions and using video to ensure hat campaign messages are being received as intended.

Accessibility

While the free and broad dissemination of videos means that sometimes candidates appear in videos that they would rather not, the open nature of the medium allows for extensive access to political information and the ability to create and share playlists, bookmark and re-watch favorite videos, post video responses, link to other videos and related websites, and most important for democratic dialogue, discuss the videos. The ability to select and track the videos of politicians and to subscribe to selected content feeds puts constituents at the center of the political experience[32] and the constant accessibility allows the public to have more information regarding the nation's political dialogue.

In 2008, all of the major party candidates used their YouTube channels to connect with potential voters; however, no campaign seemed to achieve a feeling of laid-back accessibility as well as the Obama campaign. The campaign posted multiple videos everyday on topics ranging from policy discussions to requests for donations. However, what set the Obama campaign apart was that its videos made the viewer feel as if the campaign was personal.[33] The campaign's basic plan was document Obama on the road by uploading video clips of speeches, public meetings, and informal footage of Obama working with his staff, the result was footage that was raw, immediate, and intimate, ultimately making a connection with the viewers. The videos made the viewers feel as if they were an integral part of the campaign, often thanking the viewers for their hard work. For example, in one video, David Plouffe, Obama's chief campaign manager, said to the viewers, "because of the organization that you helped us build, we think we have a good opportunity; this is what you should feel very proud about and responsible for."[34] Videos such as this helped to cultivate a sense of community amongst viewers and make supporters feel as if they were on the campaign trail with Obama, thus making Obama both visible and accessible.

McCain's campaign attempted to connect with potential voters through similar means; however, unfortunately the attempts made by Rick Davis, McCain's general campaign manager, translated more into discussions of political strategy and did not achieve political connectedness. Davis's videos served mostly to inform viewers about the campaign's general election strategy and often equated to narrated slide shows where the viewers could only hear Davis's voice and not see his face, [35] serving to make McCain visible, but seemingly inaccessible.

Even Congress and the Library of Congress have established themselves on YouTube by launching independent pages. While some congressional members already had existing YouTube channels, the launch of House Hub and Senate Hub enabled members to create and control videos on their respective hubs. The site also funnels users to their individual representatives through a use of a Google Map that allows users to click on their home state and easily connect with the channels of their state's representatives, making representatives visible and easy to access.[36] Following his election, President Obama continued using YouTube to announce the development of organizations, such as Organizing for America, discuss salient issues, such as economic recovery, and discuss his selection of Supreme Court nominee Sonia Sotomayor. While some tensions still remain between the "buttoned-up culture of Washington and the more organic, free-wheeling style of YouTube,"[37] the desire of political institutions to establish themselves on YouTube indicates an understanding of the need for visibility and accessibility that the American public has come to expect from its politicians.

The Participatory Class

Understanding how to enhance the influence of citizens, both during and in between elections, is something political philosophers and politicians have been struggling with since the early 19th century.[38]

Although many steps toward deliberative democracy have been taken, the political emergence of YouTube is significant because it encourages regular people to engage in pubic discourse.

The participatory class emerged during the 2008 presidential elections, with videos such as "I got a crush on Obama" and the "Vote Different" Orwellian clip becoming practically instant Internet sensations and demonstrating the ability of average users to have significant political impact. While these two examples do not even scratch the creative surface of the videos posted during the election, they are indicative of the power of online collectives and proof that Internet technologies can allow users to harness manifest creativity to disseminate both information and propaganda through social interaction.[39]

YouTube offers many tools and services that promote user's democratic engagement through participation and a redefinition of what it means to be democratically engaged. The CNN-YouTube Presidential Candidate Debates encouraged political participation and deliberation by allowing the public to upload video questions for possible inclusion in two nationally broadcast presidential candidate debates. For the first time in the history of American presidential debates, the audience's participation was not just courted, but vital. Although only 39 videos were selected for the broadcasts, the nearly 8,000 videos that were submitted, and the quality of the questions asked in the submissions, indicated that, when given the opportunity, the American public was both willing and able to engage political leaders in national political conversation.[40]

By facilitating the creation of communities of shared interests, which often span multiple communities, YouTube has provided an arena for political discourse to occur. Through the development of user-user subscriptions, where users subscribe to video feeds from other users, and video-video relatedness, where a video is regarded as related to another video by the site's search engine,[41] YouTube users can connect not only with each other, but with videos that they may not have located on their own. These tools support the consultative model of e-democracy by stressing the importance of the communication of citizen opinion[42] and by offering multiple arenas for public deliberation that are spontaneous, flexible, and for the most part, self-governed,[43] which can be used to encourage democratic discussion, and provide better policy and administration for the benefit of the public.

The tools provided for selection and discussion also allow for the dissemination of political conversation. YouTube provides space for each video to be linked to five other Internet pages, a tool which allows users to expand their knowledge beyond the video clip by exploring other, related sites. This tool allows politicians to provide links to sites that increase user knowledge or that provide support to campaigns, such as recruiting volunteers or helping raise contributions. YouTube enables key word searches making desired videos easy to locate, and users can not only watch, but also leave comments on videos they view. Many users take advantage of the ability to leave text-based comments as well as video-based responses. During the CNN-YouTube debates, video responses to the candidates' debate answers were a popular way of maintaining political dialogue during and after the debates. In 2009 YouTube released a tool making and uploading video responses even easier: a one-click video response icon. After viewing a video, users simply have to click an icon, which will turn on their webcam and allow them to record and upload a video-based response in seconds. Tools, such as these, contribute not only to user-to-user dialogue, but also provide a venue where the public can freely participate in deliberation away from controlling influences of the state, media corporations, and some of the structures of social inequality,[44] both which are vital components of a healthy and participatory democracy.

Changes in Control

While visibility, accessibility, and citizen participation are beneficial in opening the lines of political communication, the increase of these factors comes with a price: a changing locus of control over political messages and images. The elimination of entry barriers and the open-source nature of YouTube allow anyone, supporter or opponent, to create a YouTube channel about a politician; ultimately, giving partial control of political messages over to ordinary citizens. For example, in July 2009 there were 5,250 YouTube channels dedicated, in one way or another, to Barack Obama; however, only one of those channels was officially sponsored and maintained by Obama affiliates. In addition, unlike politicians who cannot legally falsify information in political advertising, the same standards do not hold true for YouTube video creators; as long as the users do not violate YouTube's terms of use, they have ultimate control over the content of their channels. This changing control structure can make it difficult for politicians to promote and control their platform[45] and can lead to skewed perceptions of political messages.

The introduction of YouTube onto the political scene has also forced politicians to be more conscious of what they say and do in public. The possibility of being filmed at any time, at any location, has forced candidates to be more natural, direct, and honest.[46] Competing campaigns often dispatch "video trackers" in the hopes of catching opponents' missteps on camera.[47] The context of these videos is often changed through creative editing and the videos may depict false moments and viewpoints, resulting in a significant impact on the public perception of political figures.[48] Although, as mentioned earlier, YouTube allows politicians methods for responding to negative messages, the ability of YouTube videos to quickly become part of the national conversation[49] and the difficulty in controlling viral video messages,[50] have altered the process of controlling political messages. These factors make it necessary for politicians to not only project a strong YouTube presence, but to be aware of the presence that has been created for them on YouTube.

Conclusion

What is so exciting is that we have just begun to realize the possible connections between YouTube and American politics. There is little doubt that the constant development of new applications and tools, coupled with the movement of new individuals and new institutions into the YouTube environment, that the possibilities for the future political impact of YouTube are limitless. This future will take the public deeper into both local and international politics, and in directions we cannot even begin to imagine yet. As YouTube continues to mature, the possibilities of communicating in more accessible and informal ways will continue to develop and the dominance of the medium, as evidenced by the substantial number of uploads occurring every minute of every day, will continue to provide an evolution for the ways in which we think about, talk about, and share political information.

Notes

[1] Smith, Aaron. "The Internet's Role in Campaign 2008." Pew Internet & American Life project,
http://www.pewinternet.org/~/media//Files/Reports/2009/The_Internets_Role_in_Campaign_2008.pdf (accessed May 23, 2009).

[2] Smith, 2009

[3] Smith, 2009

[4] Fox, Susannah. "Participatory Democracy, Participatory Medicine." Pew Internet and American Life Project,
http://www.pewinternet.org/Commentary/2009/April/1--Participatory-Democracy-Participatory-Medicine.aspx. (accessed July 26, 2009).

[5] Hollihan, Thomas. *Uncivil Wars: Political Campaigns in a Media Age.* New York: St. Martin's Press, 2001.

[6] Parameswaran, Manoj and Andrew Whinston. "Social Computing: An Overview," *Communications of the Association for Information Systems* 19 (2007): 762-780.

[7] Vargas, Jose. "The Newest YouTube Stars: Campaign Managers." *The Washington Post*, July 29, 2008.

[8] Fox, 2009

[9] Vargas, Jose. "YouTube Twists on Politics." *The Washington Post,* July 29, 2007, B03.

[10] Smith, 2009 PAGE NUMBER?

[11] Croal, N'Gai. "All the President's Tweets: How to Plug Americans into the White House." *Newsweek,* February 3, 2009.

[12] MacAskill, Ewen. "U.S. election 2008: Hillary and the democrats choose Web as the new deal: Party hopefuls signal their White House intentions with videos on Internet." *The Guardian*, January 2, 2007.

[13] Parameswaran and Whinston, 2007

[14] Anderson, Lindsay, "YouTube's Political Director Discusses Value of Social Media Websites in Iran Crisis." Harvard Kennedy School,
http://www.hks.harvard.edu/news-events/news/articles/youtube-iran.   (accessed July 15, 2009).

[15] Douglas, Nick. "YouTube's dark side: How the video-sharing site stifles creativity." *Slate*, July 18, 2007. Prescott, LeeAnn. "YouTube: 50% More Traffic than Other Video Sites Combined." Hitwise, http://weblogs.hitwise.com/leeann-prescott/2007/06/youtube _50_more_traffic_than_o_1.html (accessed October 8, 2008)

[16] Lubis, Diyanah. "The Sociological Impact of YouTube." Adholes,
http://adholes.com/postings/7a29982f59f5cbc1a775f6d00a53c538. (accessed July 10, 2009).
Ramirez, Jessica. "Many of the Biggest Battles of the 2008 Campaign Played out on YouTube. A Look at How the Channel Became the Most Important Political Venue of the Year." *Newsweek*, November 10, 2008.

[17] Parfeni, Lucian. "20 Hours of Video Uploaded to YouTube Every Minute." Softpedia, http://news.softpedia.com/news/Twenty-Hours-of-Video-Uploaded-To-YouTube-Every-Minute-112157.shtml (accessed June 10, 2009).

[18] TechPresident. "YouTube Stats." Techpresident,
http://www.techpresident.com/youtube (accessed March 13, 2008).

[19] Ramirez, 2008

[20] Kohut, Andrew. "Social Networking and Online Videos Take Off: Internet's Broader Role in Campaign 2008." The Pew Internet and American Life Project, http://www.pewInternet.org/pdfs/Pew_MediaSources_jan08.pdf. (accessed March 1, 2008).

[21] Ramirez, 2008

[22] Ramirez, 2008

[23] Steinhauser, Paul. "The YouTube-ification of Politics: Candidates Losing Control. CNN,
http://www.cnn.com/2007/POLITICS/07/18/youtube.effect/index.html   (accessed July 25, 2007).

[24] Gueorguieva, Vassia. "Voters, MySpace, and YouTube," In *Politicking online: The Transformation of Election Campaign Communication,* ed. Costas Panagopulos, 233-248. Pitcataway, NJ: Rutgers University Press, 2009.

[25] Gueorguieva, 2009

[26] Ricke, LaChrystal. "A New Opportunity for Democratic Engagement: The CNN-YouTube Presidential Candidate Debates." Paper presented at the YouTube and the 2008 Election Cycle in the United States, Amherst, Massachusetts, April 16-17 2009.

[27] Ricke, LaChrystal. "Technology, Civic Engagement, and Debates" (Ph.D. diss, University of Kansas, 2008).

[28] Ricke, 2009

[29] Vargas, 2007

[30] YouTube. "YouTube Channels: Politicians." YouTube, http://www.youtube.com/members?s=mv&t=a&g=8 (accessed July 13, 2009).

[31] Ramirez, 2008

[32] Vargas, Jose. "Beyond YouTube, Video Puts Users at the Center of the Campaign." *The Washington Post*, June 19, 2008.

[33] Ramirez, 2008

[34] Vargas, Jose. "The Newest YouTube Stars: Campaign Managers." *The Washington Post*, July 29, 2008.

[35] Vargas, "The Newest YouTube Stars: Campaign Managers"

[36] Vargas, Jose. "Congress Gets Down with YouTube"

[37] Vargas, "Congress Gets Down with YouTube"

[38] Chadwick, Andrew. *Internet Politics: States, Citizens, and New Communication Technologies,* New York: Oxford University Press, 2006.

[39] Parameswaran and Whinston, 2007

[40] Ricke, 2009

[41] Vargas, "Beyond YouTube, Video Puts Users at the Center of the Campaign"

[42] Chadwick, 2006

[43] Dalgren, Peter. "The Internet and the Democratization of Civic Culture." *Political Communication* 17 (4) (2000): 334-340.

[44] Chadwick, 2006

[45] Panagopoulos, Costas. "Technology and the Modern Political Campaign: The Digital Pulse of the 2008 Campaigns. In *Politicking Online: The Transformation of Election Campaign Communication*, ed. Costas. Panagopoulos, 1-17. Pitcataway, NJ: Rutgers University Press, 2009.

[46] Lizza, Ryan. The YouTube Election. *The New York Times,* August 20, 2006.

[47] Steinhauser, Paul. "The YouTube-ification of Politics: Candidates Losing Control. CNN, http://www.cnn.com/2007/POLITICS/07/18/youtube.effect/index.html (accessed July 25, 2007).

[48] Burkardt, et al. 2007

[49] Ramirez, 2008

[50] Panagopoulos, 2009

POPULAR CULTURE AND POLITICS COLLIDE

ALIAS AMERICA:
9/11 AND THE TELEVISUAL QUEST
FOR A NATIONAL IDENTITY

KAREN K. BURROWS

We cannot speak of the current state of American politics without also speaking of their defining event: the terrorist attacks of September 11. Nearly a decade has passed at the time of this writing since 9/11, but its influence on the contemporary political environment remains easily seen, if less easily defined. More subtle, perhaps, yet no less pervasive, is the effect of the attacks on the representation of politics in popular culture, especially on television. Most of America – indeed, most of the world – experienced September 11 via the medium of television, watching in real-time as America was suddenly forced to seek its place in a new world order. It seems appropriate, then, to analyze that search for the new American identity through two television programs whose protagonists are themselves on an identity quest. *La Femme Nikita* (USA Network, January 1997-March 2001) and *Alias* (ABC, September 2001-March 2006) share a definite kinship: both tell the story of a female spy who seeks to discover her place in the world while simultaneously juggling the demands of national identity, family politics, and divided loyalties. As their air dates make clear, the two programs neatly bookend 9/11, the importance of which is evident in a close analysis of the differences between the shows and their demands of their viewers. In *Alias*, the shared themes are defined by and add to the insular political climate prevalent in America post-9/11.

While most television shows disguise their political leanings, the spy genre is inescapably political by virtue of its subject matter; the proliferation of spies in popular culture during the Cold War, from Bond in fiction and film to John Steed and Emma Peel, marks the beginning of the public's deep fascination with the figure. On television, spy shows reflect the level of engagement the contemporary audience has with its country's politics.[1] Prior to 9/11 there was a definite pro-Western slant to the aims of the spy genre, but the lessening of targeted tension following the end of the Cold War allowed the concept of national security to become amorphous and undefined.[2] In this atmosphere in the late 90s, *La Femme Nikita* (*LFN*) can focus on an autonomous intelligence operation known only as Section One, which provides a successful commentary on the politics of its era without having to tether itself to one country's ideological standpoint. This ensures a measure of safety for the show by freeing the narrative to make both negative and positive judgments without having to deal with accusations of bias. Nevertheless, it also marks a departure from the hyper-nationalism of the espionage genre that often drives the viewer-character identification process. Typically, viewers are drawn to a spy show through the desire to see their own country protected: *LFN* challenges this desire, forcing viewers to question where their identity and interest lie. *Alias*, however, marks a return to the insistence on national identity, revealing the shift in character of the post-9/11 American audience.

Spy Barbie Goes to Washington: Nationality, Family, and Identity of the American Spy

LFN and *Alias* re-imagine the mythological quest structure through the conventions of the espionage genre.[3] Both have as their protagonist – the character who the viewer is meant to emulate, and who stands as metaphor for America itself – a young woman who has been recruited and trained by an elite organization in order to save the world, or at least her part of it. Nikita (Peta Wilson) from *LFN* and Sydney Bristow (Jennifer Garner) from *Alias* both struggle with the demands of their job and their desire to integrate what they learn of their families and their selves into a cohesive identity. However, the methods and the revelations of their respective discoveries vary greatly.

The quest structure as developed in both shows draws the viewer into alignment with the show's desires. In broad terms, spy shows promote a feeling of ultimate security, whereby the viewer comes to believe their point of identification will triumph. *LFN* challenges this endpoint by forcing the viewer to question the morality of the show's characters, serving as a reminder that the extreme nationalism of the Cold War has lapsed. Sending the international, anti-national Nikita on an identity quest justifies the nonexistence of *LFN*'s national alignment, suggesting that the absence of a clear national allegiance adds to her lack of identity and forces her to search for substitute components of her self. Sydney, in contrast, has a concrete national identity, but her personal, familial identity is politicized. She marks a return to uncompromising Cold War-era nationalism, perhaps an even more extreme version. Where Nikita works for a faceless organization, Sydney is loyal above all else to the CIA and thus to America: the Agency houses her family and her lovers, promoting the attachment viewers are meant to feel to their country. Threats to America are threats to Sydney's loved ones.

Read on its own, *Alias*'s pro-Americanism is unremarkable. Read next to the examination of national and family identities of its 'sister show' *La Femme Nikita*, *Alias* promotes the new political and ideological self towards which the American public is meant to struggle.

Your Only Loyalty is to Section: National Identity (and the Lack Thereof) in *La Femme Nikita*

The creators of *La Femme Nikita* deliberately sought to emphasize that their spy agency, Section One, and its operatives were independent agents not loyal or answerable to any one nation. This determination to anonymize the characters affected even the casting process. Although the show was created by USA Network, only one of the four main characters was played by an American actor: the director of Section One, Operations, played by Eugene Robert Glazer. The other actors were chosen in part for the worldliness that their non-American accents lent to the show:[4] English-Canadian Alberta Watson as Second-in-Command Madeline, French-Canadian Roy Dupuis as operative Michael, and, of course, Australian Peta Wilson as Nikita. The international aspect of the cast emphasized that Section One operated beyond borders and drew upon resources wherever and whenever it wished; it also displayed that Section One operatives, no matter where they were from, renounced even their nationality when they became agents. They belonged only to Section One.

If the show is in any way nationalistic, it is in its emphasis on the moral superiority of the West. More often than not, when a target is threatened it is the West that requires protection from the forces of evil. Even so, the show lacks the immediacy of associating the country in which it is (primarily) viewed with the country that the characters protect. Much of the action is anonymous: the location of Section One's headquarters, where the bulk of the episodes take place, is not revealed until the third season, and the revelation positions it, not in the States or even North America, but in Paris.[5] Operatives' homes are similarly indeterminate: Nikita's neighbors' accents range throughout the series from middle American to south London without explanation. Too, while the moral weight of the show is on saving lives in the West, not all of the threats are Eastern, nor are Eastern lives worthless. Many of the villains – be they terrorists, drug dealers, slavers, or others – are Western, particularly white

Western businessmen with literally cutthroat corporate instincts. Taking them and other threats out often involves agency-sanctioned loss of lives, but Nikita challenges that assumption, seeking to spare civilians regardless of whether she is in downtown America or out in the countryside of the former Eastern Bloc. Section One's mission is to save those whose innocence is defined not by their country's actions, but by their own.

The agents of Section One have no loyalty to anyone outside the agency, and often little to those within it. Their only concern is the success of their missions. Nikita is chastised constantly for her naïveté and willingness to compromise the mission in order to save lives, be they civilian or agent. Regardless of her scruples, she is compelled to follow orders, and though she is never comfortable with the fact, she kills dozens over the course of her career as a spy. This amorality is meant to trouble the viewers: they are not even granted the comfort of Nikita's innocence, as she becomes complicit in the cold-blooded slaughter.

Nikita has no country to doom by virtue of her actions; similarly, however, she has no easy, patriotic excuse for the deaths on her conscience. Her anti-nationality is a sharp contrast to the Americanism of *Alias*.

The Superiority and Survival of America: National Identity (and the Importance Thereof) in *Alias*

Unlike Nikita, the grubby street kid who Section One recruits by force, Sydney is deliberately all-American, a fresh-faced college co-ed who chooses to enter the world of espionage of her own accord, in order to serve her country. Not until she has been working as a spy for seven years does her father, Jack Bristow (Victor Garber), reveal that SD-6, the organization she believes to be an off-the-books section of the CIA, is in fact an enemy of America and has deceived her and her co-workers into working against American interests. Sydney's determination to espouse the American fight for justice is only strengthened when she discovers the truth: she becomes a double agent for the real CIA in order to help dismantle SD-6, a role that her father shares. As a result, by the end of the pilot episode the unapologetically patriotic bent of *Alias* is clear. The CIA is not only portrayed as the bastion of national security and the workplace of true American heroes: it is set against the self-serving evil of SD-6, whose greatest crime is that it co-opts would-be American patriots and robs them of the chance to serve their country. The spies at SD-6 who believe, as Sydney originally did, that they are working for a secret division of the CIA are referred to as "bad guys who think they're good guys,"[6] defined not by their beliefs but by their actions. Thus characters can cross the dividing line between 'good' and 'bad' as long as their allegiances are acceptable – that is, to America. Arvin Sloane (Ron Rifkin), for example, who headed SD-6, works with the CIA in later seasons: his mission and methods are the same as they were when he worked for SD-6, yet because he is now serving America, they have been legitimized. Sydney never truly trusts him, but is willing to work with him for the good of her country.

In contrast to the rejection of national identity seen in *La Femme Nikita*, *Alias* deliberately orients itself around the importance of American nationalism. Sydney and the other 'good guys' work for the CIA, on the side of truth, justice, and the American way – regardless of their country of origin. According to official bios, both Sydney's father Jack and her love interest Michael Vaughn (Michael Vartan) were born outside of the United States, Jack in Canada and Vaughn in France.[7] Both must have become American citizens in order to be eligible for CIA recruitment: additionally, they must have demonstrably discharged any 'conflicts of interest' in terms of their national loyalties. Where Section One displays a course of assimilation, depriving their operatives of nationalism, the CIA requires a rebranding, ensuring its agents demonstrate a glossy sheen of American patriotism. No evidence of outside forces having shaped them remains: despite their foreign origins, both Jack and Vaughn speak with an unremarkable American accent.

Many of the series' recurring characters have foreign accents; those who do are almost inevitably marked as Other. These include Vaughn's duplicitous wife Lauren Reed (Melissa George); Julian Sark (David Anders), a sometime associate of Sloane; and, of course, Syd's KGB-officer mother and aunts, Irina, Katya, and Elena Derevko (Lena Olin, Isabella Rossellini, and Sônia Braga). Very little effort goes into demonstrating specifics of each character's foreign origins. With the exception of David Anders, whose natural accent is American, all the actors cast as foreign characters have foreign accents. None of the actors share a nationality with their characters, however, nor is any attempt made to ensure they sound as if they do. Australian Melissa George plays British-educated Lauren, for example, and not only are the actresses who play the Derevko sisters not Russian, their accents are not even similar to each other: Lena Olin is Swedish, Isabella Rossellini is Italian, and Sônia Braga is Brazilian. The lack of attention given to 'matching' accent with nationality demonstrates the attitude *Alias* promotes: non-Americanness does not have to be specific to be unforgivable. Conveniently, all the foreigners ultimately fall to the CIA, further proving that it's always best to put one's faith in America.

Alias is in a position not only to justify the necessity of the CIA but also to teach the audience the importance of accepting the inconveniences caused by post-9/11 anti-terrorism measures such as the USA PATRIOT Act, promoting the value of being American not just for Sydney but for the viewers. The demonstrations of American might and right fit into two categories: first, they enable the important work the CIA does, legalizing the wiretaps Sydney plants or ensuring that suspects can be kept in custody – rather straightforward explanations of how the government is working to keep America safe; second, they show the effects of these new measures on 'ordinary' citizens. It is not just the bad guys who are tripped up by the new legislation: Sydney is handicapped by it as well in 1.17, "Q and A," when she is questioned by the FBI over a believed threat to national security and must escape to avoid being detained indefinitely. On the surface, this portrayal of the PATRIOT Act is not a positive one, as it nearly keeps our heroine from saving the world. It serves several different purposes outside of its narrative function, however. Applying it to Sydney – who is both a white female and the audience avatar – refutes the arguments of racial profiling that dogged the application of the new laws.[8] Similarly, Sydney's acquiescence signals to the audience the way they should act: she is threatened and imprisoned despite the work she does for her country, but though she is annoyed, she accepts that the legislation is necessary for the greater good.

Sydney is a marker of the new American idealism: her fight for her country is implicitly presented as America's fight for survival. The threads of nationhood and destiny bind Sydney to the CIA and establish her bright American heroism as a commendable example, prompting the audience to emulation or at least adulation.

Seeking an Identity: The Creation of Family in *La Femme Nikita*

In *La Femme Nikita*, divorcing Section One from national identity allows it to embrace a certain level of amorality without having to worry about insulting a particular ethnic or national group. The shades of grey espoused by Operations and Madeline, as well as top operative Michael, can be laid at the feet of Section One's corporate structure rather than attributed to malice. Nikita's innocence is similarly ambiguous: she does not act out of any national pride, nor privilege the lives of one ethnicity over another. Nevertheless, Nikita and Section One are shown to be lacking. Loyalty is coerced, not freely given, which results in Section One having to counter internal betrayals as often as external attacks; it has no national identity to bind it into a cohesive working model. The bureaucracy at Section One's core can excuse its amorality but cannot provide it with the type of holy mission that the CIA enjoys in *Alias*, where nationality and family are conflated into a sense of true American belonging. Instead, *LFN* attempts to escape the bonds of nationality by replacing them with a re-constructed family group: in many ways, Nikita's 'family' within Section One supplants the national identity that the show lacks.

As with nationality, Section One closely manages familial attachments. Once an operative enters Section One, he or she is dead to those left behind – often literally, as Section One specializes in faking funerals – and prohibited from ever contacting them again. The only exceptions are those that Section One itself orchestrates: Michael, for example, engages in a long-term assignment wherein he marries and fathers a child with the daughter of a terrorist whom Section One wishes to destroy. Family is so tightly controlled because it appears to reveal an operative's true self. All of the main characters have arcs dealing with their blood relationships despite the fact that those relationships are effectively forbidden from existing at all. Operations keeps an eye on his wife and son despite their belief that he died in Vietnam and the fact that he has an intensely sexualized relationship with Madeline. Michael remains protective of his son even after his 'fake' marriage is dissolved. Madeline confronts her dying mother and reveals that her extreme emotional control stems from the way she was treated as a child. All of these encounters portray the characters in a way that offsets their normal coldness: the audience wants to believe that Operations is a good father, that Michael can love (and might love Nikita), that Madeline is the product of a disturbed childhood rather than a remorseless bureaucratic psychopath. Nevertheless, family always turns out to be a luxury operatives cannot afford, one that becomes entangled with their missions. Operations fakes the death of Madeline's husband for decades and forces Madeline to kill the man once his survival is revealed; Madeline manipulates Operations' ex-wife into killing a terrorist Section One is targeting. Michael's son is used as leverage – by Section One as often as by terrorist groups – to force him into actions that endanger others. Family is a liability for everyone except Nikita.

Section One is initially portrayed as not only a replacement for, but also an improvement on, the family Nikita had before she was recruited: an absent father, an alcoholic mother who did not attend her own daughter's funeral (faked by Section One), and a solo life on the street. In

Section One, the operatives care about each other because they are not allowed to care about anyone else. Madeline is introduced as Nikita's "new mother,"[9] and in many ways she fulfils the role, teaching Nikita makeup techniques and bolstering her sense of self-worth (if only to make her more effective as a 'Valentine' agent). Operations takes the role of the all-powerful patriarch, overseeing and directing the actions of his family. Nikita has Walter, the crazy uncle; Birkoff, the annoying little brother; and, of course, Michael as love interest: a twisted family, but more functional than her own had been.

Where other operatives' families are outside Section One, splitting their loyalty and drawing them away from their mission, Nikita's family, real and constructed, only serves to draw her more deeply into the inner workings of the agency. The metaphor of Section One as family is literalized in 4.08, "No One Lives Forever," when Madeline stops Nikita from assassinating Operations by claiming he is Nikita's father. The possibility provides a vaguely Oedipal slant to the end of Season Four, when Nikita deposes Operations and tries to shut Section One down. Like so much in the series, however, the truth about Nikita's family is not so easily revealed: in Season Five, she learns she has a sister working for Center, the agency in charge of Section One. Ultimately, Nikita discovers her father is Center's top man, 'Mr. Jones,' and the reason she was recruited: before she can even learn his real name, he sacrifices himself to save Michael's son, leaving Nikita to fulfill his dying wish and run Section One. Despite disapproving of Section One's amorality and its casual manipulation of operatives' lives, Nikita develops a type of loyalty to the agency as it supplants the family she never had.

As nationality is replaced, Nikita's family identity draws her deeper into the world of Section One. Nevertheless, in the absence of nationality she has no ultimate self: her final identity – beneath all the layers, official and unofficial, that she discarded during the series – is that of the consummate spy.

Building a Country: Conflating Nation and Family in *Alias*

In *Alias*, the intermingling of national loyalty and family identity is further developed and takes a much more complicated form. According to creator JJ Abrams, *Alias* is at its heart the story of a dysfunctional family, told using the trappings of the espionage genre.[10] Moreover, it is a show about the importance, in this tumultuous era, of the traditional family unit to the continuation of America as a nation. Sydney's identity constantly undergoes extreme shifts following revelations about or by her family members; these admissions are inevitably tied to her sense of national identity. Syd's father Jack admits that he is a spy at the same time as he delivers the plot twist that defines the series – the discovery that SD-6 is not the CIA. Only by re-defining herself as a double agent can Sydney process the destruction of what she thought she knew about her own identity; hiding in the hyper-national identity of a CIA agent allows her to regain a personal sense of self. On *Alias*, the concepts of family and nation are intertwined: threats to the family are equated with threats to the nation because the strength of one depends on the strength of the other.

The saga of Sydney's mother demonstrates the conflation of the traditional American family with America itself that occurs throughout the series. Initially Sydney believes her mother was Laura Bristow, a professor of literature who was killed in a car crash when Sydney was six. As the show progresses, she learns first that 'Laura' was really Russian citizen Irina Derevko; second, that Irina was a KGB agent assigned to spy on and seduce Jack; and third, that Irina is still alive. Irina quite literally represents the threat of Mother Russia when she re-enters Sydney's life – and Jack's – in Season Two. By reframing the world in which Sydney operates using the vocabulary of the Cold War, *Alias* achieves two simultaneous aims: it makes the post-9/11 struggle familiar, contextualizing it using a battle in which the West won; and it provides a scapegoat without resorting to the racial profiling for which other shows, such as *Spooks/MI-5*, have been criticized.

Irina's presence also emphasizes that nation and family depend on each other: "She betrayed our marriage, and she betrayed this country," Jack says of Irina,[11] not specifying which offense is worse. Irina's disappearance was predicated, years before, by Jack's desire to leave the CIA to spend more time with his family, a move that would have made him worthless as Irina's mark. By attempting to abandon his country, Jack destroys his family, and only by displaying his uncompromising patriotism can he atone for his mistakes. On one mission, Jack asserts his control over Irina using the trappings of their husband-and-wife disguise, by 'gifting' her with a necklace laced with C4 explosive to which he holds the detonator.[12] Later, Irina and Jack work together to use the necklace as a weapon against a terrorist group. Accepting Jack's dominance and assisting in his crusade allows Irina to become an ally, if one whose loyalty is a point of contention through the bulk of the show. The threat of the foreign woman cannot be allowed to go unpunished, however: Irina is revealed as a power-hungry terrorist in the series finale, which is a complete reversal of her character's development but perfectly in keeping with the pro-

American bent of the series. Sydney's ultimate battle is with Irina, and Sydney triumphs over the threat to her country by revenging the betrayal of her father.

Sydney's entire family is involved in spy games on one side of the fence or another: her parents, of course, but also her two aunts, Katya and Elena; her half-sister Nadia (revealed in Season Four as Irina's child by Arvin Sloane); and her eventual husband Vaughn. Only those who work within the bounds of the American family can succeed: Nadia is doomed as a child conceived out of wedlock, Katya and Elena fall, unmarried, to the CIA, and Irina is defeated by her Americanized daughter. The traditional family is constructed as the nation's protector, and subsequent generations are brought up in the tradition and literally trained for their futures. When Sydney was a child, Jack enrolled her in a program codenamed Project Christmas that taught skills necessary for espionage. Similarly, Sydney's two children with Vaughn, Isabelle and Jack, are seen in the series finale to demonstrate the same aptitude, emphasizing their future ability to keep America safe. Only once she has become a wife and mother is Sydney truly freed from all the layers of deception that had characterized her life, both professional and personal: having retired from active duty, she no longer has to don any of the parade of 'aliases' for which the show was named, nor must she lie to her friends about the nature of the work she does.

Becoming a part of the reproductive family whose duty is to ensure the safety and continuation of America reconstructs Sydney's fractured identity. Since the viewer identifies with Sydney, her path to happiness tells us what we ought to accept from, or in service to, the nation.

The Quest Concluded: America Must Succeed

In classical mythology, women who go on identity quests rarely survive, much less achieve their mission. In a way, Nikita embodies this stereotype: though she discovers the truth about her parentage that she had been seeking, she is not able to achieve a true self-identity. Instead of being able to escape the agency, preferably with Michael, she ends the series in control of Section One but not of her own life. She remains a spy, forced to endlessly don disguises and live a lie in the service of an amorphous public, not of her own free will but because her father demanded it of her. Though she is a point of identification for the audience, she does not stand as a rallying call in the same way that Sydney does: she cannot, because she has no national identity to draw others in. In her failure, she embodies the collapse of all national agencies under the weight of their own self-excused amorality, a pointed comment on, and a call to transcend, the actions of both sides during the Cold War.

In *Alias*, however, Sydney must be presented as a success to ensure the positive portrayal of America and all it stands for. She is ultimately able to define a new identity for herself because of her service to her country; the marriage of her national and familial identities conveys an important message predicated on Sydney's survival. Her identities are portrayed as organic, arising out of her existence as an American without examining the fact of America's own construction. Sydney, as audience avatar, is allowed to complete her identity quest because her achievements signal the audience how to support America as it re-imagines its self in an era of new threats. *Alias* demonstrates, via Sydney's family unit, the relationship between the continuation of the traditional family and the survival of America as a nation: when examined in light of its relationship to Nikita, the show clearly reveals the political drive towards self-protection and self-aggrandizement that characterized American politics after 9/11.

Notes

[1] Kellner, Douglas. 1990. *Television and the Crisis of Democracy*. Boulder: Westview Press, 61.

[2] Fratanuono, Lee. 2005. "Man on a Mission." *Cinefantastique*. February/March, 175.

[3] *Ibid.*, 173

[4] White, Rosie. 2007. *Violent Femmes: Women as Spies in Popular Culture*. London: Routledge, 119.

[5] *La Femme Nikita* 3.16, "I Remember Paris"

[6] *Alias* 2.13, "Phase One"

[7] Ruddits, Paul. 2005. *Alias: Authorized Personnel Only*. New York: Simon Spotlight Entertainment, 13.

[8] E.g., Siggins, Peter. 2002. "Racial Profiling in an Age of Terrorism." Paper presented at the Markkula Center for Applied Ethics, March 12, 2002, in Santa Clara, California.

[9] *La Femme Nikita* 1.01, "Nikita"

[10] Gross, Edward. 2005. Man on a Mission." *Cinefantastique*. February/March, 34.

[11] *Alias* 2.08, "The Passage: Part I"

[12] Brown, Simon and Stacy Abbot. 2007. "Can't Live with 'Em, Can Shoot Em: *Alias* and the (Thermo)Nuclear Family." In *Investigating Alias: Secrets and Spies*, ed. Stacey Abbot and Simon Brown. London: I.B. Tauris, 94.

PARANOIA AND PREEMPTIVE VIOLENCE IN *24*

JACOBUS VERHEUL

Introduction

In the seventh season of *24* (USA: Joel Surnow, 2001-2009), Jack Bauer (Kiefer Sutherland) is subpoenaed to appear before a Senate hearing. He has to account for his actions as a CTU-agent (Counter Terrorist Unit) regarding the illegal use of torture to prevent terrorist attacks. Although this use of torture defined the first six seasons of *24*, Bauer's preemptive tactics are being challenged throughout the entire seventh season. Nevertheless, the show redeems its hero by representing the use of torture as necessary rather than optional; and those who can not stand the heat, are advised to stay out of the kitchen.

I believe that *24*'s representation of violence is symptomatic of a larger social-political tendency. In this essay, I will discuss *24*'s representation of what I would like to call the use of "preemptive violence." By focusing on *24*, a television show that is heavily influenced by the tragic events of 9/11 and its aftermath, I want to argue that, since 9/11, popular culture has been characterized by a paranoia that ideologically and morally justifies the use of preemptive violence. I will construct this thesis around three arguments. First, I will analyze of *24* as a paranoid text and argue that it corresponds to what Richard Hofstadter has called "The Paranoid Style in American Politics." Second, I will argue that *24* uses this paranoia to support an ideology of preemption (the "Bush Doctrine of Preemption") in particular. Finally, I will discuss how the relationship between paranoia and this doctrine morally and ideologically justifies the use of torture as a form of preemptive violence.

The Paranoid Style in 24

In his seminal essay on paranoia, "The Paranoid Style in American Politics," Richard Hofstadter defines paranoia as "a way of seeing the world and of expressing oneself." [1] Because of its expressive nature, paranoia is first and foremost a "style," that is, it represents the way in which ideas are believed and advocated and it is less concerned with the truth and falsity of those ideas. Hofstadter identifies two different styles of paranoia. On the micro-level, there is "clinical paranoia," a particular individual's fears of a conspiratorial world targeted specifically against him. On the macro-level, there is a "political paranoia" that concerns a world of hostility and conspiracy against a nation, a culture, and a way of life. Because of its patriotic nature, political paranoia constitutes a style that can be used to get at a political pathology, that is, "it represents an old and recurrent mode of expression in our public life which has frequently been linked with movements of suspicious discontent and whose content remains the same even when it is adopted by men of distinctly different purposes." [2] The universality of the paranoid style of politics is illustrated by a contemporary popular cultural text such as 24.

24 contains all the basic elements of Hofstadter's paranoid style. Its plots are always structured around a national or international conspiracy that tries to undermine and destroy the American way of life. This premise, William Palmer argues, also constitutes the category of the "terrorist film." According to Palmer, the terrorist film is characterized by a paranoid style in that it is a "genre" that responds to the "chaos of the wide world from which America had always held itself aloof intruding upon our previously safe domestic life." [3] Often, *24*'s conspiracies involve high-ranked US government officials and terrorists who are always represented as irrational, emotionally unstable, and fundamentalist individuals and shadow organizations that can not be brought to reason through diplomacy. Characterized by a strong apocalyptic undertone, *24* always represents American civilization at a turning point in history, that is, these conspiratorial forces always envision the end of the American way of life. This apocalyptic undertone intensifies sentiments of patriotism and militancy, and, with time running out – as symbolized by the show's real-time format – Jack Bauer and his Counter Terrorist Unit's (CTU) start an "all-out crusade" to defeat this transcendent evil. [4]

24's paranoid hero, Jack Bauer, is a militant leader. As illustrated by his conflicts with politicians, government officials, and bureaucrats, he rejects any notion of diplomacy or compromise. Instead, he stands for swift and brutal action against the conspiratorial forces. Because his battle is one of absolute good – the United States and its human values – against evil – corrupt government officials or terrorists – he will not compromise on the outcome of the battle, that is, the enemy has to be totally exterminated before Jack is able to settle down. This goal of complete elimination is, however, obstructed by failures – e.g. the unfortunate death of a colleague, friend, or relative or by the detonation of a bomb – and by bureaucrats and government officials who are frequently questioning Jack's moral judgments in the face of extreme situations. These obstacles leave Jack with a sense of powerlessness, which in turn reinforces his patriotic sentiments as well as his sense of righteousness. [5]

In *24*, Jack's enemy is, in apocalyptic terms, a sort of antichrist, a demonic agent who actively shapes history in that he always tries to change the course of history in an evil way in order to enjoy the benefit from the misery he has produced. In 24, the enemy can be a president who collaborates with terrorists in order to secure his reelection, or a terrorist organization that tries to attack America's ideals of freedom and democracy in order to destroy its political and economic hegemony. Furthermore, *24*'s paranoid style is characterized by a personal interpretation of history, that is, "decisive events are not take as part of the stream of history, but as the consequences of someone's will." [6] *24* never contextualizes terrorism as the reaction of the East to destroy the historic oppression by the West. Instead, terrorism is represented as the strategy of an evil agent who possesses some sort of special power. Either the enemy is a psychotic president who controls the army and the national security agencies and who is able to manipulate the press, or he is a terrorist who possesses a nuclear device. Finally, in *24*, the enemy is often characterized by a lack of humanity. In addition, the enemy represents political values that, from a puritan and Western ideology, can be easily condemned. For example, the villains in *24* use their sexuality to achieve particular goals, they consistently lie to and betray each other, and they show no mercy. [7]

The paranoid style of *24* is also characterized by the figure of the renegade from the enemy cause, that is, a person from inside the enemy organization who manages to escape or who, after being disillusioned in the enemy's cause, volunteers to help Jack and CTU. Because the paranoid style is characterized by an emphasis on the secrecy of the enemy cause, the figure of the renegade is awarded with special authority. Not only is he is able to provide Jack and CTU with inside information, he also confirms Jack's suspicion towards a potential enemy. Thus, the figure of the renegade justifies his paranoia. Furthermore, the renegade in *24* also signifies what Hofstadter calls "a deeper eschatological significance" because he holds a promise of redemption and victory through his rejection of evil and his decision to join the American cause. This is most overtly illustrated by the character of President Logan. Although President Logan previously collaborated with the enemy, he volunteers to use his inside knowledge to help Jack and CTU to overcome the terrorist threat. Hence, President Logan is redeemed because his assistance turns out to be extremely valuable for Jack's struggle with the terrorists. In addition to Hofstadter, I want to emphasize that this move itself creates a new level of paranoia as well in that Jack has to ask himself the question whether he can trust President Logan or not. [8]

Finally, Hofstadter also discusses the paranoid style's reliance of verifiable facts:

> The very fantastic character of its [the paranoid style's] conclusions lead to heroic strivings for "evidence" to prove that the unbelievable is the only thing that can be believed. (…) What distinguishes the paranoid style is not then, the absence of verifiable facts (…) but rather the curious leap in imagination that is always made at some critical point in the recital of events. [9]

Although Hofstadter is referring to paranoid scholarship, I believe this attention to detail also characterizes *24*'s paranoid style. Jack's actions are continuously obstructed by politicians and bureaucrats because they do not understand the seriousness of the situation nor do they believe Jack's explanations. As a result, a fair amount of time is devoted to Jack's gathering of evidence in order to turn to the undeniable into the believable, that is, in order to support his paranoid theory. As Hofstadter argues, this process is characterized by the hero's belief that his evidence will not convince the hostile environment he is struggling against. Hence, in *24*, Jack gathers evidence as a defensive act. Because he knows that he is fighting for the right cause, he has to gather evidence in order to convince his supervisors, who do not understand the reality of the paranoid threat. Once they believe the undeniable, they will legalize the actions Jack has to take in order to eliminate the enemy. Hence, in *24*, the paranoid's obsession with the gathering of evidence becomes a means to an end. [10]

Paranoia and the Ideology of Preemption in 24

Now that I have argued that *24* constructs a paranoid style of politics, I want to argue that the show uses this paranoia in order to promote an ideology of preemption. Cynthia Weber contextualizes the "Bush Doctrine of Preemption:"

> On 1 June 2002 President George W. Bush articulated his administration's primary justification for the Second Gulf War, what become known as the Bush Doctrine of Preemption. This doctrine holds that it is politically, legally and morally defensible for the United States to use force against a perceived foreign foe in order to prevent future harm against itself, even though that perceived foreign foe has not yet attacked the United States. [11]

I want to argue that *24*'s paranoia both represents and actively constructs this doctrine of preemption. To construct this argument, I will analyze the relationship between paranoia and ideology. As Richard Hofstadter argues in "The Paranoid Style in American Politics,"

> (...) the paranoid disposition is mobilized into action chiefly by social conflicts that involve ultimate schemes of values and that bring fundamental fears and hatreds, rather than negotiable interests, into political action. Catastrophe or the fear of catastrophe is most likely to elicit the syndrome of paranoid rhetoric. (...) The paranoid tendency is aroused by a confrontation of opposed interests which are (or are felt to be) totally irreconcilable, and thus by nature not susceptible to the normal political process of bargain and compromise.[12]

In *24*, the paranoid disposition is indeed mobilized for political action, that is, to support the Bush Doctrine of Preemption. The catastrophe of 9/11 generated a set of social-political values that are characterized by a fear of new terrorist attacks and a subsequent mistrust of the (non-Western) Other. As Ray Pratt argues in *Projecting Paranoia*, such conditions generate a paranoia that becomes a binding force for the whole American nation in that cultivates "a mind-set encouraged by national political leadership and the mass media." [13] *24* expresses a paranoia that represents the anxiety of a nation that perceives itself as becoming more and more powerless in the face of global terrorism.

Thus, paranoia in *24* signifies a "collective nightmare" of terrorism. However, as Pratt argues, we should not forget that a paranoid text like *24* is not an isolated cultural phenomenon. That is, it is also a popular cultural text projected *into* a market that is already characterized by anxiety and a fear of terrorism and the Other. Thus, *24*'s paranoid style is characterized by a dialectic between a *reflection* and a *production* of the ideology of preemption. Popular cultural texts such as *24* "reflect, embody, reveal, mirror, symbolize" that ideology by "reproducing (consciously or unconsciously) the myths, ideas, concepts, beliefs, images of an historical period." [14] This is the process of "discursive transcoding," whereby the images that are being produced constitute a cultural system that constructs a social reality itself. As Douglas Kellner argues, popular cultural texts such as *24* "take the raw material of social history and of social discourses and process them into products which are themselves historical events and social forces." [15] Hence, *24* projects rather than reflects a particular reality, that is, it produces an ideology of preemption through its representation of a reality in which a doctrine of preemption is now widely accepted. [16]

In *Power and Paranoia*, Dana Polan also emphasizes this relationship between paranoia and ideology. He refers to paranoia as a "*social* concept, for it allows a mediation between the externalities of social existence – the impositions and prescriptions of a culture – and their internalization in the form of a particular ideology and psychic economy." [17] Following Carl Freedman, Polan argues that paranoia is not a reaction to established positions of power and knowledge but a social concept in that it represents a condition to which power and knowledge are responses. In *24*, the discourse of preemption represents a reaction to a paranoid social reality, that is, the never-ending threat of terrorism. The show represents the doctrine of preemption as a state ideology that guarantees a position of security and reestablished authority. Hence, "culture becomes a sort of tool for state policy and authority." [18]

Now that I have discussed the relationship between paranoia and ideology, I want to argue that *24*'s paranoid ideology supports a doctrine of preemptive violence. As Dana Polan argues in *Power and Paranoia*, "The initiating violence of the narrative works (…) to center Americans around a single goal, a shared ideological vision." [19] Referring to the Japanese attack on Pearl Harbor, Polan claims that a surprise attack, such as the terrorist attacks of 9/11, provides the media with the possibility of representing America as a strong and unified nation. What is more, Polan also suggests that, "Such a representation further suggests that the next time the outcome will be quite different. A forewarned America won't be so strongly hit." [20] Here, Polan implies that representations of surprise attacks, such as *24*, often advocate an ideology of preemption.

Torture as Preemptive Violence in 24

In this section, I want to argue that *24*'s paranoid fear of unexpected terrorist attacks operates to morally and ideologically justify the use of preemptive violence and torture in particular. Given that the first six seasons of *24* contain numerous scenes in which torture occurs, it is fair to claim that torture as a preemptive strategy plays a central role in the show's narrative. On an ideological-political level, state torture institutionalizes methods of torture in order to diminish the moral resistance to such psychological and physical abuses. This institutionalization turns torture into something "natural" and "normal," that is, torture becomes a policy that "normalizes" preemptive violence in order to enhance disciplinary control. [21]

As John Fiske argues, in order to make such a thing as torture socially acceptable – that is, to normalize it – ideology creates "common sense out of dominant sense." [22] According to Fiske, a television show such as *24* normalizes an ideology of preemption by representing a concept such as torture as normal and socially acceptable; therefore manipulating the audience into believing that preemptive action is required and successful. Hence, *24* reinforces the hegemony of the Bush Doctrine of Preemption and turns it into a worldview that supports torture as an acceptable means of fighting terrorism.

24 stimulates this normalization of torture through its use of what Patricia Pisters calls "the deadline-effect," that is, its "ticking-time-bomb-scenario" [23] , which centers on a terrorist who knows of a large-scale threat but refuses to reveal it. Following Hofstadter's paranoid style, this ticking-time-bomb-scenario represents torture as "ethical" because it could save thousands of lives. The problem, however, is that this scenario is based on paranoid facts and assumptions, which, as illustrated by Hofstadter, are fallacious. Not only does *24* take the absolute authority of the Counter Terrorist Unit for granted, its paranoid ticking-time-bomb-scenario also relies entirely on the knowledge of the terrorist. Hence, the occurrence of such a paranoid scenario is most unlikely and is often based, as argued by Hofstadter, on a "curious leap in imagination." [24]

Nevertheless, *24* uses the ticking-bomb-plot to propagate a preemptive strategy of torture. Not only does the ticking-time-bomb-plot define the very core of *24*'s real-time concept, it also reinforces Hofstadter's paranoid notion of "time running out" through its continuous movement of the clock – both during the show and in between commercial breaks – that literally counts the seconds until the potential disaster.

Within this context of "time running out," the preemptive use of torture is ideologically justified in three different ways. First, torture is presented as a way of determining innocence or guilt, a way of finding out *if* the suspect has any information in the first place. Second, torture is represented as an acceptable strategy to gain vital information concerning national security. Third, the use of torture is used as a metaphor to justify, on a macro-level, the preemptive "war on terror" itself. That is, the show implies that if the US wants to win this "war on terror," preemptive action is not optional but necessary. Following the paranoid style as described by Hofstadter, the terrorists in *24* are presented as ruthless enemies who require Jack to do "whatever it takes" to prevent their evil conspiracy from happening. The only way to defeat the terrorists is to fall back on their morally ambiguous methods; therefore forcing Jack and CTU to torture in the name of national security. This blurring of the ethic boundaries between the hero and the villain constitutes a crucial segment of the paranoid imagination. As Hofstadter argues, "A fundamental paradox of the paranoid style is the imitation of the enemy." [25]

24 represents paranoia as a social reality to morally justify the use of preemptive violence such as torture. As Elizabeth Swanson Goldberg argues in "Splitting Difference: Global Identity Politics and the Representation of Torture in the Counterhistorical Dramatic Film," "in the context of mass cultural circulation of images of wounding, torture, and death, the wounded body is at once a historical referent testifying to historical atrocity and a generic signifier of fear, suspense, desire, even humor, depending upon the interpretive signals of its narrative container (…)." [26] In *24*'s narrative, the representation of torture prioritizes the Western subject position over the other cultural and national subject positions represented. As Goldberg argues, "The body of the [tortured] victim becomes the signifier of the relative safety and security of the Western body from such acts." [27]

Furthermore, *24* is also characterized by a moral revision of the traditional Western representation of torture. Whereas Goldberg argues that the acts of the torturer, usually a non-Western Other, mark the difference between the West – governed by the rule of law and morality – and the Other – who represents an oppressive, violent brutality – *24* signifies an ideological shift in that is turns this juxtaposition upside down through the process of what I have previously referred to as the normalization of preemptive violence. With Jack Bauer torturing people without any legal consequences, it is no longer the Other who commits crimes against humanity. Thus, without overestimating its social and cultural value, *24* signifies the Bush Administration's era of moral and ideological decay, which has, through the processes of normalization and naturalization, also defined the accepted social values associated of that era.

This moral ambiguity is reinforced by the show's narrative process of character-identification as well. That is, *24* morally justifies torture by forcing the audience to identify with Jack – the torturer – and not with the tortured Other who experiences the bodily pain. On the one hand, as mentioned before, *24* always justifies Jack's actions in that he has to do "whatever it takes" to prevent a potential attack from happening. While doing so, the show privileges Jack's personal dilemmas as well as his personal "trauma" generated by these morally ambiguous actions. On the other hand, however, we never get an insight into the emotions, thoughts, and feelings of the tortured Other. And when *24* does provide the spectator with some information on the experience of the tortured Other, his/her experience of pain is often constructed as natural and desirable, which not only reduces the Other to a level of "inhumanity" but also – following the tradition of Hofstadter's paranoid style – signifies him/her as a "transcendent evil." This moral and ideological contrast between the Westerner and the Other is also reinforced by the show's juxtaposition of the Western and non-Western experience of physical and psychological violence. That is, when Jack is tortured, *24* wants the spectator to identify with his experience of bodily pain and its subsequent psychological trauma, whereas the experience of the Other is mostly reduced to some sort of masochistic pleasure. Hence, the use of torture in *24* provides what Goldberg has called "a reassuring account of Western political supremacy and individual safety." [28]

Finally, following Frantz Fanon's *Black Skin, White Masks*, Darius Rejali relates the use of torture to the construction of masculinity: "Only real men will have the courage to torture. (…) [He, the real man] wants to be recognized for making the right, manly decision and so being the proper moral agent in democratic life." [29] In *24*, the contrast between Jack Bauer and the Other – that is, between the torturer and the masochist – creates what Fanon has called a crisis of white democratic masculinity. One the one hand, Jack's use of torture encourages supremacist feelings of sadistic aggression toward the tortured Other. On the other hand, his use of torture also works to restore his manhood in that it rejects the weak values associated with democracy. As mentioned before, *24*'s paranoid style of the ticking-time-bomb leaves no room for negotiation or compromise. Because *24* represents politicians and bureaucrats as "weak" or "incompetent" in that they do not understand the seriousness of the terrorist threat, Jack has to take the right into his own hand and torture potential terrorists in order to gain vital information. This emphasis on Jack's sense of "personal responsibility" and decisiveness establishes him as the ultimate, masculine action hero. [30]

Hence, torture constructs the "hero's" masculinity, which, according to Rejali, in turn accounts for the power of the scenarios he produces. In the case of *24*, Jack has to ask himself the question if he would torture when he knows that a terrorist has planted a bomb and hundreds of innocents are going to die if he does not prevent it from happening. Jack Bauer decides to torture and he proves himself a man because he, as a result of that strategy, personally "saves the day." The bureaucrats and politicians, on the other hand, are represented as weak personalities in that they advocate "weak" values such as democracy, enlightenment, and idealism. Thus, in *24*, paranoia justifies Jack's use of torture, which in turn constructs his masculinity. As Rejali argues,

> Behind the ticking time bomb scenario is the judgment (…) that civilization has somehow made us weak in the face of the challenges ahead of us. The ticking time bomb scenario in turn is a test of will and

manhood, a test to entertain and engage in impossible thoughts despite one's socialization, and learn one's true nature. [31]

This concept of a masculinity based on torture is deeply rooted in *24*'s paranoid style. As Rejali argues, "The conception of masculinity that informs the judgment, "Yes, I would torture," is based on deep doubts about the life one is living, about the values one is allegedly defending trough torture, and ultimately, about one's own masculinity." [32]

Conclusion

In this essay, I illustrated that *24* is a paranoid text that uses a paranoid style to support an ideology of preemption. Furthermore, I argued that this relationship between paranoia and the Bush Doctrine of Preemption morally and ideologically justifies Jack Bauer's use of torture as an acceptable preemptive strategy. Hence, without overestimating its impact, I do believe that 24 reflects the anxieties of its era and that it is symptomatic of a larger social-political tendency, as illustrated by other popular cultural texts that advocate the use of preemptive torture, such as *Lost* (USA: J.J. Abrams, 2004-2009) or *The Dark Knight* (USA: Christopher Nolan, 2008).

The danger of *24*'s preemptive ideology is in the message it interpellates to its audience. *24* represents torture as a means to and end; that is, in times of threat to national security, torture is represented as a necessary, inevitable, and successful preemptive strategy that protects and secures the American way of life. This ideology of preemption, also symptomatic of other popular cultural texts, is dangerous because it normalizes torture and suggests that it has been integrated into the realm of the socially acceptable. As a result, torture becomes more and more an acceptable means of fighting terrorism and less and less a crime against humanity.

Notes

[1] Richard Hofstadter, "The Paranoid Style in American Politics." *The Paranoid Style in American Politics*, (New York: Vintage Books, 2008), 4.

[2] Hofstadter, 6.

[3] William J. Palmer, *The Films of the Eighties*, (Carbondale: Southern Illinois University Press, 1993), 15.

[4] Hofstadter, 29 – 30.

[5] Hofstadter, 31.

[6] Hofstadter, 32.

[7] Hofstadter, 32-34.

[8] Hofstadter, 34-35.

[9] Hofstadter, 36-37.

[10] Hofstadter, 35-38.

[11] Cynthia Weber, "Securitising the Unconscious, The Bush Doctrine of Preemption and *Minority Report*," *Geopolitics*. Volume 10 Number 3 (Autumn 2005), 482.

[12] Hofstadter, 39.

[13] Ray Pratt, *Projecting Paranoia, Conspiratorial Visions in American Film*, (Lawrence: University Press of Kansas, 2001), 9.

[14] Stuart Samuels, "The Age of Conspiracy and Conformity: *Invasion of the Body Snatchers* (1956)," *American History/American Films, Interpreting the Hollywood Image*, John E. O'Connor and Martin A. Jackson, eds., (New York: Unger, 1979), 204 – 205.

[15] Douglas Kellner, "Hollywood Film and Society," *The Oxford Guide to Film Studies*, John Hill and Pamela Church Gibson, eds., (London: Oxford University Press, 1998), 355.

[16] Pratt, 31-45.

[17] Dana Polan, *Power and Paranoia: History, Narrative, and the America Cinema, 1940-1950*, (New York: Columbia University Press, 1986), 14.

[18] Polan, 16.

[19] Polan, 61.

[20] Polan, 58.

[21] Zygmunt Bauman, *Modernity and the Holocaust*, (Ithaca: Cornell University Press, 2001).

[22] John Fiske, "The Discourses of TV Quiz Shows, or Shool + Luck = Success = Sex," *Television Criticism, Approaches and Applications*, L.R. VandeBerg and L.A. Wenner, eds., (White Plains: Longman, 1991) 447.

[23] Patricia Pisters, *Lessen van Hitchcock (Lessons from Hitchcock)*, (Amsterdam: Amsterdam University Press, 2004), 74-75.

[24] Hofstadter, 35.

[25] Hofstadter, 32.

[26] Elizabeth Swanson Goldberg, "Splitting Difference: Global Identity Politics and the Representation of Torture in the Counterhistorical Dramatic Film," *Violence and American Cinema*, J. David Slocum, ed., (New York: Routledge, 2001), 247.

[27] Goldberg, 251.

[28] Goldberg, 257.

[29] Darius Rejali, "Torture Makes the Man," *South Central Review*, Number 24.1, (Princeton University Press, Spring 2007), 154.

[30] Frantz Fanon, *Black Skins, White Masks*, Charles Lam Markmann, trans., (New York: Grove Press, 1967).

[31] Rejali, 163.

[32] Rejali, 164.

MICHAEL MOORE'S POLITICAL DOCUMENTARIES: POPULAR POLITICS WITH A VENGEANCE

BETTY KAKLAMANIDOU

Introduction

In his teaser for his last documentary, *Capitalism: A Love Story*, which was released on October 2 2009, Michael Moore found once again a way to astonish audiences of selected theatres in Los Angeles and Chicago on June 14 2009.[1] Appearing on a close-up, and sporting his trademark cap and his full of sarcasm and irony talk, he urged the spectators to donate money to "needy banks and corporations" as it would make them "feel… good." Indeed, ushers with white T-shirts that wrote "Save Our CEOs" came down the aisles and collected money from those members of the audience who did find Moore's plea engaging and sardonic at the same time. But what compelled those people to reach into their pockets and do what was asked of them – asking no questions in turn? How did Moore manage to persuade those American citizens with such effortlessness? One would readily attribute the audience's active participation and predominantly positive reaction to the filmmaker's commercial and artistic success as Moore is already the proud holder of an Oscar and a Palme d'Or[2]. However, this explanation proves to be rather premature since there are many other awarded and celebrated documentarians who do not enjoy Moore's recognition, international popularity or even controversy nor have impact on the American popular politics and audiences.

The reason why American citizens were so willing to indulge the filmmaker lies partly in Moore's inscription in the American popular culture and popular politics for that matter ever since *Roger & Me* hit the screens in 1989. A totally uneducated filmmaker at the time, Moore managed to create a personal and powerful documentary about his hometown, Flint, Michigan, which was hailed as "one of the most subversively comic political films in memory"[3] in addition to changing the documentary landscape and causing numerous debates among scholars and critics regarding its nature and limits. In fact, after being attacked for tampering with chronology through editing, thus distorting actual events at the expense of the 'truth' and to the benefit of his personal agenda, "Michael Moore has consistently disavowed the appellation 'documentary' and the ethical baggage it entails – while shamelessly exploiting documentary's cultural capital in favor of a guilt-free notion of 'factual entertainment'."[4] However, even though the critics' accusations were valid, we should not forget that "An unreliable documentary is still a documentary. Just as there are inaccurate and misleading news stories, so there are inaccurate and misleading documentaries."[5] Yet, what is more significant is that Moore's success with *Roger & Me* and his ensuing political films has increased what Bourdieu calls 'symbolic power', "a power of constituting the given through utterances, of making people see and believe, of confirming or transforming the vision of the world [...]", a power created by "the belief in the legitimacy of words and of those who utter them. And words alone cannot create this belief."[6] Indeed, Moore did not only use words, but all the arsenal of the film medium (moving images, sounds, music, etc.) in his undying effort to stir his fellow citizens. And it is this symbolic power combined with the 'symbolic capital' Moore accumulated through the years that made the audience of those theatres last June act on his word, validating also his position as a contributor to American popular politics.

Michael Moore is not a politician per se; yet his discourse and his film texts are deeply political and for twenty years now have been part of American as well as international popular culture as both seem much more inclined to believe in individuals who speak the language of the people, by the people and for the people while regarding politicians and official state public figures with skepticism and distrust. Therefore, the goal of this essay is to determine how Moore has become such an important pop culture icon and consequently an unofficial regulator of American popular politics, based primarily on Pierre Bourdieu's theory of the different forms of capital and symbolic power. I will also discuss the use of popular signs encountered in Moore's four political documentaries which were distributed internationally (*Sicko*, 2007, *Fahrenheit 9/11*, 2004, *Bowling for Columbine*, 2002 and *Roger & Me* 1989)[7] in order to highlight the filmmaker's unique blend of artistry and political activism.

Acquiring the Necessary 'Capitals' in the Market
of Popular Film

Trying to differentiate the ways power relations are constructed and operate in social life, Bourdieu[8] argues that next to Marx's 'economic capital' there also exists the 'cultural capital', which includes knowledge, abilities, cultural achievements, et. al. and the 'symbolic capital', which is the 'value' of the cultural capital and involves attention, prestige or social status. Moore's cultural capital was already 'active' in his community since his early twenties as he was the editor of the local newspaper, *Michigan Voice*, for ten years. When he was hired in San Francisco in the mid-eighties, the closure of the *Voice* made it to the local TV news. In other words, even before his worldwide recognition, Moore was already enjoying what Bourdieu calls 'symbolic capital' in his chosen 'field' of action, the popular print media, prior to embarking on his journey in the wider cultural 'market' of film.

Both the print media and film constitute a great part of today's popular culture which Hall defined in 1981 as an "an arena of consent and resistance", a place "where hegemony arises, and where it is secured" but also "one of the places where socialism might be constituted."[9] Since popular film is one of the widest markets of this culture, Moore endeavored to actually use *Roger & Me* as a wake-up call for politicians and citizens alike in an effort to save his town from financial demise, thus confirming the claim that political action can be part of popular culture .

After taking a rather unsuccessful stab at running a San Francisco tabloid, Moore returned to Flint. His homecoming coincided with the massive layouts decided by General Motors, the driving economic force of the town ever since the 1930s. Enraged by the ability of a multinational corporation to command and destroy the lives of his townsmen and with no film knowledge whatsoever, Moore decided to shoot a documentary to voice his opinion about injustice, the working class, his town and his ineffective efforts to meet with GM's 'ruthless' CEO, Roger Smith. His endeavor was not only motivated by the injustice he witnessed taking place around him, but also his 'habitus', a term used by Bourdieu to designate an agent's "systems of durable, transposable *dispositions*, structured structures predisposed to function as structuring structures, that is, as principles of the generation and structuring of practices and representations which can be objectively "regulated" and "regular" without in any way being the product of obedience to rules […] collectively orchestrated without being the product of the orchestrating action of a conductor".[10] As Moore makes it clear in the opening sequence of *Roger & Me*, all the members of his family have been employed at one time or another by GM. Therefore, since his childhood his habitus was inculcated and structured by his working class environment. Since these dispositions are also durable, and generative, Moore reveals in the film's DVD commentary that he set out with the ideal that he could save Flint on some level, and thus created a personal story. The first sequences of the documentary verify this statement as the film starts with Moore's voice over narration of events from his childhood, accompanied by personal home videos and snap shots. Moore's habitus is present in his voice over, his intonation, his sarcasm and his overall demeanor since it "provides individuals with a sense of how to act and respond" as well as orienting "their actions and inclinations."[11]

Mixing Pop Culture with Real Issues

The most obvious characteristic of Moore's oeuvre is that his documentaries concentrate on issues of American politics. It has already been noted that *Roger & Me* attacks the immoral capitalistic ideology of American conglomerates which do not hesitate to implement inhumane strategies, always aided by governmental policy, in order to maximize their profits. *Bowling for Columbine* examines the issue of gun possession which claims 11,127 American citizens annually, *Fahrenheit 9/11* criticizes vehemently the Bush administration before, during and after the September attacks while meticulously investigating the financial relationship between the Bush family and the Bid Ladens. Finally, *Sicko* explores the American health care industry and its more than often fatal inadequacies. Besides the examination of social and political problems, Moore essentially attacks, albeit with his distinct irreverently humorous and caustic disposition, the core of the liberal American ideology which is based on the least possible governmental intervention and on the "cult of the individual", which dictates that "a resilient resourceful individual with personal courage and ingenuity overcomes the odds and succeeds without help against the grain of an oppressive environment often depicted as the government."[12]

Moore is not only the writer and director of his films but also their main attraction.

His presence is the key to the narrative, the comprehension and the success of the film. According to Rosenthal[13], a successful documentary needs "a *key*, or *handle*, an angle from which to tell the story in the most interesting, riveting, and entertaining fashion." Moore is transformed into the basic key of *Roger & Me*, because his extensive on-screen appearance as well as his voice over echo purely personal opinions, notwithstanding based on concrete evidence (company records, news footage, interviews with GM's executives, former workers, etc.) that confirm his positions. It was his presence, albeit not intentional in his first film that mainly led to its commercial and artistic success, increased Moore's popularity and recognition – his cultural and symbolic capital – and placed him at the centre of his next projects. Indeed, in *Fahrenheit 9/11*, Moore did not even have to show any credentials as was asked in *Roger & Me*, because he was even recognized by George W. Bush among a pool of reporters in a public appearance. His name had already become synonymous to frankness, directness and democratic belief but also demagogy and threat to those who stood to lose from the release of his films.[14]

Operating in the cultural arena of popular film, Moore often places popular songs, as well as footage from TV shows and films of the past in strategic narrative moments, aiming to make a travesty of socially and politically critical situations, associate the past with the present, or simply mock political figures as when R.E.M.'s "Shiny Happy People" is linked with photos of the Bushes with the Bin Ladens in *Fahrenheit 9/11* or when The Staples Singers' "I'll Take You There" accompanies Hilary Clinton's ineffective efforts to improve health care in *Sicko*. In *Roger & Me*, Moore discusses the repercussions of unemployment with an old schoolmate, who narrates his nervous breakdown as he was driving and listening to Beach Boys' "Wouldn't It Be Nice". The joyous and lighthearted melody accompanies derisively the next sequence; a travelling along the empty – filled with deserted and dilapidated houses – streets combined with a simultaneous shot alternation of news footage reports on the distressing condition of Flint and its residents. In *Bowling for Columbine*, Moore associates one of the most optimistic songs of all times, "What a Wonderful World", in its first performance by Louis Armstrong in 1968, with archival footage of the full of interventions history of the U.S.A. Armstrong's familiar voice accompanies some of America's darkest moments; from the overthrow of President Mossadeq in Iran in 1953, the installation of the Shah's dictatorship, and the Vietnam War, to the revelation that the U.S.A. trained and funded Osama Bin Laden in 1980, and the death of nearly 3,000 American citizens on September 9, 2001. The "Wonderful World" comes in direct contrast with reality and the historic events crash with the most categorical way the myth of America as the land of promise. The selection of these songs is anything but random, since the "music track can also play a crucial role in the establishment of a political point of view and the cultural positioning of the spectator. Film music has an emotional dimension: it can regulate our sympathies, extract our tears or trigger our fears."[15] The blatant contrast of these popular melodies with the archival footage of violence, desertion, atrocity, and injustice forces the spectator to recognize chapters of the American history he/she was never taught at school as well as become aware of the repetitive mistakes of a 'consistent' governmental policy that continues to blemish the nation and target its citizens.

In addition to music, Moore also uses footage from TV shows and films especially from the 1950s – the affluent and optimistic post-war decade which "witnessed a great expansion of mass and popular culture, especially through the vehicle of television"[16] – as ironic connections with the reality he wants to castigate. He tries to prove that the image of the 1950s as the incarnation of the American dream was nothing more than a carefully constructed illusion, through the contrast of the deceptively impeccable past and its detrimental consequences in the present he examines. *Bowling for Columbine* starts with a black and white commercial of the National Rifle Associate which comes in direct contrast with the anti-gun opinions voiced in the documentary whereas in *Fahrenheit 9/11*, the interview of a retired FBI agent that criticizes the American government for helping members of the Bin Laden family leave the US after the attack is followed by footage of the popular TV show *Dragnet* (NBC, 1951-1959) which glorified police officers. The antithesis between the fictional positive representation and the inability and possible corruption of the real American public officers is made clear while the writer/director is also attacking the power of the television medium to erroneously shape the collective conscience, guided by governmental mandates and corporate profit.

The use of these popular references not only help create a distinctive filmic style but affirm the filmmaker's inclination towards what Bourdieu[17] calls 'popular taste', as opposed to 'legitimate' and 'middle-brow' taste. Tastes function as markers of class, and even though popular tastes "are dismissed as natural, naïve and simple"[18], Moore makes sure that his points will be widely understood since "a work of art has meaning and interest only for someone who possesses the cultural competence, that is, the code, into which it is encoded."[19]

Prompting Action

Moore has been accused of many things; yet no one has been able to accuse him of social inertia or indifference. He may have failed in his don quixotic attempt to save Flint in *Roger & Me* or alter the national election result with *Fahrenheit* but he did manage to waken part of the American and international audience. Renov[20] claims that the unexpected success of *Fahrenheit 9/11* underlines "the efficacy of the documentary as a vehicle for igniting politically charged and highly public debate" as well as opening the door to many new documentarians.[21] More importantly, however, Moore's films did achieve tangible results. For instance, with the aid of two teenagers who survived the 1999 Columbine High School shootings, in *Bowling for Columbine*, he succeeded in forcing Kmart stop selling ammunition. In a country where there are banks that give away guns with each new account, where kids can buy bullets at a super market – the two students responsible for the massacre had more than 900 bullets in their possession the day of the shooting – and where the mass media reinforce a sentiment of fear and unrest, this small victory on the part of Moore and his two teenage friends proves that social action can be caused by a film text by a popular filmmaker.

In *Sicko*, the outcome came after the mere mention of the director's name. When Moore asked for HMO stories on his web site, Doug's nine-month-old daughter was on the verge of losing her hearing and in need of two ear-plants. However, the family's HMO had decided to only provide one. Upon reading Moore's call, Doug sent a letter to his health care provider informing them about the new documentary. The response was immediate and his daughter's second ear-plant was readily approved since even during the pre-production period, Moore was already a household name and a 'threat' for every major corporation or ineffective for the citizen governmental policy. It is true that *Sicko* did not change the nation's health care system, but the impact it had on the life of that little girl or the three 9/11 volunteers who were medically treated in Cuba with little cost and no bureaucracy cannot be overlooked or covered under the many accusations that follow Moore.

Epilogue

Having briefly outlined some of Michael Moore's film characteristics, it seems quite evident why he has become one of American's most popular and controversial political filmmakers. His habitus, directly influenced by his working class background, led him to create filmic 'essays'[22] which the audience could easily identify with, understand and ponder on. Moore's voice-over is not the all-knowing, authoritative 'voice of God' that prevailed in the documentaries of the 1930s and 1940s[23]. Instead, it is the voice of the man next door, a man who does worry about the social and political difficulties his country faces, a man who accepts his share of responsibility and asks that the audience does the same.

Nevertheless, it is equally true that although his unique on-screen presence and sharp commentary against the American social and political institutions increased his domestic as well as international cultural and symbolic capitals, they also made him the target of unnecessary attacks, mainly as far as his personal interest and the 'demotion' of the documentary genre are concerned . It has already been stated that Moore does not accept the term of documentary for his work, maybe because he does know that while he uses authentic, archival material and the by definition documentarian method of the interview with people that represent all the sides of the subject he investigates, he 'plays' with the editing, the music score, and his voice-over commentary to 'make' the spectator identify or even assume his position.

Williams[24] underlines that this new documentary truth is "subject to manipulation and construction by docu-auteurs who, whether on camera [...] or behind, are forcefully calling the shots." However, Izod and Kilborn[25] appropriately observe that "documentaries may well give us privileged access to empirically observable reality, but this is far from suggesting that they can reveal important truths about that reality." Ideological 'baggage' cannot escape but penetrate even in the documentarian form which by definition supports the objective treatment of its theme. What Moore has tirelessly been trying to achieve for two decades now is not only to make his audience reflect deeply on thorny issues but to also 'do' something to right the wrongs, to "get the world back in our hands."[26] And it is this honest effort that resonates with not just the American audience but the global as well. It is his truth – unashamedly accompanied by his ideological and political convictions – that made him an important pop culture icon. And to quote Oscar Wilde, another highly controversial figure of the late nineteenth century the truth "is rarely pure and never simple."

Filmography

Michael Moore, *Roger & Me*, U.S.A., 1989.
Michael Moore, *Bowling for Columbine*, U.S.A., 2002.
Michael Moore, *Fahrenheit 9/11*, U.S.A., 2004.
Michael Moore, *Sicko*, U.S.A., 2007.

Bibliography

Arthur, Paul. "Extreme Makeover: The Changing Face of Documentary." In *Cineaste* Vol. XXX No. 3, 18-23, 2005.

Bordwell, David and Kristin Thompson. *Film Art: An Introduction*. New York: McGraw Hill, 2008.

Bourdieu, Pierre. "Distinction." In *Literary Theory: An Anthology*, edited by Julie Rivkin and Michael Ryan, 1028-1036. UK: Blackwell, 1998.

—. *Language and Symbolic Power*, edited and introduced by John B. Thompson, translated by Gino Raymond and Matthew Adamson. UK: Polity Press, 1994.

—. *Outline of a Theory of Practice*, transl. Richard Nice, Cambridge: Cambridge University Press, 1989.

Franklin, Daniel R. *Politics and Film*. USA: Rowman and Littlefield Publishers, 2006.

Hall, Stuart. "Notes on Deconstructing "the Popular"." In *People's History and Socialist Theory*, edited by R. Samuel, 227-241. London: Routledge and Kegan Paul, 1981.

Hinson, Hal. Review of *Roger & Me*. In *Washington Post Online*, http://www.washingtonpost.com/wp-srv/style/longterm/movies/videos/rogermerhinson_a0a906.htm (accessed December 12, 2008).

Hollows, Joanne and Mark Jancovich (eds), *Approaches to Popular Film*, UK: Manchester University Press, 1995.

Izod, John and Richard Kilborn. "The documentary." In *The Oxford Guide to Film Studies*, edited by John Hill and Pamela C. Gibson. 426-433. USA: Oxford University Press, 1998.

Neiwert, David. "Michael Moore asks audiences to donate so we can "Save Our CEOs"." http://crooksandliars.com/david-neiwert/michael-moore-wants-you-help-save-ou (accessed July 1, 2009).

Nichols, Bill. *Issues and Concepts in Documentary*. USA: Indiana University Press, 1993.

Pinel, Vincent. *Film Schools, Movements and Genres*, edited by Christos Dermentzopoulos, translated by Marilena Karra. Athens: Metaixmio, 2004. (in Greek).

Renov, Michael. "The Political Documentary in America Today." In *Cineaste* Vol. XXX No. 3, 29-30, 2005.

Rocher, Antoine du. "*Fahrenheit 9/11* Takes Cannes' Palme d'Or." In *Culture Kiosque* 24 May 2004.
http://www.culturekiosque.com/nouveau/cincma/michael_moore.html) (accessed December 8, 2008).

Rosenthal, Alan. *Writing, Directing and Producing Documentary Films and Videos*, USA: Southern Illinois University Press, 2007.

Schester, Danny. "The Political Documentary in America Today." In *Cineaste*, Vol. XXX No. 3, 31-32, 2005.

Stam, Robert and Louise Spencer. "Colonialism, Racism, and Representation: An Introduction." In *Film Theory and Criticism* edited by Leo Braudy and Marshall Cohen, 877-891. Oxford: Oxford University Press, 2004.

Williams, Linda. "Mirrors Without Memories: Truth, History and the New Documentary." In *Film Quarterly, Forty Years – A Selection*, edited by Brian Henderson and Ann Martin, 308-328. USA: University of California Press, 1999.

Young, William H. *The 1950s*. Westport: Greenwood Press, 2004.

Notes

[1] Neiwert, David. "Michael Moore asks audiences to donate so we can "Save Our CEOs"." http://crooksandliars.com/david-neiwert/michael-moore-wants-you-help-save-ou (accessed July 1, 2009).

[2] *Bowling for Columbine* won the Oscar for Best Documentary in 2003 and *Fahrenheit 9/11* is only the second documentary in the history of the prestigious Cannes Film Festival to win the coveted Palme d'Or in 2004, after Jacques Yves Cousteau's *The Silent World* (1956) (du Rocher 2004) and is also considered the most commercially successful documentary of all times grossing more than 200 million dollars worldwide according to the internet database boxofficemojo.com.

[3] Hinson, Hal. Review of *Roger & Me*. In *Washington Post Online,* http://www.washingtonpost.com/wp-srv/style/longterm/movies/videos/rogermer hinson_a0a906.htm (accessed December 12, 2008).

[4] Arthur, Paul. "Extreme Makeover: The Changing Face of Documentary." In *Cineaste* Vol. XXX No. 3, 18-23, 2005, p. 20.

[5] Bordwell, David and Kristin Thompson. *Film Art: An Introduction*. New York: McGraw Hill, 2008, p. 339.

[6] Bourdieu, Pierre. *Language and Symbolic Power*, edited and introduced by John B. Thompson, translated by Gino Raymond and Matthew Adamson. UK: Polity Press, 1994, p. 170.

[7] I should note that the chapter was written in the summer of 2009 which explains the exclusion of *Capitalism: A Love Story*, although Moore's last doc does share the director's narrative trademarks.

[8] Bourdieu, Pierre. *Outline of a Theory of Practice*, transl. Richard Nice, Cambridge: Cambridge University Press, 1989.

[9] Hall, Stuart. "Notes on Deconstructing "the Popular"." In *People's History and Socialist Theory*, edited by R. Samuel, 227-241. London: Routledge and Kegan Paul, 1981, p. 239.

[10] Bourdieu, Pierre. *Outline of a Theory of Practice*, transl. Richard Nice, Cambridge:
Cambridge University Press, 1989, p. 72.

[11] Bourdieu, Pierre. *Language and Symbolic Power*, edited and introduced by John B. Thompson, translated by Gino Raymond and Matthew Adamson. UK: Polity Press, 1994, p. 13.

[12] Franklin, Daniel R. *Politics and Film*. USA: Rowman and Littlefield Publishers, 2006, p. 25.

[13] Rosenthal, Alan. *Writing, Directing and Producing Documentary Films and Videos*, USA: Southern Illinois University Press, 2007, p. 66.

[14] Michael Moore had problems upon completion of *Fahrenheit 9/11* as Miramax Films refused to distribute the film because of its attack against George W. Bush (see Franklin 2006, 1-2). *Fahrenheit* also provoked his opponents' immediate response with two films: *Celsius 41.11: The Temperature at Which the Brain... Begins to Die* (2004) and *Stolen Honor: Wounds That Never Heal* (2004), among numerous print and internet articles accusing the filmmaker of exploiting the film medium for the increase of his personal wealth as well as at the expense of the truth and the reliability of the documentary as a film genre.

[15] Stam, Robert and Louise Spencer. "Colonialism, Racism, and Representation: An Introduction." In *Film Theory and Criticism* edited by Leo Braudy and Marshall Cohen, 877-891. Oxford: Oxford University Press, 2004, p. 889.

[16] Young, William H. *The 1950s*. Westport: Greenwood Press, 2004, p. xi.

[17] Bourdieu, Pierre. "Distinction." In *Literary Theory: An Anthology*, edited by Julie Rivkin and Michael Ryan, 1028-1036. UK: Blackwell, 1998, pp. 1028-1033.

[18] Hollows, Joanne and Mark Jancovich (eds), *Approaches to Popular Film*, UK: Manchester University Press, 1995, p. 5.

[19] Bourdieu, Pierre. "Distinction." In *Literary Theory: An Anthology*, edited by Julie Rivkin and Michael Ryan, 1028-1036. UK: Blackwell, 1998, p. 1029.

[20] Renov, Michael. "The Political Documentary in America Today." In *Cineaste* Vol. XXX No. 3, 29-30, 2005, p. 29.

[21] Schester, Danny. "The Political Documentary in America Today." In *Cineaste*, Vol. XXX No. 3, 31-32, 2005, p. 31.

[22] According to Pinel (2004, 241), filmic essays are narratives which are based on "the free and subjective in-depth analysis of a topic, that the author does not claim to have exhausted."

[23] Nichols, Bill. *Issues and Concepts in Documentary*. USA: Indiana University Press, 1993, p. 34.

[24] Williams, Linda. "Mirrors Without Memories: Truth, History and the New Documentary." In *Film Quarterly, Forty Years – A Selection*, edited by Brian Henderson and Ann Martin, 308-328. USA: University of California Press, 1999, p. 313.

[25] Izod, John and Richard Kilborn. "The documentary." In *The Oxford Guide to Film Studies*, edited by John Hill and Pamela C. Gibson. 426-433. USA: Oxford University Press, 1998, p. 428.

[26] These are Moore's words spoken at the end of *The Corporation* (2003).

THE EULOGY EFFECT:
THE IMPACT OF A CANDIDATE'S DEATH
ON MEDIA COVERAGE DURING CAMPAIGNS

CHAPMAN RACKAWAY, KEVIN ANDERSON, MICHAEL A. SMITH AND RYAN SISSON

Introduction

"Rick Hardy, a political scientist at the University of Missouri-Columbia… told The Associated Press this week that Ashcroft now has three opponents - the late governor, Jean Carnahan and the news media. The media, Hardy said, are 'providing so much coverage to the Mel Carnahan-Jean Carnahan story, and who can blame them? It's fascinating.'" [1]

How does the American news media deal with the death of a candidate? Mediated news presents a systematic bias in the material presented to newsreaders and viewers. In television, radio, print, and electronic journalism, the media sets the public agenda and determines the structure within which the public will discuss political issues. While that structure may or may not drive voting choice, the fact that news can be presented in a skewed fashion is significant for political scientists.

This paper proposes the concept of a "eulogy effect." The term refers to the boost in positive media coverage toward a candidate who dies in the midst of a political campaign. Such circumstances are very rare in the United States, hence this paper's focus on only three cases. We hypothesize that in such a situation there will be a significant boost in media stories featuring a positive tone toward the deceased. We further hypothesize that for a time, these stories will go unanswered with others showing the more damaging aspects of the now-deceased candidate's campaign. Finally, we investigate the eulogy effect's duration: did it last through election day, or did it begin to fade earlier? A review of literature on media framing and cognitive information processing shows that the eulogy effect can potentially be significant in the process of opinion-formation.

Media Effects

In political campaigns, media effects are legion. Early studies suggested that media effects were only present when individual voting choices changed as a result of media exposure.[2,3] As a result, those early voting studies overlooked many effects the media presentation can have on voter perceptions. Later studies began to open doors to different perceptions. For example, media influence can come without changing vote choice.[4] Issues of trust and knowledge regarding government, elected individuals, and candidates can change under pressure from mediated news.

The mediated messages viewers and readers receive can substantially alter political context, even if they do not change an individual's opinion. Voters can be primed simply by what they see on television, for example: fears of nuclear war increased after ABC television aired "The Day After", a fictional account of post-nuclear-attack Kansas City.[5] Media determine the public agenda in both what they cover and what they do not cover.

Nelson and associates find that the media can set the public agenda simply by choosing different frames for the same event or issue. In particular, Nelson et al. present experiment subjects with two different news stories relating a Ku Klux Klan rally. One story frames the event as a disruption of the public order, while the other presents a free speech angle. Public tolerance increased when viewing the story relating the rally as a free speech expression.[6]

The American media tend to oversimplify the context that surrounds a story. Framing the news is a fairly common practice among news producers that can have effects on voters. The effect of such coverage on public opinion is hard to measure. Most studies which do so rely on experimental data. However, the mere fact that news becomes distorted in the telling, is a significant area for research.

One reason that news descends into framing practices deals with the limited time allotment for television news. Iyengar refers to television news as a "one minute headline service" that boils news down to its essential elements and therefore must be placed into a simplistic frame. Brief time spans for news accounts breed oversimplification. Indeed, they require it. The dominant perspective on election campaigns is a news frame: the "horse race". News reports on Presidential election campaigns feature news on which candidate is ahead and which is behind in public opinion polls. The horse race coverage leads to beliefs that all candidate activities are crass attempts at boosting poll numbers instead of sincere presentations of political ideology.[7]

Iyengar studies the results of news frames. His results are telling. According to Iyengar, news coverage of terrorism focuses viewer attention on two factors. First, the media portray the personal qualities of terrorists as the dominant cause for their acts. Second, they suggest the preventative weakness of sanctions. In the issue of poverty, news frames focus on individual responsibility for one's status rather than upon pressing societal forces. During the Iran-Contra affair, Iyengar's content analysis suggests that Americans held Ronald Reagan personally responsible for the illegal arms deal. Iyengar concludes that media effects are most significant when they have a reinforcing effect on the viewer's attitudes. This, in turn, occurs primarily when they media frames are close to existing attitudes held by that viewer.

Frames show how journalists, editors, and supervisors view the political world, and frames are pervasive.[8] For example, framing effects are visible in Public Broadcasting Service (PBS) news coverage. This occurs even though PBS is popularly viewed as being above the standard commercial and deadline pressures plaguing the rest of the industry. PBS news broadcasts show a majority of news packages using a horse-race frame in campaign coverage.[9]

Even when voters decision-making processes are not affected, the information ascertained from media can be biased through the frame. A separate study showed that human-interest stories inspired more emotional thoughts on recall, and actually resulted in a lesser ability to recall information. News frames can set the agenda within which voters make up their minds, controlling the decision-making process from without.[10]

Thomas Patterson takes the media to task for these simplistic news frames. He argues that the media cover events, not complex phenomena or the rules and dynamics of political systems.[11] Such events include the sensational—Patterson points to the all-too-familiar example of politicians' extramarital affairs, which crowd out more "boring" stories about the complicated phenomena such as legislation moving through Congress, for example, or the promises and limits of the president's powers in our political system. Patterson ultimately grounds his argument in the work of Lipmann, who in turn argues that media coverage forms a "picture in our heads" which substitutes for real-time observation of actual events.[12] Lipmann observes that this coverage generally tends to personalize news by identifying historical occurrences with certain names and faces instead of deeper phenomena. Patterson points out that Lipmann's observations are as true today, in the age of television and "sound bytes", as they were when Lipmann wrote in the 1920s.

To summarize the literature's contribution to our theory, we hypothesize that the media and the public will rally behind Carnahan's and Wellstone's families and campaigns (as well as thier successors) after the crashes. Ashcroft and Coleman, the opponents, will understand the public's expectations and will cease campaigning until it is deemed appropriate. If parties or candidates do not violate expectations, unifying coverage will renew vigor and create enthusiasm for Jean Carnahan and Mondale and the public will become motivated to return to their earlier active role in the campaign. On the other hand, if the campaigns return too early (or fail to adjust), the public becomes uncomfortable, which leads to negative outcomes for the living candidate. Depending upon who violates the expectations of appropriate behavior, such emotions could cause greater support for Jean Carnahan and Walter Mondale.[13]

The circumstances of Edward Kennedy's were very different. The Senator had been reelected in 2006 and thus was not in the middle of a campaign, the diagnosis of cancer was made public almost immediately, thus removing the shock from the news of his death, and the candidates vying to replace him were neither direct family members nor individuals that had been vetted and selected by the family. All of these factors contribute to a new and unique investigation of the power of the Eulogy Effect.

The 2000 Missouri Senate Campaign

News media political staff generally report campaign activities during an election, and they rarely write obituaries. The 2000 Missouri Senate campaign presented a typical election contest until October 16th. The events of that day were momentous. Traveling between campaign stops in inclement weather, Democratic Senate nominee Mel Carnahan's plane crashed south of St. Louis. The crash claimed the lives of Carnahan, his son Roger "Randy" Carnahan, and campaign operative Chris Sifford.

Prior to the crash, the race had been fairly contentious. The campaign proper had begun more than a year prior to Election Day, and the campaign became the most expensive statewide race in Missouri history. Throughout a pervasive negative campaign on both sides, opinion polls remained virtually tied within the margin for error, with some showing a slight lead for Ashcroft. Carnahan's death completely altered the scope of the campaign.

Campaigns are difficult to run without a candidate, and so a quasi-campaign emerged from the Missouri Democratic Party in the aftermath of Carnahan's death. Both the Carnahan campaign and incumbent opponent

John Ashcroft suspended their operations, but a fateful decision by Carnahan's gubernatorial replacement Roger Wilson would change the entire course of the campaign.[14]

The Missouri Governor is empowered with choosing a replacement candidate in the event that an elected candidate dies. Lieutenant Governor Roger Wilson, also a Democrat, became governor upon Carnahan's death. On October 23rd 2000, Wilson announced that if Missouri voters elected Mel Carnahan on November 6th, he would use his appointment powers to place Carnahan's widow, Jean, in the office.

Ashcroft's campaign was suddenly faced with campaigning against two people: a popular governor and his widow. Several days after Governor Carhanan's funeral, Jean Carnahan announced she would accept acting-governor Wilson's nomination if her late husband won the race posthumously. Shortly afterward, she appeared in one television advertisement. Ashcroft suspended campaign activities (including advertising) until after the funeral, arguing that it was a sign of respect for the deceased. He also attended the funeral. Ashcroft later turned to ads stressing his Senate experience and work on behalf of the state. On November 6th, Missouri voters chose the deceased governor, and his wife was subsequently appointed to the Senate.

Many pundits and commentators underestimated the Carnahan passing's effects on the emotions of voters and their mobilization by those feelings. As voters heard of Jean Carnahan's entry as her husband's replacement, many became more optimistic and enthusiastic about sending her into office as a symbol of their commitment to her husband's legacy, and they became more engaged and active participants in the campaign, consistent with Marcus and Mackuen's findings about links between emotion and action.[15] Indeed, the Missouri Democratic Party sent out free buttons to reinforce the "maintaining a legacy" frame that read simply "Still With Mel."[16]

The 2002 Minnesota Senate Campaign

Two years after Mel Carnahan's replacement was voted into the U.S. Senate from Missouri, a shockingly similar tragedy happened in Minnesota. Running for a third term in the U.S. Senate, Paul Wellstone was facing a strong fight from former St. Paul mayor Norm Coleman. Wellstone's death would come in circumstances all-too-fresh in the minds of Missouri voters.

Eleven days before the 2002 election, Wellstone was traveling with his wife Sheila, daughter Marcia Wellstone, two pilots, and three campaign staffers. Despite having a scheduled fundraiser in Minneapolis with former Vice President Walter Mondale and Senator Edward Kennedy, Wellstone's entourage began a flight north to Eveleth, where a Minnesota House member's father was to be buried. Nearing Eveleth, the plane crashed in dense forest, killing all eight persons on board.

Prior to the crash, the race had been contentious: quite possibly as contentious as the Carnahan-Ashcroft race two years prior. Wellstone had never won more than 51% of the statewide vote in two tight races with Republican Rudy Boschwitz, so Wellstone was accustomed to the prospect of a close race. An April 16 poll by the Saint Paul Pioneer Press had Wellstone at only 42% support.[17] A Zogby poll released October 14 of that year showed Wellstone up to 46%, while Coleman was at only 37%. However, 10% of the respondents were not sure, making a significant swing vote.[18]

The Wellstone-Coleman race was negative, if not suffused with the personal animosity that characterized the Ashcroft-Carnahan tilt. Coleman-favoring interests did run attack ads against Wellstone claiming he levied taxes on the dead, while Wellstone attacked Coleman on questionable campaign donations he had received. Polls remained close, and the election looked to go down to the final day.[19]

Wellstone's death on October 26 changed the Minnesota Senate campaign, closer to Election Day than Carnahan's death in 2000. A further dissimilarity between Carnahan and Wellstone's legacies was provided in varying state laws. In Missouri, the candidate's name remained on the ballot while the governor was allowed to appoint a surrogate in the event Carnahan won. Minnesota, by contrast, required Wellstone's name to be struck from the ballot. The Minnesota Democrat Farmer Labor (DFL) Party would be allowed to name a replacement, who would be placed on the ballot instead of Wellstone. The party subsequently chose one of the men Wellstone was to have joined at his Minneapolis fundraiser: former Vice President Walter Mondale, himself a former two-term senator from Minnesota.

Initially, the news media handled Wellstone's death in a similar manner as they had responded to Carhanan's. National media flocked to the state, spontaneous memorials arose, and it was impossible to read a newspaper or watch television without seeing images of tragedy and grief reinforced. Public officials underscored the image of grief, as well:

Senator Tom Harkin of Iowa breaking down at a press conference commemorating his closest Senate friend. Similarly, Pete Domenici's aide had to recover the call from his boss on the air when the Senator broke down, leaving only silence on the other end of the phone. Emotional and deeply respectful images of Republicans and Democrats were repeatedly shown, unified in grief and remembrance of a politician who was greatly admired. In addition, remembrances of the other seven victims simply amplified the impact of the tragic event.[20]

The eulogy effect may in fact be caused by the intense media coverage above and beyond that of the campaign's normal coverage. After the plane crash that killed Wellstone, polls showed that Wellstone's slight lead over Republican challenger Norm Coleman translated almost unchanged to his replacement. In fact, Jasperson mentions that:

> [P]rivate polls in the days after the plane crash for the Mondale campaign showed a larger percentage lead than experienced by Wellstone. Pundits and practitioners on both sides conceded that Coleman was "in between a rock and a hard place" as the sympathy vote from Wellstone's death would likely propel Mondale into office. . . In the context of political tragedy, these emotions of grief and sympathy operate to unite the public, similar to the emotional reaction in the wake of the 9-11 tragedy when the public demonstrated a "rally around the flag" in the context of national crisis.[21]

Coleman did not formally suspend his campaign immediately following Wellstone's death, but did alter the negative tone that had characterized their contest previously. News reports gave the Wellstone campaign free advertising time by airing the final spot of the campaign, one that the Senator had written himself. Coleman joined in the grief and memorializing, saying:

> This is a terrible day for Minnesota. Paul Wellstone and I were political opponents and that was it...I had the greatest respect for his passion, he was a fighter. The people of Minnesota are going to miss that...I am going to miss that. We have suspended all campaign activities....this is a time for folks to pray, and pray and mourn. Again, we are very, very, very saddened...Our focus is solely on bending our knees, and being very reflective and very prayerful.[22]

Coleman's strategy was significantly different from that of Ashcroft, who basically went into hiding following Carnahan's crash. Ashcroft issued a press release rather than holding a press conference, in effect placing a funeral veil around his campaign.

Because of Ashcroft's fate, the Coleman campaign decided that their candidate would not drop completely out of sight. He would present himself to the public as a mourner who commiserated with the loss for Minnesota. In fact, one DFL strategist referred to Coleman as "the Mourner in Chief" because of his remaining presence in this context on television over the next several days. Analysis of media coverage showed that Norm Coleman did receive a small amount of airtime. Five percent (or 22 stories out of the 410) showed Coleman speaking as a mourner.

The campaign's turning point may have been Wellstone's public memorial service, which some turned into a quasi-campaign rally. Some of Wellstone's supporters couldn't resist booing Senate Majority Leader Trent Lott at the event, and at least one speaker admonished Republicans to elect Wellstone's replacement—a comment widely believed to be inappropriate at such a time. Coleman attempted to rise above the fray by eschewing the partisan nature of the campaign.

Mondale's late entry and the partisan memorial service failed to seal an easy victory for Coleman, but neither did the sympathy factor propel Wellstone's replacement to victory. Coleman did win the election, but by less than sixty thousand votes, a margin of three percent over Mondale.

With many cases of tragedy, the replacement candidate is a spouse or family member such as Jean Carnahan in 2000. According to interviews, neither of the Wellstone's two surviving sons was considered for the race.

While Mondale was not a Wellstone family member, he was a prominent figure in the Minnesota DFL and an integral part of Wellstone's career in Minnesota. Just after the plane crash, news reporters showed touching images of Wellstone and Mondale walking and talking together. While Mondale's intention to run was not officially released in writing to the press until the day after the Wellstone memorial, it was generally understood by Sunday that Mondale would succeed Wellstone.

The link between Wellstone and Mondale was strongly forged through constant news coverage and video images that began immediately after the plane crash. Also, the fact that the Wellstone sons chose Mondale was an immediate focus of media stories. One reporter opened his story on the 5pm news Sunday by saying, "As Democrats celebrate Wellstone's memorial, Wellstone's family chooses the man they want to carry his message forward." In a clear tie to Mondale, the report framed the candidacy in terms of Wellstone's legacy and that many were looking to Mondale to carry on for him.

We speculate that because Mondale was not part of the Wellstone family, his presence in the campaign was framed very differently from that of Jean Carnahan. Instead of being crowned as heir-apparent to Wellstone, Mondale was evaluated on his own. These evaluations included some negative frames, for example, his service in the one-term Carter Administration, and his landslide defeat in the 1984 Presidential election. Some reports also mentioned Mondale's advancing age—74 as of 2002—and younger voters' lack of name recognition for him.

Precedent

The state of Missouri seems unusually ill-fated in regards to candidate deaths. In 1976, twenty-four years before Carnahan's plane would crash, popular Democratic member of the U.S. Congress, Jerry Litton, won the August Democratic primary for U.S. Senate. While flying to a Kansas City victory celebration that night, Litton's plane crashed. The crash killed Litton, his wife, and their two children.

Litton's death was a significant shock, and sent the state Democratic Party into chaos. Litton had won a hotly contested three-way race for the Democratic Senate nomination over former governor Warren E. Hearnes and U.S. Representative James Symington. The Missouri Constitution offers little in the way of guidelines or expectations for the succession of candidates who have died while on the campaign trail. In the case of Litton, the state Democratic Party convened a sixty-member committee to choose his successor.

The committee eventually chose primary runner-up Hearnes to succeed Litton on the ticket for the general election. However, in previous instances of candidate death, the party has bypassed the runner-up in the primary and chosen somebody else. In the general election, Republican nominee John Danforth beat Hearnes. Litton's tragic death would not be the last time such an event would visit Missouri politics.[23]

On June 22, 1996, nine-term U.S. Representative Bill Emerson died of lung cancer. The filing deadline had passed for the Missouri Eighth District he represented. Therefore, the primary and entire election process was thrown into turmoil. Emerson's wife, Jo Ann, wished to file for the primary to succeed her late husband, but Secretary of State Rebecca McDowell Cook informed Emerson's widow that since the filing deadline had passed, she could not enter her name in the Republican primary.

Richard Kline, a virtual unknown, won the primary in Emerson's absence, but Jo Ann Emerson circulated petitions to include her name on the November ballot. Emerson's widow would run as an independent backed by "Team Emerson," her late husband's political following. She won. Final vote totals were: 50% of the vote for Emerson, 37% for Democrat Emily Firebaugh, and 11% for Kline. In a strange coincidence, the wives of two of Missouri's highest-profile deceased candidates both came from Washington D.C. backgrounds: Jo Ann Emerson and Jean Carnahan. Indeed, their Beltway upbringing may have well prepared them for assuming the reigns of their husbands' campaign machinery.[24]

The phenomenon of deceased candidates may be rare, but it is not limited to Missouri politics. When Louisiana political boss and U.S.

Representative Hale Boggs died in an Alaska plane crash in October of 1972, his wife Lindy took over his seat, won a special election to succeed him, and won re-election to eight subsequent terms in Congress. After two-term Congressman Salvatore "Sonny" Bono died in a vacation accident in January 1998, California's Secretary of State called for a special election. Urged by GOP leaders to run, Bono's widow contested the election in April and won handily with 64% of the vote. In a strongly Republican district, Mary Bono won 60% of the general election vote and took the seat in her own right.[25]

Candidate death is likely to produce positive coverage in the media. Human nature seems to automatically extend sympathy toward the bereaved, so the positive effect may help the candidate posthumously in eulogy-like press coverage. Furthermore, the remaining candidate becomes straitjacketed by the circumstances. Note the Richard Hardy quote that opens this paper. Hardy contends that Ashcroft had to campaign against Mel Carnahan, his widow, and the press. Furthermore, there was concern that if Ashcroft were to run negative ads against a dead man or his widow, the public opinion backlash would guarantee defeat. Thus Ashcroft's campaign no longer had the option of attacking the opponent, usually a tried-and-true campaign tactic.

Senator Edward Kennedy

Edward M. Kennedy, senior Senator from the state of Massachusetts, brother of former President John F. Kennedy, and former Attorney General, Senator, and Presidential candidate Robert Kennedy, was first elected to the United States Senate in a 1962 special election, and served until his death in 2009. He was noted as a passionate liberal advocate as he championed Education, Civil Rights, Immigration and the issue he called the "cause of his life," universal healthcare. While noted for his political advocacy, Senator Kennedy first became a national figure due to his famous brothers and the significant events of his own life.

His rise as a Senator and the perception of him as caretaker of the Kennedy name in the wake of the assassinations made him a standard bearer of the liberal legacy of his family. He was touted as potential future Presidential candidate. This image of him as a successor was damaged in 1969 by the Chappaquiddick Incident that resulted in the death of Mary Jo Kopecne. This incident appeared to destroy any possible Presidential ambitions the Senator held, although he did consider running in 1976 and ultimately did seek the Democratic Presidential nomination in 1980 against incumbent Jimmy Carter. Kennedy lost a hard-fought primary as he attempted to define himself as the progressive champion against a President thought to be too moderate by some, and too weak against a resurgent Republican party led by former California Governor Ronald Reagan.

Kennedy's stature as the 'liberal lion' in the Senate grew as he championed legislation to advance progressive causes, and he did so in a bipartisan fashion. Included among his legislative accomplishments was the passage of a number of incremental changes in health care such as the COBRA Act of 1985 which extended employer based health benefits after leaving a job. He then worked with President George H.W. Bush to help pass the Americans with Disabilities Act in 1990 and continued to work with Republicans to pass the Health Insurance Portability Act in 1996 (with Kansas Republican Nancy Kassebaum), Health Care extension to children in 1997, (The program known as SCHIP), and the expansion of insurance coverage with the Mental Health Care Parity Act also in 1997. These laws illustrate the commitment to advancing universal healthcare as a defining goal of his political career.

The Senator was struck with a seizure in May of 2008 that led to the diagnosis of a cancerous brain tumor. He began an aggressive form of treatment that allowed him to continue to serve in the Senate, and to speak at the 2008 Democratic Convention, in which he was able to reprise his most famous speech, the 1980 Democratic convention concession address, by stating: "The Work begins anew, The hope rises again, and the dream lives on". The Senator was able to see Senator Obama elected and inaugurated and took part in some of the early discussions of the healthcare proposal being put together by the administration, yet as the policy was shaped and prepared for Congress, his health deteriorated. On August 25, 2009, he died in Hyannis Port, Massachusetts. His death, while personally mourned by friends and family, created the circumstances for both a special election to replace him as a Senator, and the national political question regarding a key policy issue that touched on his political legacy; healthcare.

The Race to Succeed Kennedy

On January 19, 2010, Republican Scott Brown defeated Democrat Martha Coakley in a special election to fill the remainder of Kennedy's term in the U.S. Senate. Brown, a state senator, won 52% of the votes, while Coakley, the state's attorney general, won 47%. The race featured a third candidate, an independent labeled by the news media as a conservative. Ironically, this third candidate was named Joe Kennedy, but he was not related to the late senator. This Kennedy garnered only 1% of the vote; not enough to act as a spoiler.[26] Massachusetts is a Democratic, or "blue" state, where voters had given President Obama 62% support just two years earlier.[27] Writing shortly after the election, Newsweek blogger and veteran political analyst Andrew Romano offered this explanation for the election's outcome, "the answer, I think, is actually pretty simple: the Coakley campaign took the voters of Massachusetts for granted."[28] Is that what happened? Our answer is: probably so. More importantly, Scott Brown's campaign did not take the voters for granted. Finally, our analysis finds no evidence of a "eulogy effect" in the Coakley-Brown vote totals.

Massachusetts law now provides that a special election be held when a U.S. senator dies in office. Shortly after Kennedy's death, Coakley announced her candidacy for the seat, sparking rumors that members of Kennedy's family were offended that she hadn't waited longer.[29] Paul Kirk, appointed to the seat immediately upon Kennedy's passing, did not make himself a candidate. Coakley easily defeated other Democrats to win the party nomination for the special election. Early polls seemed to show Coakley leading handily.[30] Yet, the charismatic Republican Scott Brown campaigned doggedly, using stump speeches and television advertisements to burnish his image as a pickup truck-driving, suburban everyman.[31] Meanwhile, Coakley did not campaign during the Christmas holidays.[32] Later, when she did become more visible, she made several high-profile "gaffes." These included a suggestion that a popular, former Boston Red Sox baseball player was a fan of the arch-rival New York Yankees. Evidently not a sports fan herself, Coakley also implied that it would not be worth the effort to campaign outside sports venues in cold weather.[33] These gaffes were not only reported in the news, but also featured in the entertainment media, including Comedy Central's popular "Daily Show with Jon Stewart."

On the weekend of January 9-10, new poll results were released showing the race to be a virtual tie. Earlier polls had shown Coakley leading by as many as 15 points.[34] With a week and a half to go, Democrats lurched into action, with former President Clinton, Kennedy's widow Vicki, and, finally, President Barack Obama all stumping for Coakley. The candidate herself leapt into action, with an intense schedule of campaigning around the state. But, Brown continued his own aggressive campaigning. For example, during a debate with Coakley, Brown corrected commentator David Gergen when Gergen referred to "Teddy Kennedy's seat" in the Senate. Brown responded sharply, "it's not the Kennedys' seat, it's not the Democrats' seat, it's the people's seat."[35] The

Democrats' last-minute efforts on the part of Coakley were insufficient, and Brown won a significant victory on Election Day.

News media commentators offered an array of explanations for the Brown victory. Most of them centered on two themes: the aforementioned argument that Coakley took victory for granted, and a second one, that Brown's victory represents "voters' anger."[36] Brown won the support of the nascent, conservative "Tea Party" movement, and the national news media framed the election as a referendum on the health-care legislation championed by President Obama and the late Senator Kennedy.[37] Commentator Elanor Clift offered a different explanation: the Coakley campaign overemphasized her gender and underplayed connections to the state's blue-collar voters.[38] Adding to the fray, a New York Times writer suggested that Brown won many independent voters.[39] National news media outlets also stressed that Brown's victory meant the end of a theoretically filibuster-proof, sixty seat strong Democratic caucus in the U.S. Senate.[40] Most immediately, this would affect the chances of passing the health-care bill, which Brown had vowed to oppose.[41] Other explanations for Brown's upset victory included unusually high voter turnout for a special election, with the New York Times reporting that some polling places ran out of ballots while others featured long lines.[42] Finally, anecdotal accounts surfaced about "Democrats for Brown."[43]

Many of the factors cited by commentators may indeed have affected the election, including Coakley's lackluster campaign style, Brown's effective campaigning, and the fact that high-profile Democrats including Clinton, Vicki Kennedy, and Obama waited until very late to stump for Coakley. Likewise, the strong Republican reaction against the health care bill and the outspoken "Tea Party" movement's support for Brown may, in part, explain Brown's ability to deliver nearly every McCain-voting Bay Stater back to the polls on a cold January Tuesday. Finally, the Times is partially correct in citing high turnout for a midterm, special election-- there was unusually high turnout among Republican voters.

We speculate that some of the explanations, such as the "angry voter," and Coakley's gaffes, are exaggerated. The simplest explanation for the figures in the above table is that Republicans were able to mobilize their voters to the polls, while Democrats were not. Nor can we find more than scattered evidence of possible "Democrats for Brown." We find no evidence of a eulogy effect in the vote totals, which reinforces the idea of the eulogy effect primarily as one of a media framing and informational one. The question remains, was there a eulogy effect in the media coverage?

Method

We must begin with a note regarding our previous work in this area. Smith, Rackaway, and Anderson used content analysis to determine that the death of Mel Carnahan created a media boost for his campaign, which we termed a eulogy effect.[44] The original eulogy effect work used content analysis to determine that the tone of campaign coverage in state metropolitan daily newspapers changed in response to the tragic passing of Governor Carnahan. Stories about Carnahan's death crowded out reportage of campaign tone, issues, and events. Furthermore, the number of articles that referred to Carnahan alone, without compensatory references to Ashcroft, skyrocketed.

While we used content analysis for the original eulogy effect work, we abandon that practice here. The Wellstone-Coleman race was more complex with the additional presence of Mondale and the controversial memorial service, which made the 2002 coverage less suitable for content analysis. Instead, we have chosen a method which has greater benefits: word counts.

Rather than assigning individual coders articles and seeking levels of intercoder reliability, we have chosen to choose a series of words that would suggest a number of different tones. For instance, we have two primary sets of terms, one which we will call "campaign-relative" and the other "memorial-relative". The memorial relative words are: eulogy, memorial, tribute, funeral, honor, celebrate, grief, grieve, mourn, somber, remember, tragedy, pain, and life. The campaign relative terms are campaign, controversy, raucous, partisan, poll, race, attack, snipe, debate, rival, negative, and nasty.

Theoretically, some terms could be used in both contexts. Two words are of particular note here: "controversial" and "nasty." In the case of Carnahan's passing, the weather was inclement during the fateful plane ride. Therefore, we may expect to see a mention of "controversial" decisions to fly. The weather, furthermore, may have been deemed "nasty" in subsequent stories. To test the relationship between words, we performed a correlation of the terms "controversial" and "nasty" with two sets of two words indicative of the campaign and funeral themes: memorial and remember for the eulogy terms, and race and funeral for the campaign themes (taking Wellstone's service into account). Results in Table 1 show that the only statistically significant relationship was between the two terms in question and the campaign theme, reinforcing our decision to place them in the campaign terms.

Table 1: Term Correlations

Term	Memorial	Remember	Funeral	Race
Controversial	.096	.425	.371*	-.040
Nasty	.087	.011	.046*	.033*

* significant at the .01 level

Finally, we include variables for each relevant name: Wellstone, Coleman, Mondale, Carnahan (Mel and Jean), and Ashcroft. We included both sets of names in the 2002 data set, but omitted Wellstone, Coleman, and Mondale from the 2000 data due to their irrelevance to the race at that time. Carnahan's death established a precedent and context for the 2002 race, so it is vital to include the 2000 candidates' names in the 2002 set.

Our research design takes articles from the two metropolitan daily newspapers in each state: The Kansas City Star and Saint Louis Post-Dispatch in Missouri, and the Minneapolis Star-Tribune and Saint Paul Pioneer Press in Minnesota. Working backwards from Election Day, we start the analysis at such a point that each candidate's death occurs halfway between the beginning of our analysis and Election Day. In the case of Wellstone, who died eleven days before the election, we take every article on the race from October 26, 2002 to election day, and an equal number of days prior to October 26. Therefore, the Wellstone data begins on October 14. For the Carnahan-Ashcroft race, our data begins on September 28, 2000. Carnahan's October 16th passing marks the halfway point between September 28 and Election Day, November 7.

Results

In the original Eulogy Effect study, we examined weekly trends in tone changes, and so we begin with the same method of analysis here. Carnahan's death occurred in Week 4 of the campaign, and so we look at that week as the "pivot point" upon which campaign tone changed. Consistent with our previous work, memorial-related terms tend to squeeze the campaign related terms out of coverage. Some words were mentioned only in the week of Carnahan's death: "controversial" and "nasty." In each instance, the article referenced the previous tone of the campaigns from both camps. Other campaign relative words faded from use. The word "attack" was used less frequently in the two weeks following Carnahan's death than in the week leading up to it. Similarly, the term "partisan" stayed very stable after Carnahan's death. As other campaign-relative terms would normally increase, as exemplified by terms

Figure 1: Memorial Relative Terms by Week, 2000

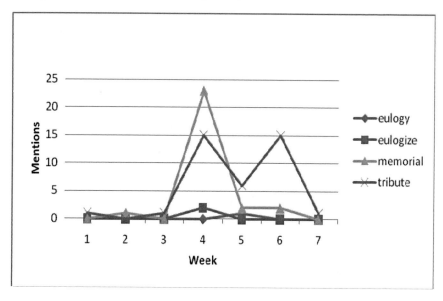

Figure 2: Campaign Relative Terms by Week, 2000

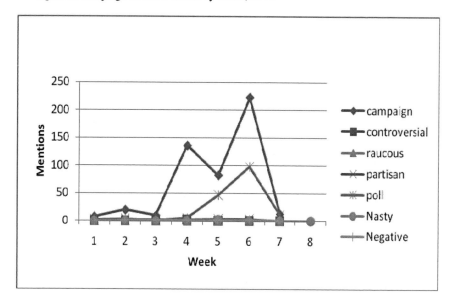

like "campaign" and "poll," the more virulent words such as "nasty" and "controversial" never appeared after Carnahan's passing.

As expected, the number of memorial relative terms increased significantly after Carnahan's death. "Tribute," "funeral," and "grieve" were not used frequently prior to Carnahan's passing, but "tribute" was used 22 times after week 4, and "grief" was printed 26 times. "Tragic," "pain," and "remember" each appeared more than ten times after October 16th, 2000.

The most significant finding is name mentions, again consistent with our earlier work. In an era of sensitivity to the Fairness Doctrine, we would expect that candidate names would be mentioned with some degree of parity. Indeed, the first three weeks of our data confirm that suspicion. In actual fact, John Ashcroft's name is mentioned slightly more each week than Carnahan's. While Ashcroft does receive more mentions that Carnahan, the widest disparity is 65 Ashcroft mentions compared with 46 for Carnahan, a difference of only 19 times over an entire week.

Carnahan's death and funeral had the expected effect of increasing his relative mentions to those of Ashcroft, but in astronomical proportions. In Week 4, that of Carnahan's death, mentions of him outnumber those of Ashcroft 770 to 95. Carnahan is mentioned nearly nine times for every single reference to Ashcroft. The effect remains throughout the balance of campaign, although it diminishes until week 7. Carnahan mentions are just over twice those of Ashcroft in week 5, and just one-and-a-half times Ashcroft references in week 6. By week seven, though, Ashcroft mentions are more than those of Carnahan, 35-22.

For 2002, we are faced with a compressed time frame, and only four weeks of data to analyze. In fact, only one week of campaigning followed Wellstone's passing, so weekly trends are difficult to extrapolate from the data. Campaign terms, which would normally just become high in the final two weeks of a campaign, do in fact begin to trend upward in week 3, the week after Wellstone's plane crashed. With the exception of "partisan," though, the eulogy effect of news coverage causes all the campaign-relative terms to drop down to pre-candidate death levels.

Figure 3: Candidate Name Mentions by Week, 2000

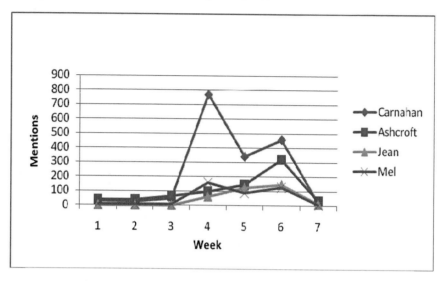

Figure 4: Memorial Relative Terms by Week, 2002

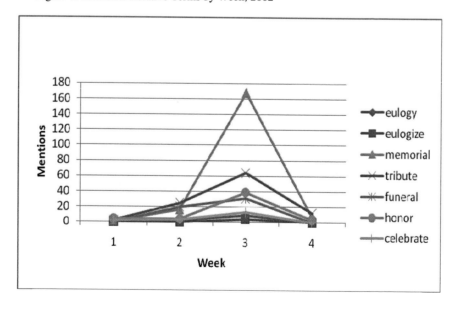

Interestingly, the weekly numbers of memorial-relative terms also drop significantly in the final week, even after an upward spike in weeks 2 and 3. The number of mentions for "memorial," "honor," and "grief" are all five times their previous levels during week 3, but all mentions drop significantly in week 4.

The eulogy effect displays a similar pattern in name mentions for Wellstone as for Carnahan. Coleman mentions register at slightly more than those for Wellstone prior to his passing: 159 to 129. In week 2, though, near the end of which Wellstone's plane crashed, Wellstone's name is mentioned five times as often as Coleman's, 773-146. The effect continues in Week 3, 972-485, a doubling of the Wellstone mentions over Coleman. Mondale's entry into the race exacerbates the disparity, with another 736 references to the replacement nominee. Combining Wellstone and Mondale references, they appear almost four times as often as Coleman's name did in week 3. Finally, in week 4, the combined Wellstone-Mondale references still outstrip Coleman's, 345-229.

There is a decided shift toward greater coverage of Mondale, as opposed to Wellstone, in the late days of the Minnesota campaign. Mondale was not related to the decesased and could be evaluated on his own terms, not as an heir to Wellstone's legacy. Even the Minnesota laws contributed to this separation of the new nominee from the old. Missouri law allowed the deceased's name to remain on the ballot and the governor to name a replacement after the election, in the event of the deceased's victory. By contrast, Minnesota featured a frantic process in which old ballots were recalled and new ones printed with the correct DFL nominee's name. Absentee voters who favored Wellstone had to re-vote on a "Mondale" ballot, or risk not having their choice recorded. On the political front, Coleman's campaign eulogized Wellstone and focused their fire upon Mondale, whom they dismissed as being old and out of touch. The data show a clear growth in the coverage of Mondale as opposed to that of Wellstone alone. In Missouri, it was the deceased's name who remained on the ballot, and his heir apparent was his own wife who shared his popular name.

We can see from the weekly data that the eulogy effect exists, although its primary benefit appears to be an increase in name mentions for the candidate. Still, some evidence points to a decline in the eulogy effect over time, suggesting that the effect may in fact decay prior to an election.

Figure 5: Campaign Relative Terms by Week, 2002

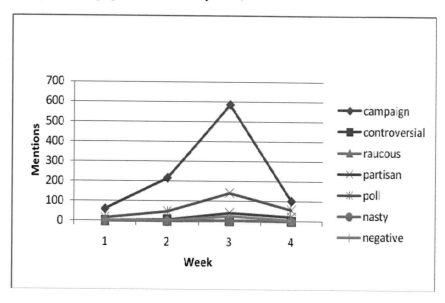

Figure 6: Candidate Name Mentions by Week, 2002

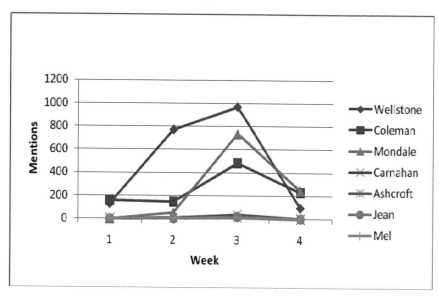

Turning to campaign relative terms, and the death of one candidate in 2000 appeared to squelch most mentions of the type.   Except for poll, race, and campaign, neither the Post-Dispatch nor Star reference many of the terms typically associated with campaigning. The use of "partisan" and "attack" both decline seriously after Carnahan's death.

Finally in 2000, the same weekly trend carries forth in name mentions. From Carnahan's death until the eve of Election Day, Carnahan's mentions exceed those of Ashcroft ranging from nine times Ashcroft's mentions, at first, to twice the references near Election Day. Clearly, the Eulogy Effect creates an "event" around the candidate's death which separates it from typical campaign coverage.

As we turn to 2002 and the Wellstone-Coleman race, we can see that the upward trend in memorial-related references does not decay as quickly as that of the Carnahan-Ashcroft race. The terms "mourn", "life", "pain", and "remember" increase in frequency after Wellstone's death and only begin to decay in the final days of the campaign. Another second stage effect is noticeable with the word "memorial", because of the partisan nature of Wellstone's service. As "memorial" stays higher in frequency that most mentions of its type, the term "partisan" from the campaign-relative terms also stays high. The Eulogy effect is clearly dampened by the memorial service, which re-introduced campaign politics to the remembrance of Paul Wellstone.

As a result, campaign relative terms do not decline in reference frequency to the same degree in 2002 as in 2000. Mentions of "race" and "attack" stay consistent throughout the memorial period, and references to "negative" increase significantly. The data suggest that campaign politics simply subsumed the death of Wellstone into it, rather than allowing the tragedy to place politics aside, if even briefly.

Name mentions follow a consistent trend, where mentions of both Wellstone and Mondale are very high in the post mortem period. Some disparities between Wellstone and Coleman mentions are as wide as 20-1 (Wellstone 401-Coleman 26), and do not equalize until the campaign's final four days, when again combining Wellstone and Mondale references exceed Coleman references consistently. But here again, Mondale references grow substantially relative to those of Wellstone, making the campaign more focused on Coleman vs. Mondale, not the memorializing of Wellstone. Regardless of intervening factors, the Eulogy Effect does press deceased candidate mentions above those of the opponent.

The 2009 instance of the Eulogy Effect presents an opportunity to further place the effect in context because the circumstances are significantly different from the other two instances of candidate death.

First, Kennedy's death was not a surprise since his cancer diagnosis. The surprise and shock of Carnahan and Wellstone's deaths may have played in to the eulogy effect in each candidate's case. Without the shock factor, the eulogy effect may be lessened. Second, the time frame between the death of the candidate and the election is extended: twenty-one weeks gives us the opportunity to trace any fading of the eulogy effect over the scope of an entire campaign. Third, one core issue in the subsequent campaign involving Brown and Coakley was an issue synonymous with Kennedy: the debate and subsequent passage of health care reform legislation. The centrality of the health care issue may overshadow the eulogy effect because Kennedy's legacy was entwined with the passage of the bill.

Because of the length of the campaign for Kennedy's seat after his death, we separate the 2009 data into two sets: one set of 55 articles on Kennedy's death and funeral, another set of 44 articles on the Brown vs. Coakley campaign. We searched for the same terms in each set of articles. For memorial relevant terms, we counted five terms: Honor, Remember, Tribute, Memorial, and Legacy. Campaign relevant terms were encompassed by four terms: Campaign, Issue, HealthCare, and Anomaly.

For the Kennedy articles, Figures 7 and 8 show the memorial and campaign relevant terms. As news coverage related to the late Senator Kennedy, there is a pronounced two-stage development consistent with the eulogy effect. As figure 8 shows, the early days of Kennedy coverage focused on campaign-relevant terms. Most attention focused on the campaign to replace him and focused on the effect of Democrats possibly losing the seat and its effect on the filibuster-proof majority commonly seen as a guarantee of health reform passing. Not surprisingly, the campaign-relevant terms dip in between the immediate aftermath of Kennedy's death and the election.

An intriguing result is the delay in memorial-relevant terms that pinpoint the eulogy effect. Rather than beginning with a spike in eulogy coverage, the spike in memorial relevant terms do not come immediately after Kennedy's death but immediately before the election. Figure 7 shows a pronounced eulogy effect but shows it at the end of the campaign. Eulogy effects do occur, certainly. However, there is an interaction of campaign and eulogy coverage that relates to the passage of time. The Carnahan and Wellstone instances, with their compressed time frames, did not allow us to see the decay of one form of coverage (campaign-relevant) and the rise of the other (memorial-relevant).

Figure 7: Memorial Relevant Terms for Kennedy by Week, 2009

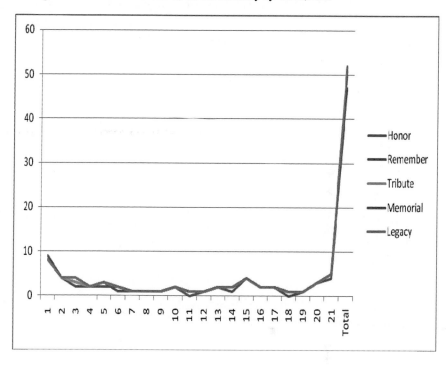

Figure 8: Campaign Relevant Terms for Kennedy by Week, 2009

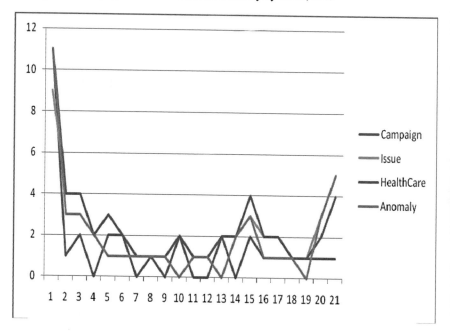

The Coakley and Brown coverage, by comparison, show a form of eulogy effect very consistent with the Carnahan and Wellstone instances. Both memorial and campaign coverage increased as time passed. Figures 9 and 10, show a longer-building but still significant eulogy effect over time. Even with Kennedy's death an instant spike of memorial-relevant coverage did not occur. However, the memorial coverage did increase significantly as the election came closer. The memorial coverage did increase along with a commensurate spike in campaign-relevant mentions, as well. The eulogy effect did occur, but the longer time frame and different circumstances allow us to say that the eulogy effect can come at any time between a candidate's death and the subsequent election for the seat they held or pursued.

Figure 9: Memorial Relevant Terms for Coakley & Brown by Week, 2009

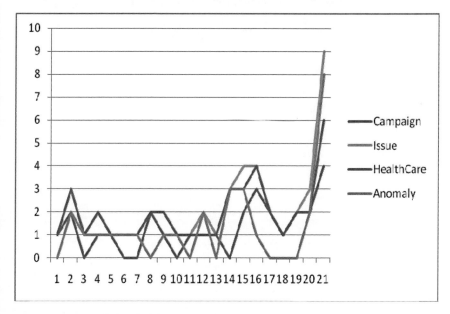

Figure 10: Campaign Relevant Terms for Coakley & Brown by Week, 2009

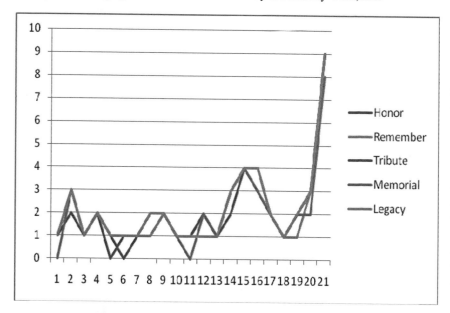

In the Carnahan and Wellstone instances, we also focused on the number of candidate name mentions during the scope of the post-candidate-death campaigns. We culled name mentions for Kennedy, those affiliated with Kennedy such as his family and close associates, Coakley, and Brown for first the Kennedy dataset and then the Coakley & Brown dataset. Consistent with the eulogy effect shown by the word counts, we see a two-stage eulogy effect here. Figure 11 shows Kennedy's name being mentioned more than any other, consistent with previous examples. Whereas the Carnahan and Wellstone deaths were so close to the election that there was no time for the eulogy effect to reduce, the eulogy effect did seem to fade in the weeks after Kennedy's death only to re-emerge close to the election. We also tracked names of those closely associated with the late Senator, such as Kennedy's brothers and sister. While not as many mentions were evident as for Kennedy himself, the pattern of many mentions followed by a period of few to no mentions, and then a spike as the election drew near remains apparent.

Figure 11: Name Mentions in Kennedy Articles, by Week, 2009

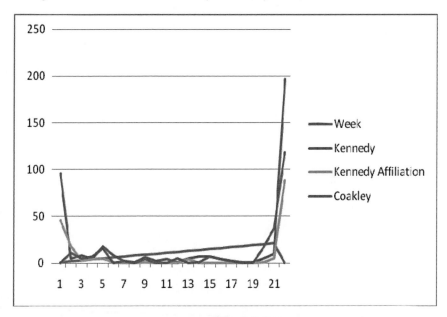

Turning to Figure 12, and the eulogy effect is less evident. Mentions of Senator Kennedy and those affiliated with him are not as consistently present in the dataset as they were the Coakley and Brown set. However, except for two brief spikes in mentions of Coakley as the race became competitive, there was generally little coverage of the race and mentions of all candidates were consistently low.

Figure 12: Name Mentions in Coakley & Brown Articles, by Week

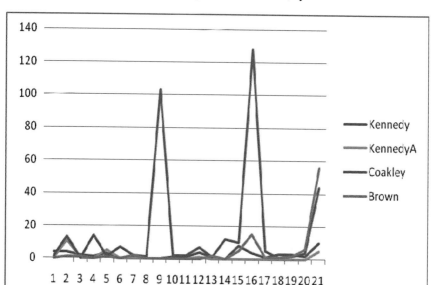

Discussion

The preceding data points to the conclusion that the eulogy effect is an endemic part of press coverage in campaigns when a candidate dies. Mentions of the deceased candidate and his replacement always exceed those of the remaining opponent. Furthermore, the eulogy effect has a dampening effect on the campaign related terms that would otherwise be used in reporting on debates, advertisements, speeches, and debates. Memorial relative terms increase sharply and then fade, but still have the effect of reducing traditional campaign coverage. While we cannot say positive or negative coverage changes relative to the deceased candidate, we do notice an overall shift in the tone of campaign coverage.

(1) Eulogy effects change the terms of campaign discussion. Each candidate death resulted in a noticeable change in the terms used during reporting on the two candidates. Memorial-relative terms, which would be close to non-existent in typical campaign coverage, jump to high levels after one candidate dies. Even after the eulogy effect fades, the terms still appear with greater frequency than prior to the candidate's death.

As the campaign accelerates into its final stages, we should expect campaign relative terms to jump up in the same dramatic fashion we see with memorial relative terms after the candidate dies. However, the eulogy effect appears to stanch that flow, keeping campaign relative terms from dominating news coverage. Campaign coverage does still appear, but not to the same ratio one would expect.

(2) Wellstone's eulogy effect was shorter than Carnahan's. Despite the shocking similarities between Carnahan and Wellstone's passing, their coverage was quite different. Wellstone's effect lasted for a shorter time frame than Carnahan's did. Three primary factors explain the difference in our estimation: a) The time frame was shorter. The Minnesota DFL had only eleven days to run Mondale's entire campaign, whereas the Missouri Democrats had three weeks; b) the campaign organizations themselves were primed having learned the lessons of the Carnahan death and its aftermath; and c) the lack of blood relation in replacement of Wellstone. Jean Carnahan was named Mel's replacement, which instantly allowed journalists and voters alike to express sympathy for the deceased with a vote. Mondale's accretion to the ticket followed very differently, owing to the loss of Wellstone's wife and the vagaries of Minnesota state law.

(3) Two varieties of eulogy effect. In the case of Mel Carnahan, his death was an event in and of itself, separate from the Senate campaign which went on in his absence. Therefore, we call the Carnahan eulogy effect a "death as unique non-campaign event". By contrast, Wellstone's death seemed to fit into the overall campaign. A partisan memorial service failed to establish separation between Wellstone's death and the campaign, leading to a weaker eulogy effect. Wellstone's eulogy effect was a "death as campaign event."

(4) The eulogy effect occurs no matter how much time passes between candidate death and the election. With twenty-one weeks between Kennedy's death and the election for his seat, it was possible that an initial increase in memorial relevant coverage would fade over time and not sustain until the election. However, the longer time frame seems to have merely delayed the eulogy effect.

Conclusion

Not only do the media cover events, as Patterson argues, they also cover events within events. The death of a popular governor or senator who is also seeking office is clearly a major such event which draws heavy press coverage. That heavy press coverage, in turn, shifts the terms of the political campaigns that must go on despite the grief. This paper clearly establishes the presence of a eulogy effect in media coverage of both the

2000 Missouri and 2002 Minnesota Senate races. Yet the eulogy effect varies with circumstances.

Mel Carnahan's death drew media attention which focused on his life, the grief experienced by his family (and the state), and his contributions as governor—classic eulogy coverage. The death and mourning became an event unto themselves, not an event in the context of a political campaign. This eulogy effect has clearly begun to fade by Election Day, but it was nevertheless sufficient to salvage a campaign that some had seen as a lost cause in the days immediately following the tragedy. That cause, of course, was the election of Jean Carnahan in her husband's place. By contrast, Paul Wellstone's death was not accompanied by such a sharp separation of "campaign" media coverage from "eulogy" coverage. The tragedy occurred in the midst of a hotly-contested political campaign which returned with surprising rapidity into... a hotly-contested political campaign. Clearly, much coverage focused upon the death and the memorializing of the Wellstone family as well as the others on the ill-fated flight. But this coverage tended to either return to the "campaign" frame quickly, or meld the discussion of Wellstone's death with more-traditional coverage of polls, political position-taking, and the like.

The fact that Wellstone's wife did not survive to take his mantle was a likely factor in this, as was the oft-debated memorial service. In sum, eulogy effects happen, and they do fade between the date of death and Election Day. However, circumstances of the campaign may force eulogy coverage to compete with more-traditional campaign "horse race" coverage, and that, in turn, may dilute the eulogy effect's impact by the time Election Day comes. The longer a campaign runs, the likelier the eulogy effect will be delayed until the election itself. This dynamic of the eulogy effect squaring off with more-traditional campaign coverage is affected by the circumstances of the tragedy itself (such as whether or not close family members survive to take the deceased place on the ballot), state law, the events that take place afterwards, and the opposition's campaign strategy.

As a result of the eulogy effect's decay over time, the aftermath of Senator Kennedy's death reveals one more important point: the eulogy effect only predicts media coverage changes – it does not necessarily reflect election outcomes. Carnahan's case, where the late candidate's wife ran in his place, bears notice here. When a replacement candidate with the same last name is on the ballot, the connection between media eulogizing the late candidate and the electoral stakes for the replacement is sharper. In the other two cases, the eulogy effect faded either through time or other campaign events and the result was no overall impact on the election outcome.

Notes

[1] Kansas City *Star*, November 1, 2000.

[2] Lazarsfeld, Paul, Bernard Berelson, and Hazel Gaudet. 1944. *The People's Choice.* New York: Columbia University Press

[3] Berelson, Bernard and Paul F. Lazarsfeld. 1954. *Voting.* Chicago: University of Chicago Press.

[4] Campbell, Angus, Warren Miller, Philip Coverse, and Donald Stokes. 1960. *The American Voter.* Chicago: University of Chicago Press.

[5] Graber, Doris. 1993. *Mass Media in American Politics.* Washington: CQ Press.

[6] Nelson, Thomas E., Rosalee Clawson, and Zoe. M. Oxley. 1997. "Media Framing of a Civil Liberties Conflict and its Effect on Tolerance." *American Political Science Review* 91:3, 567-84.

[7] Iyengar, Shanto. 1991. *Is Anyone Responsible?* Chicago: University of Chicago Press.

[8] *Ibid.*

[9] Kerbel, Matthew and Sumaiya Apee. 2000. "PBS Ain't So Different." *Harvard International Journal of Press/Politics* 5:4, 8-33.

[10] Valkenburg, Patti M. and Hollee Semetko. 1999. "The Effects of News Frames on Readers' Thoughts and Recall." *Communication Research* 36:5, 55-57.

[11] Patterson, Thomas E. 1993. *Out of Order.* New York: Kropf.

[12] Lipmann, Walter. 1997 (orig. 1922). *Public Opinion.* New York: Free Press.

[13] Jasperson, Amy. 2003. "The Sympathy Vote: Real or Illusion?" Paper presented to the American Political Science Association Annual Meetings.

[14] Kropf, Martha, Anthony Simones, E. Terrence Jones, Dale Neuman, Allison Hayes, and Maureen Gilbride Mears. 2001. "The 2000 Missouri Senate Race." Brigham Young Symposium on Outside Money and Election Advocacy. http://www.byu.edu/outsidemoney/2000general/contents.htm

[15] Marcus, George E., and Michael MacKuen. 1993. "Anxiety, Enthusiasm and the Vote: The Emotional Underpinnings of Learning and Involvement during Presidential Campaigns." *American Political Science Review* 87: 3, :688-701.

[16] Kropf *et. Al.*

[17] Webb, Tom and Bill Salisbury. 2002. "2002 Senate Race: Wellstone: Two polls, one number." *Saint Paul Pioneer Press.* April 16.

[18] Anonymous. 2002. "Incumbents in Trouble Everywhere." Zogby International Poll, October. http://www.zogby.com/news/ReadNews.dbm?ID=634

[19] McCallum, Laura. 2002. "Adwatch: Attack ad goes after Wellstone." *Minnesota Public Radio Report.* June 21.
http://news.mpr.org/features/200206/21_mccalluml_adwatch/index.shtml

[20] Jasperson.

[21] *Ibid.*

[22] Coleman Press Conference 10/25/02.

[23] Anonymous. 1976. "National Affairs." *Newsweek.*

[24] Anonymous. 1996. "Congressional Races Offer Hot Contests." *Saint Louis Post-Dispatch.*

[25] Nuttig, Brian and Holli A. Stern. 2001. *CQ's Politics in America 2002.* Washington: CQ Press.

[26] Rudin, Ken. 2010. "New Poll Has Brown Up; Obama Will Campaign For Coakley" *Political Junkie* January 15.
http://www.npr.org/blogs/politicaljunkie/2010/01/new_poll_has_brown_up_obam a_wi.html

[27] Cooper, Michael. 2010. "G.O.P. Senate Victory Stuns Democrats." *New York Times.* January 19.
http://www.nytimes.com/2010/01/20/us/politics/20election.html

[28] Romano, Andrew. 2010. "How Coakley Blew It In Massachusetts" *blogs.newsweek.com.* January 19.
http://blog.newsweek.com/blogs/thegaggle/archive/2010/01/19/how-coakley-blew-it-in-massachusetts-.aspx

[29] Newton-Small, Jay. 2010. "Could the Democrats Lose Kennedy's Senate Seat?" *Time* January 12.
http://www.time.com/time/politics/article/0,8599,1953034,00.html

[30] *ibid.*

[31] Cooper.

[32] Romano.

[33] *ibid.*

[34] Newton-Small.

[35] Romano.

[36] Cooper.

[37] *Ibid.*

[38] Clift, Elanor. 2010. "Coakley and 'The Woman Thing.'" *blogs.newsweek.com.* January 20.
http://blog.newsweek.com/blogs/thegaggle/archive/2010/01/20/coakley-and-the-woman-thing.aspx

[39] Cooper

[40] *ibid.*

[41] Nuss *et. al.*

[42] Cooper.

[43] Nuss *et. al.*

[44] Smith, Michael A., Kevin Anderson, and Chapman Rackaway. 2002. "The Eulogy Effect." Paper presented to the Midwest Political Science Association Annual Meetings.

Conclusion

In this volume, we examined the intersection of politics and popular culture by looking at three ways the media and politics mutually affect each other. First, we explored the role that the entertainment media play in understanding politics. We were able to see that fictional worlds allow us to consider different political ideals without the baggage of our last vote, our ideology, or real-world consequences. Thus, we can step outside ourselves and safely challenge the way we think on particular issues. Second, we explored the real world of politics as it has been shaped by technology in this new century. As powerful a medium television proved to be to politics, the latest technological breakthroughs have proved to be a seismic shift. From website to Facebook to Twitter, our politicians are able to keep in almost constant contact with their constituencies, which has vast implications for the way political discourse will progress. Our political world will never look the same again. Indeed, Thomas Jefferson would not recognize political discourse if he were to rise from the dead and walk around tomorrow. Finally, we explored what happens when the real world and media collide. Entertainment media change their messages when major political events happen. The influence goes in both directions as politicians and the political world adjust when media coverage changes. We were able to see what happens when focusing events shift the political conversation in such a way as to affect the outcome.

As this book goes to press, we move into another election cycle – the 2010-midterm elections - and we see that the effect of popular culture is pervasive. Everything we talk about in this volume is intensified for this round. For example, the candidate for the Kentucky seat for the United States Senate, Rand Paul, mentioned to a popular television talk show host that he did not endorse the totality of the Civil Rights Act. Within 24 hours this comment was blogged about, commented on, and everyone in the nation knew what Paul had said, even though only people in Kentucky will decide his political fate. When asked why he waited so long to respond, which he did the next evening, Paul said it took him a day to get on a national show. The most recent phenomenon to hit U.S. politics, the Tea Party, has used Facebook extensively to mobilize its supporters to rallies across the country. The television show *Lost* drew 13.5 million viewers for its finale, indicating that American viewers are interested in following a show for six years that deliberately engages them in a conversation about social contract theory.

Our politics have become interconnected in new ways due to popular culture. Our national politics have become a national pastime. New technologies mean that virtually no political event can occur without an immediate response from bloggers and pundits thus leaving politicians, such as Paul, with no ability to respond before most of the nation has made a decision about him. Millions of Americans sat in wonder after *Lost* trying to understand what the finale meant – and even they go to one of countless forums, blogs and news sites in an attempt to find answers and theories This collective reaction from such a large number of people indicates the vast potential of popular television programs. As we move into the future, this interconnection due to popular new media will only increase. We will be subjected to further assault by information, which will have profound influences on the way people think about politics – and scholars will need to continue to examine how these influences change the political landscape.

EDITOR AND CONTRIBUTOR BIOGRAPHIES

Editor

Leah A. Murray is Associate Professor of Political Science at Weber State University. Her research agenda includes the presidency and Congress, youth political participation and the political effects of popular culture. She was published in the area of popular culture in *The Philosophy of the Undead* by Open Court Press in 2006. She has presented papers on *The West Wing* and *Battlestar Galactica* at national conferences.

Contributors

Kevin Anderson is Assistant Professor of Political Science at Eastern Illinois University. His teaching and research interests include American Political Thought, African American Political Thought and African American Politics. His first book, *Agitations: Ideologies and Strategies in African American Politics* will be published in April 2010 by the University of Arkansas Press.

Karen K. Burrows is a DPhil student at the University of Sussex, where she is completing her thesis on the representation of the female spy in political and popular culture. Her other research interests include gender and sexuality in genre television and identity politics in American superhero films and comics.

Gerry Canavan is a Ph.D. candidate in the Program in Literature at Duke University preparing his dissertation on Anglophone science fiction and the political history of the twentieth century under the co-direction of Fredric Jameson and Priscilla Wald. His work argues that, far from occupying some literary periphery, SF in fact plays a central role in generating the discursive field in which political struggles over history, identity, justice, and empire are waged. A recipient of a James B. Duke Fellowship, he is also the co-editor of *Polygraph* 22, "Ecology and Ideology," as well as a special issue of *American Literature* devoted to science fiction, fantasy, and myth.

Dr. Jeffrey Crouch is an assistant professor at American University, where he teaches courses on American politics. His first book, *The Presidential Pardon Power*, was published by the University Press of Kansas in 2009. Dr. Crouch earned a Ph.D. from The Catholic University of America (2008) and a J.D. from the University of Michigan Law School (2000). Originally from Michigan, he currently lives in Washington, D.C.

John F. Freie is professor of Political Science at Le Moyne College. He has written extensively in the areas of political participation, civic education, and the politics of cyberspace. He is the author of *Counterfeit Community: The Exploitation of Our Longings for Connectedness* and the forthcoming book *The Making of the Postmodern Presidency*.

Lilly Goren is Associate Professor of Politics and Global Studies at Carroll University in Waukesha, WI. She teaches American government, the Presidency, the U.S. Congress, Politics & Culture, and Gender Studies. Her research often integrates popular culture, literature and film as means to understanding politics, especially in the United States. Her published works include: "Not in My District: The Politics of Military Base Closures" (Peter Lang, 2003), and "You've Come a Long Way, Baby: Women, Politics and Popular Culture" (University Press of Kentucky, 2009). She is currently revising a manuscript on the role of anger in the American electorate. She is a regular political commentator at Wisconsin Public Radio. Professor Goren earned her A.B. in Political Science and English from Kenyon College, and has an MA and a PhD in Political Science from Boston College.

Lindsey A. Harvell is currently a Doctoral Candidate in the Department of Communication at The University of Oklahoma. Lindsey's area of specialty is political communication, social influence, and mass media effects. She received her undergraduate degree from the University of Kansas in 2004 and received her Master's degree from Wichita State University in 2007.

Betty Kaklamanidou is Adjunct Lecturer at the Film Studies Department at the Aristotle University of Thessaloniki, Greece. She studied French Literature as well as journalism and completed her Ph.D. on Film and Literature in May 2005. She is the author of two books in Greek (When Film Met Literature, 2006 and Introduction to the Hollywood Romantic Comedy, 2007). Her fields of study include film and politics, adaptation theory, genre and gender, and contemporary Greek cinema.

Scott McDermott is the author of *Charles Carroll of Carrollton: Faithful Revolutionary* (Scepter Publishers, 2002). He is currently a Ph.D. student in American History at Saint Louis University in St. Louis, Missouri. His current historical work focuses on how Protestant scholastics used natural law thinking to influence American society.

Gwendelyn S. Nisbett is a doctoral candidate in the Department of Communication at the University of Oklahoma. She received a MSc in Media & Communication from the London School of Economics and a BA in Public Policy from the College of William & Mary. Having worked in campaign politics for ten years, Nisbett studies the collision of politics, campaigns, and popular culture.

Chapman Rackaway is Assistant Professor of Political Science and Director of the Political Management Program at Fort Hays State University. His teaching and research interests include political party targeting practices, electronic communication strategies of elected officials, and media framing effects. He has been previously published in the Journal of Politics.

LaChrystal Ricke is an Assistant Professor of Mass Communication at Sam Houston State University in Hunstville, Texas. Her primary area of research interest is the intersection of online and political communication; specifically, the role of YouTube in the evolving political Internet.

Richard J. Semiatin is Academic Director, Washington Semester Program at American University. His research specializes in campaigns and elections. He is the author of *Campaigns in the 21st Century* (2005) and editor of *Campaigns on the Cutting Edge* (2008).

Ryan Sission is a graduate student in the Master's Degree program at Easten Illinois University.

Michael A. Smith is Associate Professor and Associate Chair of Political Science at Emporia State University, in Kansas. His research interests include the theory and practice of representation, political decisionmaking, and reapportionment of legislative districts. Michael's curriculum vitae includes a book, *Bringing Representation Home* (Missouri, 2003), several journal articles and book chapters, and his work on several local, political campaigns in the Kansas City area.

Hugo Torres graduated from Saint Mary's College of California with a B.A. in Politics and Religious Studies. His interest in these fields continued into graduate school, where he attended Harvard Law School and Harvard Divinity School, receiving a J.D. and M.T.S. After working for a few years as an intellectual property attorney, he now serves as a prosecutor in Seattle, Washington.

Justin S. Vaughn is Assistant Professor of Political Science in the College of Liberal Arts and Social Sciences at Cleveland State University. He joined CSU in August 2007 after receiving his Bachelor of Science and Masters in Science degrees in Political Science from Illinois State University and his doctoral degree from Texas A&M University. Dr. Vaughn has been selected as a Presidential Fellow by the Center for the Study of the Presidency and has authored several studies of presidential politics, including papers recently published in *Presidential Studies Quarterly*, *Political Research Quarterly*, *Review of Policy Research*, the *International Journal of Public Administration*, and *Administration & Society*. His current projects include examinations of the role popular culture plays in shaping the presidential image, empirical analyses of management theory as applied to the inner workings of the White House, and an ongoing study of the formal and informal linkages between the presidency and the American public.

Jaap Verheul is a PhD Candidate in Cinema Studies at New York University. His research interests include cinematic violence, marxist cultural theory, politics and (early) cinema, trauma and national identity, cultural memory, European cinema, media institutions in an age of globalization, and convergence culture. He is a frequent contributor to the Belgian film journal CineMagie, for which he has written essays on the representation of trauma and memory in Sydney Lumet's "The Pawnbroker;" the "fascist" aesthetics in films by Busby Berkeley and Leni Riefenstahl; and the American films of Dutch director Paul Verhoeven.